Education in Communist China

R. F. PRICE

London
ROUTLEDGE & KEGAN PAUL

First published in 1970
by Routledge & Kegan Paul Limited
Broadway House, 68–74 Carter Lane
London, E.C.4

Printed in Great Britain by
C. Tinling and Co. Ltd.
London and Prescot

ISBN 0 7100 6784 4

WORLD EDUCATION SERIES

Education in Communist China

World education series

GENERAL EDITOR: DR. BRIAN HOLMES
Reader in Comparative Education
Institute of Education
University of London

Education and Development in Latin America

Laurence Gale

To Erika

Contents

Contents

World education series

The volumes in the *World Education Series* will treat national systems of education and, where appropriate, features of different systems within a particular region. These studies are intended to meet the needs of students of comparative education in university departments and schools of education and colleges of education and will supplement the growing volume of literature in the field. They may also appeal to a wider lay audience interested in education abroad.

As an area study of a national system each volume presents an accurate, reasonably up-to-date account of the most important features of the educational system described. Among these are the ways in which the school system is controlled, financed and administered. Some account is given of the various kinds of school within the system and the characteristics of each of them. The principles of curriculum organization and some aspects of teacher education are outlined. Of more interest, however, is the analysis which is made in each volume of the unique national characteristics of an educational system, seen in the context of its history and the sociological, economic and political factors which have in the past and continue now to influence educational policy.

The assumption behind the series is, however, that common socio-economic and educational problems find unique expression in a particular country or region, and that a brief analysis of some major national issues will reveal similarities and differences. Thus, while in each case the interpretation of policies and practices is based on the politics of education, the interpretative emphasis will vary from one country to another.

The framework of analysis for each volume is consequently the same, attention being drawn in the first section to the legal basis of educational provision, followed in the second section by an analysis of the political considerations which have and do influence the formulation, adoption and implementation of policy. The role of political parties is described where appropriate and the influence of the church or churches on policy examined. Attention too is given to the activities of pressure groups at national, regional and local levels. Changing industrial, urban and familial patterns are used to show how educational needs are in process of change and what difficulties arise when innovations are attempted. Again, each author touches on the extent to which economic resources affect the implementation of policy. The analysis relates principally to the twenty-year period between 1945 and 1965 but relevant aspects of the pre-Second World War period are described and the chains of events are seen in historical perspective.

Finally, in the third section some account is given of problems which arise within the educational system itself. Those which appear to the author of particular interest and importance have been treated in some depth. Others have been referred to so that readers may consult other sources of information if they wish. Broad problem areas in education have, however, been identified. The points of transition within a system between the first and second and between the second and third stages of education give rise to problems of selection and allocation. Under conditions of expansion, created by explosions of population and aspirations, traditional solutions are often thought to be no longer adequate. The attempts made to meet these new situations are described. So too are the relationships and debates about them, between the various types of school at different levels of education. For example what are the possibilities of transfer between academic, general and technical/vocation schools at the second stage of education? And where these different types have been replaced by some form of common or comprehensive school what kinds of differentiation exist within the single school? At the third level of higher education what relationships exist between institutions providing general education, professional training and research opportunities? In some systems a form of dual control is growing up with the universities retaining much of their traditional autonomy and the technological institutes and teacher education institutions increasingly feeling the influence of government agencies. Again, after a process of differentiation in course content in the first stage of higher education there is now a tendency for the first year (or two) of college or university work to be regarded as a preparatory year (or years) with common or somewhat similar courses of studies for all students.

Particular attention has been paid to the problems which arise in the area of teacher education. Movements in most countries are in the direction of bringing together the previously separate systems of training for elementary and secondary school teachers. Common entrance prerequisites to different training institutions may now be required. Where this is not yet the case training colleges usually make it possible for students to obtain, during the course of their studies, a certificate which grants entry to the university and highest (in prestige and status) forms of teacher education. The place of teacher education in the structure of higher education is, in short, discussed in each of the volumes. So are debates about curricular content and methods of certification.

Finally, some attention is given to the interaction of the schools and other social agencies. Among these the health services, youth organizations, the family, the Church, industry and commerce have been regarded as important. Where special note is not taken of such institutions the impact they have in the schools is dealt with throughout the volume as a whole.

The framework in short is intended to facilitate cross cultural studies through the series as a whole. Basic educational legislation is referred to in the belief that it gives the most reliable and valid source of national goals or aims in education. The problems of putting these into effective action are socio-economic-political and educational. Comparisons can be made, therefore, between the aims of education as expressed in national legislation and between the main factors which inhibit or facilitate practical provisions in accordance with these aims.

BRIAN HOLMES
General Editor

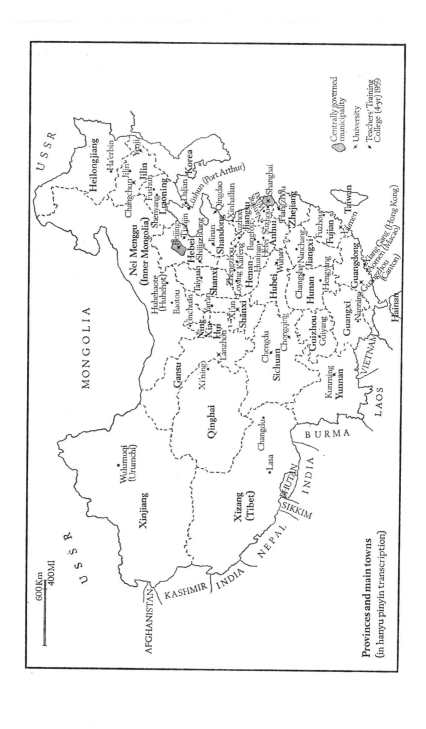

Provinces and main towns
(in hanyu pinyin transcription)

Centrally governed municipality

University

Teachers' Training College (4-yr) 1959

600 Km
400 MI

U S S R

MONGOLIA

Heilongjiang

Ha'erbin

Nei Menggu
(Inner Mongolia)

Changchun
Jilin
Jilin
Fushun
Shenyang
Liaoning
Dalian
Lüshun (Port Arthur)
Korea

Huhehaote
(Huhehot)

Baotou

Beijing
Tianjin
Hebei
Shijiazhuang
Jinan
Shandong
Qingdao
Xinhailian

Taiyuan
Shanxi

Yinchuan
Ning
Xia
Hui

Yan'an

Xi'an
Shǎnxi

Zhengzhou
Loyang Kaifeng
Henan
Bangfou
Hefei
Anhui
Suzhou
Shanghai
Hangzhou
Zhejiang
Taiwan

Lanzhou

Gansu

Xining

Chengdu

Chongqing

Hubei
Wuhan

Changsha
Hunan
Hengyang

Nanchang
Jiangxi

Fuzhou
Fujian
Amen

Guizhou
Guiyang

Guangxi

Nanning
Guangdong
Guangzhou
(Canton)
Xiang Gang (Hong Kong)
Aomen (Macao)

Hainan

Sichuan

Kunming
Yunnan

VIETNAM

LAOS

Qinghai

Changdu

Wulumuqi
(Urumchi)

Xinjiang

Xizang
(Tibet)

Lasa

BURMA

BHUTAN

SIKKIM

INDIA

NEPAL

INDIA

KASHMIR

AFGHANISTAN

U S S R

General editor's introduction

The educational system of ancient China had as its principal aim the selection and training of civil servants. The content of instruction was based to a very considerable extent on the classics, which were subjected to careful literary analysis. Much had to be memorized and attempts to moderate examinations as objectively as possible restricted the kind of questions which could be asked to those which could be marked satisfactorily. The social aims of the system of civil service examinations were to restrict nepotism and to draw into the Imperial service able young men from the villages.

The influence of this system in the educational systems of Europe has been considerable. The civil service *concours* of France and the competitive entrance examinations in England reflect this tradition. The treatment of classical literature and its central position in the curriculum in European schools represent the same kind of approach to education.

Against this background should be seen the efforts of the present leaders of China to reform the school system. It would be a mistake simply to assume that directives from a powerful central government can be passed down through the system and implemented by teachers in the classroom. The acceptance of an ideology does not mean that practice will follow it automatically. Among the obstacles preventing or slowing down reform should be counted traditional ideologies and well established schools. The Communist government in China has had to face a powerful heritage.

It was also faced with difficulties due to the size and diversity of the country and its population. Communications, still rudimentary in many areas, the variety of spoken languages, and the complications of the written language, continue to create problems for implementing policy. The traditional family structure has also to be taken into account when trying to explain the reasons for an apparently slow rate of progress towards a system of schools more closely in line with Communist theory.

It should also be remembered that during their first decade of power the Communist leaders had little time to formulate educational policy. During the last ten years more attention has been paid to education. Among Party leaders and educationists opinion has been divided. Radical and conservative points of view have been strongly expressed as part of the Cultural Revolution. Mao's contributions to these debates have been considerable. The practical outcomes of them are, at the moment, matters of conjecture. One thing is certain, however, the radical transformation of an old and respected system of education will take many decades of effort to achieve.

Mr. Price is well qualified to analyse the educational implications of the Cultural Revolution and the difficulties which face Mao in his attempts to introduce new educational policies. The author spent two years in Peking, teaching English, and had access to many documents and sources of information extremely difficult to consult outside China. His analysis of Mao's Thoughts on the nature of man, society and knowledge is against the philosophical assumptions of the classical Chinese tradition. He shows how Communist government educational policies have had to face the inertia of pre-World War II schools strongly influenced by foreign practice. In the third section of this volume Mr. Price gives detailed accounts of the full and part-time systems of education.

Like other volumes in the *World education series* this book should be regarded as a case study in the reform of education. In the case of China the problems are particularly fascinating because so many factors are involved in the analysis of tradition and change. Violent changes have occurred in the political and economic spheres of Chinese life under the Communist government. The power of the cultural heritage is considerable. The energy and skill of the people involved in the transformation of their society are well known. This volume has been written at a crucial stage in the process. Education may go in any of several directions. Readers will be in a good position to judge what these possibilities are after reading Mr. Price's careful and detailed study.

The audience for which this book is intended is wide. Comparative educationists, students of education, teachers and interested laymen should find it very useful and extremely readable. So little is known of education in China, however, that it was felt desirable to document this volume more fully than some of the others in the series. As a result it should appeal to students in the field of Chinese studies.

It admirably meets the aims of comparative education. Readers will note, for example, that China faces similar problems of reform to those which exist in Western Europe and the USSR. It also reveals many facets of the problems which arise when selective cultural borrowing is attempted. Finally some deeper understanding of the processes of education may be gained from a careful reading of the section which deals with the schools and part-time education.

The lay-out follows the usual pattern. The first section deals with policy and the important debates going on; the next section analyses the major obstacles to reform and the third section gives details of schools, how they are organized, what kind of curricula are provided, how they are financed, and how teachers are trained. The volume it is hoped will be of general interest to educationists and will provoke more studies into a fascinating system of education.

BRIAN HOLMES

Preface

Going to China was for the writer the culmination of boyhood dreams and diverse adult interests: an exciting event only marred by the political obstacles to fuller participation in Chinese life. In this book I have tried both to stand back and analyse, and to give something of my subjective feeling for China and its problems.

It was perhaps as an aid to the imagination that my stay in China was most useful, rather than for any particular information I was able to acquire. I gained the lasting advantage of a key to the interpretation of the large quantity of material which is available in the West. Made available either directly by the official Chinese news and publicity agencies, or by the excellent abstracting and monitoring services of such bodies as the B.B.C. and the U.S. Consulate-General, Hong Kong, newspaper articles, speeches and letters appear in a language guaranteed for misunderstanding. Where the English go in for understatement, the Chinese prefer colourful metaphor, often taken from their ancient literature. Certain fixed phrases are repeated endlessly so that to English ears they sound insincere and even ridiculous. In the pages ahead some of the quotations reveal this difference in the way our two languages express ideas.

When the writer first began to read about China a major difficulty was remembering the names of people and places, so short and so alike to the untrained eye. It was for this reason that an appendix was included, giving some help with pronunciation and transcriptions. A few minutes spent studying this appendix should help those readers who have similar difficulties. A map is also provided, using the same transcription as the text, frequent consultation of which should help to fix the place names in space. The time chart, which contains those people and events most closely connected with the main argument of the book, will, it is hoped, also help to make matters clearer.

Preface

Were I to name all those who have helped me, directly or in-directly, with the writing of this book the list would be very long. I can only say that I am very conscious of the debt I owe, and of the difficulty of making a worthy acquittance.

May I thank the librarians and their staffs of the School of Oriental and African Studies of the University of London, the Institute of Education of the University of London, and the Tate Library, Streatham, in the Borough of Lambeth. I am also indebted to the Society for Anglo-Chinese Understanding whose sets of bound volumes of Chinese journals published in English and other books and pamphlets proved an easily accessible store of information.

R. F. PRICE

Abbreviations

Organizations

CCP	Chinese Communist Party
CC CCP	Central Committee of the Chinese Communist Party
NCNA	New China News Agency
PLA	People's Liberation Army
YCL	Young Communist League
YMCA	Young Men's Christian Association

Publications

The following are English-language translations prepared by the United States Consulate General in Hong Kong:

CB	Current Background
ECMM	Extracts from China Mainland Magazines
SCMP	Survey of China Mainland Press

EPMC	An Economic Profile of Mainland China, being Studies prepared for the Joint Economic Committee of Congress of the United States, U.S. Printing Office, 1967.
JPRS	Translations by the Joint Publications Research Service, Washington, D.C.

Educational aims
and the thoughts of Mao Ze-dong

The Cultural Revolution of 1966

In the autumn of 1965, in the sixteenth year of the People's Republic of China, the first verbal hand-grenades were thrown in what was to become known as the Great Proletarian Cultural Revolution (*wuchan-jieji wenhua da geming*). The *Shanghai Literary Gazette* published on 10 November an attack on the writer and vice-mayor of Peking, Wu Han, which was reprinted by the *Liberation Army Daily* on 29 November, and by the *People's Daily* on the 30th. In the spring of 1966 this was widened into an attack on various writers and historians. Guided and stimulated by articles and editorials in the *Liberation Army Daily*, the *People's Daily* and *Red Flag*, what at first appeared to be just another rectification campaign moved, in the form of posters, on to the walls of the colleges and schools, and finally into the streets in the form of massive demonstrations in July 1966.

The struggle was not something which suddenly began in 1965, nor was it a question of the succession, as some foreign observers liked to suggest. While personalities, and personal interests were obviously involved, at the base there was a division on the fundamental question of how to rule. It might be described as a morality in search of an institutional structure, except that its advocates constantly stress the need for vigilance and struggle over 'decades or even centuries' (CR docs. 2, vol. 5, p. 18), and therefore show they recognize the limitations of any institutions.

During the two confused years which followed it became clear that education in its widest sense was central to the struggle being waged between Mao Ze-dong and his supporters, and that often shadowy 'handful of people in the Party taking the capitalist road'. While the debate did not raise any essentially new issues, it posed certain old ones in a particularly sharp manner and forced people to take a firm stand on one side or the other. At the same time it threw a clearer light on the events of the previous decade and a half during which the CCP had tried to transform the educational system of China to meet the new needs.

The importance of education was brought out in numerous articles during the Cultural Revolution. Very early on, in the editorial for 18 April 1966 the *Liberation Army Daily* wrote: 'we must . . . integrate ourselves with the workers, peasants and soldiers, remould our thinking, raise the level of our political consciousness and whole-heartedly serve all the people of China and of the world, with no thought of fame or profit, and without fear of hardship or death' (CR docs. 2, vol. 1, p. 16). Here were Mao's two main ideas: integration with the working people and moral-political education. On 6 June 1966 the *Liberation Army Daily* published a long article in which it amplified these points while outlining what the Cultural Revolution was about. 'Its purpose', it said, 'is not only to demolish all the old ideology and culture . . . but also to create and cultivate among the masses an entirely new, proletarian ideology and culture, and entirely new proletarian customs and habits.' (CR docs. 2, vol. 5, p. 23). The emphasis had by then moved from the intelligentsia, from historians and playwrights, to the 'masses'. Official pronouncement on the schools came later, in the Sixteen Points adopted by the CC CCP on 8 August 1966 as guidelines for the conduct of the Cultural Revolution. Point 10 read:

In the great proletarian cultural revolution a most important task is to transform the old educational system and the old principles and methods of teaching.

In this great cultural revolution, the phenomenon of our schools being dominated by bourgeois intellectuals must be completely changed.

In every kind of school we must apply thoroughly the policy advanced by Comrade Mao Ze-dong of education serving proletarian politics and education being combined with productive labour, so as to enable those receiving an education to develop morally, intellectually and physically and to become workers with both socialist consciousness and culture.

The period of schooling should be shortened. Courses should

be fewer and better. The teaching material should be thoroughly transformed, in some cases beginning with simplifying complicated material. While their main task is to study, students should also learn other things. That is to say, in addition to their studies they should also learn industrial work, farming and military affairs, and take part in the struggles of the cultural revolution to criticize the bourgeoisie as these struggles occur. (CR docs. 3, pp. 9–10).

In line with Mao Ze-dong's dictum that it is necessary to destroy the old before one begins to construct the new, most of the discussion has been in negative terms, in terms of what Mao's supporters are against. What they are for is more difficult to grasp in concrete terms. It has often been expressed in terms of 'serving the people' and 'eliminating self'. Perhaps it could not have been more specific because it is rather a question of the *way* in which things are done than *what* should be done which often divides the protagonists. Mao is deeply concerned with human relations, with sociology rather than economics. For example, his support for the rural people's communes is more for what they do to develop human co-operation than because he expects them to develop agricultural output 'faster, better and more economically', though he expects them to do that too, in the end.

At this stage it is too early to be certain about the exact nature of the opposition to Mao Ze-dong and his policies, or the extent to which it was organized. It is probable that there were several 'oppositions', and that many of the accusations made against this or that leader were applicable to a trend rather than a particular person. Perhaps that was one reason why many of the attacks were addressed to 'China's Khrushchev' or 'the top person in the Party taking the capitalist road'. In many of the articles on education Lu Ding-yi, former Director of the Propaganda Department of the CC CCP, was attacked by name as being responsible for anti-Maoist policies, usually in conjunction with 'China's Khrushchev'. (SCMP 4109 1968)

In spite of doubts about the details, the general policy of those opposed to Mao was quite clear. Their main belief was in government by the expert, by a highly trained and privileged group who would occupy the Party and managerial positions. Work was to be

3

done by administrative decision, with little emphasis on involving those who were to carry out the decisions. Mao's attempts to get the managerial and technical personnel to take part in manual labour were regarded as largely a waste of valuable time and training. In the school system this policy was represented by special schools for the children of officials, and long and highly selective courses in the universities and colleges.

The repeated accusation that the opposition was attempting to restore capitalism refers to this differentiation of the ruling group from the mass of workers and peasants. While to the European observer life might have appeared to be uniformly austere, a closer look revealed countless ways in which those holding high office were able to obtain privileges. The Maoist argument is that such small privileges lead to a differentiation of interests and a gradual development of a new exploiting class. It is in this connection that one should read the repeated attacks on the USSR, where Mao's group sees this process already far advanced.

Support for the policy of government by the expert, and emphasis on individual material incentives is generally condemned under the term 'revisionism'. But in the field of education similar attitudes are attacked as 'bourgeois'. One should not be misled by the endless clichés into thinking that the accusations have no substance.

It is important to note that this is a struggle within the Communist Party, between groups who agree on a number of fundamental questions, such as the development of co-operation in farming and trade, and on the public ownership of industry. But the deep division on the way in which government should be carried out is connected with questions like the rate of change-over from private to public ownership, the degree of centralization of this or that sphere of the economy, and the whole sphere of general and specialist education.

The ideas behind the educational policies of the 'bourgeois academics' are familiar to specialists in education everywhere. But the Thoughts of Mao Ze-dong require more detailed consideration if current attempts to reform Chinese education are to be understood.

The Thoughts of Mao Ze-dong

During the Cultural Revolution the study of the works of Mao Ze-dong, already long established as basic mass educational material,

4

was urged with astonishing vigour. The red plastic-covered volume of quotations became familiar, not only in China where it was carried, waved at meetings, studied and recited, but also throughout the world. Mao Ze-dong's Thought was proclaimed as a means of 'transforming society and nature' and as the key to solving all problems. It became clear that for some time at least Mao's writings would occupy a larger share of the curriculum throughout the school system.

Mao is held up in China as the successor to, and developer of the ideas of Marx, Engels, Lenin and Stalin, whose pictures stand opposite the Tian An Men (Gate of Heavenly Peace) on National Day. The works of these earlier writers are available in Chinese translations, but they are only read by a small percentage of the millions who read the works of Mao. Therefore only a brief attempt will be made here to compare Mao's ideas with those of European Marxism.

Mao's Thoughts will be examined under the general themes of man, society, and knowledge, followed by some of his specific comments on education. It will be argued here that many of his ideas affecting education have their roots deep in the Chinese tradition. It is therefore apposite to begin by briefly outlining his early life and education.

Mao Ze-dong was born in the village of Shaoshan in Hunan Province on 26 December 1893. His father was a peasant of moderate means and Mao Ze-dong began working on the land at the age of six. At seven he began attending the local primary school, which was one of the old classical schools in which the pupils were forced to memorize the classics without understanding them. In spite of this Mao acquired a love of reading, and soon began to devour the great novels which his teachers banned. He was especially drawn to stories of heroes and rebels, like those in *The Water Margin*, and *The Romance of the Three Kingdoms*.

When Mao was about thirteen he left the primary school and worked full-time on his father's land. At seventeen he took up studies again, going for a year to the Dongshan Primary School in his mother's native town of Xiangxiang. This school was a modern-style one, and here Mao for the first time encountered European ideas. He read political periodicals, and became influenced by Yen Fu, the great translator, and the reformers Kang Yu-wei and Liang

Qi-chao. He also read historical biographies and was greatly impressed by George Washington and Napoleon.

In 1911 he went to Changsha, the provincial capital, and here witnessed the revolution which proclaimed the Great Han Republic. Together with some friends, he cut off his pigtail, symbol of Manchu oppression, and at the end of the year he joined the revolutionary army for six months. Perhaps even more significant, he began to read newspapers, which he later described as one of 'the two most important instruments of education' (Schram, 1963, p. 214).

Coming out of the army on 15 February 1912, Mao looked around for a suitable means of further study. He considered a police school, a soap-making school, and a law school. He joined a commercial school for a month, but left when he found that much of the work was conducted in English, which he could not understand. After this he spent six months in the First Provincial Secondary School, Changsha, for whose entrance examination he had passed first.

In the summer of 1912 Mao left school and for a time studied on his own. He ate very little and spent his days reading in the Provincial Library. Whatever money he had went on newspapers.

From 1913 to 1918 Mao was a student at the First Teachers' Training School in Changsha. Officially a secondary school, it provided an exceptionally good education with a strong humanist bias. The staff included a number of outstanding men, including the teacher of ethics, Yang Chang-ji, who was later to be a professor at Peking University and Mao Ze-dong's father-in-law. Yang combined a classical education with ten years' study abroad, in Japan, England and Germany. He was a follower of the twelfth-century neo-Confucian philosopher, Zhu Xi.

At the Training School Mao continued to develop his interest in history, and was also good in geography and history. His essays, improved by the study of the Tang essayist, Han Yu, were regularly displayed on the school walls.

During 1918 Mao helped found a political discussion group, the New People's Study Society, which held weekly or fortnightly meetings and grew to a membership of eighty. He also, with other students from his school, taught in evening classes for workers and shop-assistants.

Late in 1918 he travelled to Peking where he worked as an assistant

6

in the university library to the famous Li Da-zhao. Under his influence Mao moved towards Marxism.

Returning to Changsha in 1919 Mao became a teacher at the Xu-ye Primary School, and in 1920 he was appointed Headmaster of the Primary School attached to his old Teachers' Training School. But his main interest was in politics, the politics of national revival, and revolution. He had, as he later told Edgar Snow, 'become, in theory and to some extent in action, a Marxist, and from this time on I considered myself a Marxist.' (Snow, 1937, p. 153).

Mao Ze-dong's Thoughts are presented to the Chinese public in a variety of forms, in selections ranging in time from 1926 to the present. Foreign readers have in certain cases access to the original texts (Schram, 1963; Brandt, 1952; Compton, 1952), but those works read in China today have been carefully edited to teach the required lessons. While this obscures the development of Mao's ideas it does not affect the present study which is concerned with what has been taught in China during the past two decades.

Various editions of the *Selected Works* have appeared in China, beginning in 1951. In spite of this the demand would appear to have exceeded the supply, and foreigners in China have had the embarrassing experience of being taken into the corner of the main bookshop in Peking and sold a copy from under the counter, while a few yards away Chinese were being told the edition was sold out. In 1966 the *Selected Works* were reprinted in the simplified characters, enabling them to be read by a much wider group of people.

The world-famous little red book, the *Quotations from Chairman Mao*, first appeared in May 1964 in an edition published by the General Political Department of the People's Liberation Army. It was initially circulated in various organizations, but appeared in the shops in 1966.

What had been available on a mass scale before 1966 were separate pamphlets, editions of what had been considered to be the most important articles for popular study. Most talked of were the 'three old articles': *Serve the People*, 1944; *In Memory of Norman Bethune*, 1939; and *The Foolish Old Man Who Removed the Mountains*, 1945.

The two philosophical essays, *On Practice*, 1937, and *On Contradiction*, 1937, have also been widely studied, but were regarded as much more difficult than the 'three old articles'. Together with

Reform Our Study, 1941, and other material, they were used by the Youth League in its study programme (Myrdal, 1967, p. 251).

Talks at the Yenan Forum on Literature and Art, 1942, has been reprinted a number of times, and studied particularly by those working in these fields. During the Cultural Revolution, when the nature and exercise of political power became the main issue, people were urged to study *On the Correct Handling of Contradictions Among the People*, 1957; the *Speech at the National Conference of the Communist Party on Propaganda*, 1957; *On Correcting Mistaken Ideas in the Party*, 1929; *Combat Liberalism*, 1937; *On New Democracy*, 1940; *The May 4th Movement*, 1939; and *The Orientation of the Youth Movement*, 1939.

Mao's ideas on the nature of man

Mao regards man as a product of his social class, with his ideas and habits strongly determined by his origin. But at the same time he appears to have an almost infinite belief in man's ability to rise above these limitations. Time and again in his writings he returns to education, persuasion and ideological work as a means of eradicating various errors which he identifies in the work of the Communist Party. These errors are often couched in terms of individual psychology: individualism; or subjectivism. They are often regarded as characteristics of a particular class: 'putschism' is attributed to the petty bourgeoisie and lumpen-proletariat; or 'ultra-democracy' and 'subjectivism' is attributed to the peasantry and petty-bourgeoisie. By contrast, the proletariat is always described as having a correct ideology, and members of other classes are advised to learn from it, and identify themselves with it in order to correct their own shortcomings.

Mao's exhortations to goodness are always addressed to Party members and cadres. He constantly returns to the qualities of a revolutionary. But he does not expect uniformity. At one point he remarks: 'A man's ability may be great or small, but if he has this spirit [absolute selflessness] he is already noble-minded and pure, ... a man who is of value to the people.' (Mao, 1965, vol. 2, p. 338).

Serving the people, putting the needs of others before that of self, this is for Mao the key characteristic of a revolutionary. Two of the 'three old articles' have this as their main lesson. In the first of these

8

it was a foreigner, the Canadian doctor, Norman Bethune, who died of blood poisoning while tending the Red Army wounded in 1939, who was held up as a model of 'utter devotion to others' with 'no thought of self'.

Next in importance comes persistence, working with all one's energy, patient hard work. The third of the 'old articles' hammers this home with its retelling of the ancient tale of Yu Gong, who with the aid of his sons, began to dig down the two mountains which obscured the view from his house. As in the story of Bruce and the Spider, persistence brought reward. With persistence in action should go persistence in theory. 'A communist should always and everywhere adhere to principle and wage a tireless struggle against all incorrect ideas and actions' (Mao, 1965, vol. 2, p. 33).

Finally comes modesty and the ability to learn from others. Communists should at all times 'learn from the masses as well as teach them' (Mao, 1965, vol. 2, p. 198). 'Every Communist working among the masses should be their friend and not a boss over them' (ibid). 'Communists must listen attentively to the views of people outside the Party and let them have their say' (Mao, 1965a, p. 274).

These, then, are the qualities Mao advocates for revolutionaries, for communists. But they are also the qualities he deems necessary for all cadres, who may be non-party, and indeed for all who aspire to active citizenship in the New China. In the sixties the discussion has been in terms of the qualities of 'revolutionary successors' who will 'guarantee that our Party and country do not change their colour' (Mao, 1966a, pp. 276–9). They must be genuine Marxist-Leninists; revolutionaries who serve the overwhelming majority of the people—of China and of the whole world; statesmen capable of working with those who agree, and those who disagree with them; they must be democratic and listen to the masses; and they must be modest and capable of admitting and correcting mistakes in their work. Note that 'serving the people' is now qualified to 'the over-whelming majority of the people', to be contrasted with serving the interests of a privileged stratum of society as it is alleged is the case in the Soviet Union.

That few men have these qualities Mao explicitly admits, and he patiently spells out the methods by which they can be inculcated and maintained. Everyone, he stresses, needs periodical re-education, because as circumstances change, people do not always change with them, but need education to adapt their ideas to what is new.

One form of re-education which the CCP has carried out from time to time is what it calls rectification (*zhengfeng*). Its purpose, Mao points out, is political, 'to educate Party members so that a political and scientific spirit pervades their thinking' (Mao, 1965, vol. 1, p. 112). There seems to have been some difference between the methods prescribed by Mao for carrying out rectification, and the methods employed in practice. According to Mao (Mao, 1966*c*, p. 14) certain documents should be studied, using the method of criticism and self-criticism in order to elucidate past errors and clarify future work. 'Personal shortcomings, unless they are related to political and organizational mistakes' should not be 'over-criticized' as then people become timid and overcautious, and ignore the main problems (Mao, 1966*a*, p. 263). On more than one occasion Mao warns members against using violent methods. 'In treating an ideological or a political malady, one must never be rough and rash, but must adopt the approach of "curing the sickness to save the patient"' (Mao, 1966*a*, p. 262). But at the same time Mao opens the way for the rough treatment he deplores by his distinction between the treatment of 'the people' and 'the enemy'. Force is permissible against the latter (Mao, 1966*c*, p. 25). In another place he says that the first thing necessary when reasoning with someone 'is to give [him] a good shake-up by shouting at [him], "you are ill!" so as to administer a shock and make [him] break out in a sweat' (Mao, 1965, vol. 3, p. 56). Only then will the patient be in the right condition to receive advice. The fearful 'struggle meetings' at which insults, accusations and sometimes blows are hurled at the 'struggle object', often for hours at a time, may appear to be justified by these last two points.

Under the title of thought reform, or ideological remoulding (*sixiang gaizao*) the process of rectification was carried into the universities in the early 1950s, and numerous prominent intellectuals made public confessions of past errors (Lifton, 1961).

Mao's ideas on the nature of society

Mao, the Marxist, sees society as divided into conflicting classes, constantly engaged in struggle against each other. In an early work,

Analysis of the Classes in Chinese Society, first written in March 1926, he begins: 'Who are our enemies? Who are our friends?' (Mao, 1965, vol. 1, p. 13). He returns to this question again and again, in 1957 making what has been hailed in China as a great theoretical step forward, when he differentiated two fundamentally different kinds of contradictions: 'those between ourselves and the enemy, and those among the people themselves' (Mao, 1966*b*, p. 80).

While earlier Marxists distinguished classes according to their function in the productive process, and especially whether they own property or work for others as wage labourers, Mao pays greater attention to their wealth or poverty in assessing their attitude to the revolution. The three essays which deal with this topic in detail differ slightly in the way the classes are divided, and recent editions have been rewritten in places (Schram, 1963, ch. 4). The most detailed account is given in *The Chinese Revolution and the Chinese Communist Party*, written in December 1939. As this was during the anti-Japanese war, the criterion of 'friend' was determined by a person's attitude to the war. Hence the national bourgeoisie was regarded both as an exploiter, and as an anti-Japanese ally.

The classes discussed are: (1) landlords: including their political representatives (1933), the warlords, officials, 'local tyrants and evil gentry'; (2) bourgeoisie: including the comprador big bourgeoisie and the national bourgeoisie; (3) the petty bourgeoisie: including intellectuals and students, small tradesmen, handicraftsmen, and professional people; (4) peasantry: divided into rich, middle and poor; (5) the proletariat: including industrial workers, artisans and shop assistants, and farm labourers; and (6) the vagrants, or lumpen-proletariat (1926): the unemployed, criminal groups, those who live on superstitious practices, and (1926 only) their secret societies.

Society, for Mao, is constantly changing but class struggle goes on, even though the landlords have been 'liquidated as a class' and a 'people's democratic dictatorship' been established. In the changed situation of 1957 'the enemy' are all those who oppose socialism and 'the people', among whom there are 'non-antagonistic contradictions', are all who favour socialism, who work for socialist construction. According to Mao (Mao, 6, p. 107) only a small number of even the industrialists and merchants were unwilling to undergo 'study and remoulding'.

Closely bound up with Mao's view of society is his political policy, described as 'the mass line'. This is based on his belief that the masses (*qunzhong*) are collectively rational. 'Twenty-four years of experience', he wrote in 1945, 'tell us that the right task, policy and style of work invariably conform with the demands of the masses at a given time and place . . .' (Mao, 1966*a*, p. 123). Writing about the suppression of counter-revolutionaries in the middle fifties he said:

> 'even with the mass line mistakes may still occur in our work, but they will be fewer and easier to correct. The masses gain experience through struggle. From what is done correctly they learn how things should be done. From what is done wrong they learn useful lessons as to how mistakes should be avoided.' (Mao, 1966*b*, pp. 98–9).

The mass line is Mao's concept of democracy, which he describes as democratic centralism. Policy should begin with what people feel they need at the moment, and not with something thought up from above. If the masses do not see what society as a whole objectively requires, the leaders must be patient and resort to education and explanation. Mao is confident that reason will prevail. 'If we reason earnestly and properly, it will be effective' he writes in another place (Mao, 1965, vol. 2, p. 56). He sees the relation between leader and led as a reciprocal process: the leaders learning from the masses what they want, what they think about events; then working out a policy based on these needs; returning to the masses to explain this policy and get it accepted; and finally testing the policy in action. 'If, in the interests of the people', says Mao, 'we persist in doing what is right and correct what is wrong, our ranks will surely thrive.' (Mao, 1965, vol. 3, p. 227).

Mao's ideas on the nature of knowledge

Mao's theory of knowledge is that of dialectical materialism (Mao 1966*b*, p. 135). In a short uncompleted essay of the same title he states: 'Materialism recognizes the independent existence of matter as detached from spirit and considers spirit as secondary and subordinate' (Schram, 1963, p. 122, and Doolin and Golas, 1964). Later in the same essay he emphasizes that matter is something apart from knowledge, having an independent existence in the external world.

But he stresses that Marxism, contrary to mechanistic materialism before Marx, sees thought as active. 'It shows that thinking arises from social practice and at the same time actively directs practice' (Doolin and Golas, p. 45). Marxism is a dialectical theory of the unity of knowing and doing. It is, of course, the working out of this relationship which is at the root of all education. Some writers have pointed out that Mao lays especial stress on the role of ideas, to the extent that he might be described as a voluntarist, desiring to achieve the impossible by the sheer exercise of will (Schwartz, 1958).

The most important aspect of social practice for Marxists is, says Mao, material production (Mao, 1966*b*, p. 1). But it also includes class struggle, political life, scientific and artistic pursuits, and indeed all of man's activities. By the 1960s Mao had reduced these to three kinds: struggle for production; class struggle; and scientific experiment. These he regarded as the three kinds of social practice from which alone correct ideas could come (Mao, 1966*b*, p. 134).

Mao asserts that knowledge is arrived at by two stages. First comes a stage of perception when separate aspects of things, and their external relations are seen. For Mao no concepts are involved at this stage of thinking. All is sense perception. 'Between concepts and sense perceptions there is not only a quantitative but also a qualitative difference' he writes (Mao, 1966*b*, p. 5). Then follows a second stage when man uses concepts to form judgements and inferences. Knowledge has now passed from the 'perceptual stage' to the stage of 'rational knowledge'. There is little indication in all this that Mao understands the effect of previously-held concepts on our processes of sense perception. Such a formulation may therefore put serious limitations on Chinese psychological studies, ultimately affecting education adversely. It is not sufficient for Mao to comment that while the perceptual and rational are qualitatively different they are united on the basis of practice. 'Our practice proves that what is perceived cannot at once be comprehended and that only what is comprehended can be more deeply perceived' (Mao, 1966*b*, pp. 6-7). The point is, why?

Mao goes on to say that to observe and think is not enough. Ideas must be tested by further practice. 'Generally speaking, those that succeed are correct and those that fail are incorrect' (Mao, 1966*b*, p. 135). Practice is thus both the source and the test of our knowledge. The struggle for truth, for 'correct ideas', is a protracted one in which we learn by making mistakes. Sometimes correct ideas fail because the forces of reaction are too strong. But Mao is confident that persistence will win in the end. (ibid).

Man's knowledge is never complete. Starting from practice man acquires some knowledge. Returning to practice he corrects and improves his knowledge. And this is repeated in 'endless cycles'. At any given stage man's knowledge is partial, relative. Mao quotes Engels's comment on the contradiction between man's inherently unlimited capacity for knowledge and the limited knowledge possessed by any single man. Furthermore, the external world is continually changing so that man's correct ideas of today become incorrect tomorrow.

An essential component of the Marxist theory of knowledge is the concept of contradiction. Mao developed this in his essay *On Contradiction*. It is necessary to examine the concept for two reasons. First, it forms the theoretical core of Mao's methodology, which he is trying to persuade people to adopt. Second, in so far as he is successful in this, it affects both the language and the interpretation of the subject-matter of the various school disciplines.

Mao outlined the scope of the concept of contradiction as follows:

> 'The law of contradiction in things, that is, the law of the unity of opposites, is the fundamental law of nature and of society and therefore also the fundamental law of thought. . . . According to dialectical materialism, contradiction is present in all processes of objectively existing things and of subjective thought and permeates all these processes from beginning to end . . .' (Mao, 1966*b*, pp. 71-72).

The concept is popularized in China in the slogan: 'one divides into two'.

The concept is a very complex one which is intended to describe how change is brought about in all kinds of processes. It is on the one hand a method of examination, a subjective tool, and on the other it is a model of what is objectively occurring. Mao links it with the concept of quantitative changes bringing about qualitative change when they reach a certain value. He describes two 'states of motion in all things', 'that of relative rest and that of conspicuous change'. While both of these states contain two contradictory elements interacting in some form of 'struggle', the first stage is characterized by gradual quantitative changes, while the second stage is one of 'conspicuous [qualitative] change' (Mao, 1966*b*, p. 67).

A clear example of objective contradiction is given by Mario Bunge (Bunge, 1959, p. 19). When substances change their state from solid to liquid, liquid to gas, or the other way round, the change is brought about by the interplay of two opposing trends: thermal agitation of the molecules, and molecular attraction. Quantitative changes occur over a certain range, and at critical points one trend predominates, and a change of state occurs. Taking the boiling of water as an example, one can describe it in terms of Mao's two stages. While the liquid is being heated the temperature rises, but all is outward calm. Then at the critical point the water is convulsed with bubbles, the temperature remains stationary, and the water changes into steam. When all the water has been changed to steam a new stage of 'relative rest' begins again and the temperature continues to rise as further heat is supplied.

Mao illustrates his argument with a large number of examples of contradictions, not all of them of the same kind. He devotes an important section of his essay to 'the particularity of contradiction' (Mao, 1966*b*, p. 35), pointing out the need for careful study of each particular case, and stressing that the solution of each type of contradiction will be different. Within the current Chinese situation he listed contradictions between 'all the oppressed classes . . . and imperialism; . . . between the great masses of the people and feudalism; . . . between the proletariat and the bourgeoisie; . . . between the peasantry and the urban petty bourgeoisie on the one hand and the bourgeoisie on the other, . . . [and] between the various reactionary ruling groups [themselves]' (Mao, 1966*b*, p. 38).

Not all of these contradictions exhibit the mutually determining property which has generally been taken to be a criterion of a dialectical contradiction. This is seen most clearly in the first example above. By definition the proletariat and bourgeoisie are mutually determined. One could not exist without the other. (Marx, 1942, p. 633). When Mao discusses this point (Mao, 1966*b*, p. 61) he does so in terms of subjective dialectics, of 'concepts in the human mind'. He begins by asserting 'that no contradictory aspect can exist in isolation. Without its opposite aspect, each loses the condition for its existence.' He gives as examples the opposites, life and death, above and below, misfortune and good fortune, and facility and difficulty.

Mao takes care to explain that opposites should not be taken as fixed, absolute or unchanging. On the contrary, they are 'conditional, mobile, temporary and relative; in given conditions, every contradictory aspect transforms itself into its opposite.' (Mao, 1966*b*, p. 64). He illustrates this by describing how the Guomindang changed from a progressive, revolutionary party to being counter-revolutionary in 1927, and then again became progressive to the extent that it fought the Japanese after the Xi'an incident of 1936. He predicts how in the coming revolution the old ruling landlord class would be overthrown and become the ruled, while the then ruled, 'the people', would become the rulers (ibid. p. 56). In this example both aspects of the contradiction turn into their opposites as the contradiction is resolved.

An important aspect of Mao's conception of contradiction is his distinction between the principal contradiction and various secondary contradictions within a complex process. Such a principal contradiction will 'determine or influence the existence and development of the other contradictions' (Mao, 1966*b*, p. 51). He gives as an example the contradiction between the proletariat and the bourgeoisie in capitalist society which affects the relations between all other conflicting groups.

Mao's ideas and European Marxism

Mao, who reads no foreign language, had to rely on second-hand accounts of Marxism and a very limited number of translations of Marxist works. Talking to Edgar Snow in 1936, he recalled the impression made on him by *The Communist Manifesto*, Kautsky's *Class Struggle*, and *A History of Socialism* by Kirkupp (Snow, p. 153). In his writings he refers specifically to Engels's *Anti-Duhring* and *Ludwig Feuerbach*, Marx's *Theses on Feuerbach*, Lenin's *Materialism and Empiriocriticism* (available to him only in an abridged edition), and two sections from Lenin's *Philosophical Notebooks*. According to V. Holubnychy (*China Quarterly*, no. 19, p. 16) only 4 per cent of all references and quotations in the four volumes of Mao's works refer to Marx and Engels, compared with 18 per cent for Lenin and 24 per cent for Stalin.

Lin Biao, speaking at a rally in Peking on 18 August 1966, claimed that: 'Mao Ze-dong's thought marks a completely new stage in the development of Marxism-Leninism.' This is not the place to argue about Mao's political leadership. That is well described and discussed elsewhere (*China Quarterly*, no. 1 & 2; Schram, 1963, etc.). So far as the elements of Mao's thinking which are relevant to education are concerned, they would seem to this writer to be a restatement of previous ideas, sometimes elaborated, but hardly improved upon. The essays *On Practice* and *On Contradiction* have the advantage over most of the writings of Marx and Engels that they are developed as positive arguments, rather than polemical attacks on others whose ideas are now only familiar to specialists (cf. Engels, 1962, or Marx & Engels, 1957 and 1964). And for the Chinese they have the advantage that they are put into a Chinese setting.

What is strikingly new in the writings of Mao is the repeated moral exhortation. This was lacking in the writings of Marx and Engels to such an extent that their ideas were widely regarded to be without any ethical criteria (Hook, 1962, p. 51). Both characteristics are deeply rooted in the writers' environments. Marx and Engels were determined to get away from abstract moralizing about rights and justice, and establish an ethics firmly based in the real, class-divided world (Hook, p. 51). Mao Ze-dong remains to some extent within the Chinese tradition which has always regarded moral instruction as its first duty.

Marx and Engels, like Mao, were primarily concerned with social and political questions. When they mentioned man, the individual, it was always in a historical, social context. They had no time for concepts of unchanging human nature. Man is the product of his environment, unique in the animal kingdom in his consciousness, and having the ability to change his surroundings, and himself, to the extent that he understands them.

Engels, in *Dialectics of Nature* writes: 'Man is the sole animal capable of working his way out of the merely animal state—his normal state is one appropriate to his consciousness, one that has to be created by himself.' (Engels, 1954, p. 262). And in the same book:

'Thus at every step we are reminded that we by no means rule over nature like a conqueror over a foreign people, like someone

17

standing outside nature—but that we, with flesh, blood and brain, belong to nature, and exist in its midst, and that all our mastery of it consists in the fact that we have the advantage over all other creatures of being able to know and correctly apply its laws.'

Marx links the individual and social in the *Economic and Philosophic Manuscripts of 1844*:

'. . . just as society itself produces man as man, so is society produced by him . . . Again when I am active scientifically etc., when I am engaged in activity which I can seldom perform in direct community with others, then I am social, because I am active as a man. Not only is the material of my activity given to me as a social product (as is even the language in which the thinker is active): my own existence is social activity, and therefore that which I make of myself, I make of myself for society, and with the consciousness of myself as a social being.' (Marx, 1959, p. 104).

The effect of membership of a particular class is mentioned by Engels in *Anti-Duhring*, where he quotes Marx's *Capital* on the crippling effect of the division of labour on the labourer, and then goes on to comment on members of other classes who are made 'subject . . . to the tool of their function' (Engels, 1962, p. 402).

Mao's conception of a society divided into conflicting classes is an application to China of the ideas he absorbed from *The Communist Manifesto*. Here he read: 'The history of all hitherto existing society is the history of class struggles', and the vision of the future is of a time when 'in place of the old bourgeois society, with its classes and class antagonisms, we shall have an association, in which the free development of each is the condition for the free development of all.'

Mao's ideas on the nature of knowledge were particularly influenced by Lenin and Engels. 'All ideas', wrote the latter, 'are taken from experience, are reflections—true or distorted—of reality' (Engels, 1962, p. 461). And Marx added: 'Social life is essentially practical. All mysteries which mislead theory to mysticism find their rational solution in human practice and in the comprehension of this practice.' (Marx & Engels, 1942, p. 354). Of crucial importance here is Marx's first thesis on Feuerbach, where he emphasizes the active role of the subject. Dialectical materialism was to embody the best of all previous philosophies, to unite the subject and its object in an active, ever-changing relationship in which neither was to be regarded as an absolute. (Hook, pp. 273–6). Throughout their writings Marx and Engels stress how relative is man's knowledge at each stage in his gradual understanding and mastery of nature, both his own nature and that outside of him.

Maos' conception of the two stages in the development of our knowledge is to be found in a less developed state in Lenin. Commenting on the plan of Hegel's *Dialectics*, Lenin wrote:

'First of all impressions flash by, then something emerges—afterwards the concepts of quality and quantity are developed. After that, study and reflection direct thought to cognition of identity—of difference— . . . all these moments [steps, stages, processes] of cognition move in the direction from the subject to the object, being tested in practice and arriving through this test at truth.' (Lenin, 1961, p. 319).

Elsewhere he wrote: 'From living perception to abstract thought, and from this to practice—such is the dialectical path of the cognition of truth, of the cognition of objective reality' (Lenin, 1961, p. 171).

The importance of the preconceptions which man brings into his attempts at perception was quite clearly recognized by Marx. In the *Economic and Philosophic Manuscripts of 1844* he wrote: 'The forming of the five senses is a labour of the entire history of the world down to the present', and he went on to give examples of the 'care-burdened man' who 'has no sense for the finest play', and 'the dealer in minerals' who 'sees only the mercantile value but not the beauty and the unique nature of the mineral' (Marx, 1959, pp. 108-9).

Much more important, but regrettably little known, is Marx's account of his theoretical method. He describes this in terms of a study of political economy, in a manuscript which was only found after his death and published much later (Marx, 1904, pp. 292-3). He describes what 'seems to be the correct procedure' for an investigation: 'to commence with the real and concrete aspect of conditions as they are.' He suggests taking the population of a country as the starting point of a study of its political economy. But, he warns, 'if we do, we do so with a chaotic conception of the whole, and by closer analysis we will gradually arrive at simpler ideas; thus we shall proceed from the imaginary concrete to less and less complex abstractions, until we get at the simplest conception. This once attained, we might start on our return journey until we would finally come back to population, but this time not as a chaotic notion of an integral whole, but as a rich aggregate of many conceptions and relations.'

Here is a much more fruitful description of the process of thinking than anything which Mao has provided.

The conception of contradiction used by Mao Ze-dong is a very ancient one in both the European and Chinese philosophical traditions. Marx himself wrote little which is explicit about it, but all his writing is soaked through with the concept. In an early work he commented: 'What constitutes dialectical movement is the co-existence of two contradictory sides, their conflict and their fusion into a new category' (Marx, 1892, p. 95). In *The Holy Family* he stresses the importance of seeking the causes of change within, rather than outside a process. 'The whole contradiction is nothing but the movement of both its sides, and the condition for the existence of the whole lies in the very nature of the two sides', he wrote. (Marx and Engels, 1957, p. 50).

Engels went further, and in *Dialectics of Nature* wrote:

Dialectics, so-called objective dialectics, prevails throughout nature, and so-called subjective dialectics, dialectical thought, is only the reflection of the motion through opposites which asserts itself everywhere in nature, and which by the continual conflict of the opposites and their final passage into one another, or into higher forms, determines the life of nature. (Engels, 1954, p. 280).

However, time did not allow Marx to write a projected work on dialectics (Hook, p. 61), and Engels concentrated more on other aspects of dialectics than the exact nature of contradiction. He argued at length against abstract, static views, as in this typical passage from one of his letters (Marx and Engels, 1942, p. 496).

What these gentlemen all lack is dialectics. They always see only here cause, there effect. That this is a hollow abstraction, that such metaphysical polar opposites exist in the real world only during crises, while the whole vast process goes on in the form of interaction—though of very unequal forces, the economic movement being by far the strongest, most primeval, most decisive— that here everything is relative and nothing absolute—this they never begin to see. Hegel has never existed for them.

Lenin, in his essay, *On the Question of Dialectics*, refers to 'the division of a unity into mutually exclusive opposites and their reciprocal relation'. (Lenin, 1961, p. 360). In his notes on Hegel's *Science of Logic* Lenin drew attention to the contradictions within phenomena. He noted 'the contradictory nature of the thing itself, the contradictory forces and tendencies in each phenomenon'; 'the internally contradictory tendencies (and sides) in this thing'; and 'the thing [phenomenon, etc.] as the sum and unity of opposites.' (Lenin, 1961, p. 221). Elsewhere he adds: 'Dialectics in the proper sense is the study of contradiction in the very essence of objects.' (ibid. pp. 253-4). (cf. Holubnychy, p. 30). Lenin also noted the point later developed by Mao: 'not only the unity of opposites, but the transition of every determination, quality, feature, side, property into every other [into its opposite?]' (ibid, p. 222).

These extracts are sufficient to show that Mao does not develop any essentially new ideas in his writings on contradictions, but that does not necessarily make them the less valuable. Some idea of how certain Chinese used the concept to solve practical problems is given by articles republished in the *Peking Review* in 1966 (*Peking Review*, nos. 17 and 21-5, 1966). While in a few cases the writers appear to have been strongly influenced by the idea of contradiction, mainly in its subjective form, in others it appears to have been added subsequently by the editors. What will be the result of prolonged and widespread teaching of this methodology in the schools remains to be seen. It cannot fail to be interesting.

Mao's ideas on education

Mao Ze-dong's writings are full of comments on education. Most of them are directed to Party members, or cadres. Only his first published work is directly concerned with education, and even here the aspect he chooses, physical education, is related to the political aim of strengthening the nation (Schram, 1963, pp. 94-102). But taken together his comments form a consistent view of the nature, purpose and methods of education which has not changed since Mao's early years. They are perhaps the more interesting because Mao is one of the few great political figures who has himself been a school-teacher.

Like all serious thinkers on education, Mao does not regard it as something to be confined within classroom walls, or practised only for a limited period of a person's life. Its purpose should be to enable people to develop morally, intellectually and physically (Mao, 1966*b*, p. 110) so they become 'well-educated worker[s] imbued with socialist consciousness'. Mao appears here to give equal emphasis to each aspect of education, but elsewhere he takes the more traditionally Chinese stand of putting moral-political education before all else.

While education is primarily conceived as moral-political, it is at the same time practical and social. An earlier section described the importance which Mao attaches to practice in man's struggle to gain knowledge. But practice is also the end to which knowledge must be applied. Mao castigates those party members who memorize passages from Marxist writings, without getting down to the job of solving current problems of the Chinese revolution (Mao, 1965, vol. 3, p. 19). 'It is necessary to master Marxist theory and apply it, master it for the sole purpose of applying it.' (Mao, 1966*a*, p. 307).

Education is social because while books are to be consulted, it is in social practice that man will correct his ideas and make them truly his own. 'Reading is learning, but applying is also learning and the more important kind of learning at that.' (Mao, 1966*a*, p. 308). Moreover, everyone must at the same time be a pupil and a teacher. This was developed in the revolutionary armies. 'Officers teach soldiers, soldiers teach officers, and the soldiers teach each other.' (Mao, 1966*a*, p. 168). It was also used in the literacy movement. The idea is emerging more strongly again as the Cultural Revolution draws to its close.

A large part of Mao's comments on education refer to methods of study. These are for the most part addressed directly to CCP members, and refer to political studies, but they might equally be applied to the school curriculum. The emphasis on problem-solving and a critical approach remind one of discussions nearer home. But in China they seem to be in conflict with the massive pressure for conformity. It remains to be seen how this contradiction will work out, and how seriously those in charge of education will attempt to apply this part of the Chairman's Thoughts.

Mao's clearest statement on the importance of problem-solving was contained in a speech he made at the opening of a Party school in 1942 (Mao, 1965, vol. 3, p. 38). There he spoke at length about the uselessness of reading Marxist works endlessly and not relating what was read to the current problems of the Chinese revolution, Chinese history, and Chinese economics. He recommended that the Party school should grade its students, not according to the amount read, but according to the success with which the student could solve Chinese problems. This appears in the *Quotations* as 'It is necessary to master Marxist theory and apply it . . . If you can apply the Marxist-Leninist viewpoint in elucidating one or two practical problems, you should be commended and credited with some achievement. The more problems you elucidate and the more comprehensively and profoundly you do so, the greater will be your achievement.' (Mao, 1966*a*, p. 307).

Mao deals at great length with the way in which problem-solving should be tackled. In a report to a cadres' meeting in 1941 he spoke of the need 'to study conditions conscientiously and to proceed from objective reality and not from subjective wishes' (Mao, 1965, vol. 3, p. 18). He cited Marx's method, 'to appropriate the material in detail and subject it to scientific analysis and synthesis', against people in the Party who paid 'no attention to the study of objective conditions, often rely on sheer enthusiasm and substitute their personal feelings for policy' (Mao, 1965, vol. 3, p. 21). In 1944, at a meeting of senior cadres in Yan'an (Yenan), to discuss certain questions of Party history, Mao returned to the same question. In order to learn from the past, and unite the Party leadership, errors were to be thoroughly examined: 'the content of the errors and their social, historical and ideological roots' (Mao, 1965, vol. 3, p. 164). Lenin was quoted approvingly for saying that the concrete analysis of concrete conditions was the soul of Marxism, and then Mao went on: 'Lacking an analytical approach, many of our comrades do not want to go deeply into complex matters, to analyse and study them over and over again, but like to draw simple conclusions which are either absolutely affirmative or absolutely negative.' He also castigated those cadres who 'the moment they alight from the official carriage' give their uninformed opinions on this and that (Mao,

1966*a*, p. 230). And as always in Mao, we return to the moral: 'Knowledge is a matter of science . . . what is required is . . . honesty and modesty.' (Mao, 1966*b*, p. 8).

Marxism for Mao is a method to be studied in order to learn how to solve problems. 'It is not just a matter of understanding the general laws derived by Marx, Engels, Lenin and Stalin from their extensive study of real life and revolutionary experience, but of studying their standpoint and method in examining and solving problems' (Mao, 1966*a*, p. 306). Lin Biao makes the same point when he says that Mao's works should always be read with problems in mind. It is the same with all book learning. It is the combination of reading and practice which matters. 'Those experienced in work must take up the study of theory and must read seriously', Mao advised in 1942. 'Only then will they be able to systematize and synthesize their experience and raise it to the level of theory, only then will they not mistake their partial experience for universal truth and not commit empiricist errors' (Mao, 1966*a*, p. 308).

Objective conditions are to be studied by using the eyes and ears, by carefully listening to what other people have to say, and then thinking about it. Quoting Mencius's saying: 'the office of the mind is to think', Mao went on to say: 'We should always use our brains and think everything over carefully. A common saying goes, "Knit the brows and you will hit upon a stratagem" ' (Mao, 1965, vol. 3, pp. 174–5). Elsewhere he wrote: 'Communists must always go into the whys and wherefores of anything, use their own heads and carefully think over whether or not it corresponds to reality and is really well founded; on no account should they follow blindly and encourage slavishness.' (Mao, 1965, vol. 3, pp. 49–50). All this is summed up in the often-quoted phrase: 'without investigation there is no right to speak' (Mao, 1965, vol. 3, p. 23).

But it is not enough to look and listen, and to ponder over what has been observed. It is necessary to learn by doing. Writing about military strategy in 1936 Mao said: 'A revolutionary war is a mass undertaking; it is often not a matter of first learning and then doing, but of doing and then learning, for doing is itself learning,' (Mao, 1966*a*, p. 309). In the conditions of the 1950s Mao developed this idea in relation to schooling. 'Qinghua University has factories', he observed. 'Social sciences can't have factories. Students of art, literature, economics, social sciences must take society as their factory; contact workers and peasants, know industry and agriculture, otherwise they are no use as graduates. Law students must understand criminals, how and why they are guilty' (Mao, 1967).

Mao's attitude to traditional Chinese studies, and to foreign learning is subject to his criterion of application. Writing in 1940 on 'a national, scientific and mass culture' in his long essay, *On New Democracy*, Mao argued for critical assimilation of whatever is useful to China. He described how it should be done. 'We should not gulp any of this foreign material down uncritically, but must treat it as we do our food—first chewing it, then submitting it to the working of the stomach and intestines with their juices and secretions, and separating it into nutriment to be absorbed and waste matter to be discarded' (Mao, 1965, vol. 2, p. 380). Similarly with the 'splendid old culture [which] was created during the long period of Chinese feudal society . . . To reject its feudal dross and assimilate its democratic essence is a necessary condition for developing our new national culture and increasing our national self-confidence'. But he went on to warn: 'As far as the masses and the young students are concerned, the essential thing is to guide them to look forward and not backward.'

The need to 'learn from the good experience of all countries, socialist or capitalist' was repeated in 1957, in a passage praising the help given to China by the USSR. But the succeeding paragraph attacks the 'doctrinaire attitude' of 'transplanting everything, whether suited or not to the conditions of our country', and advocates 'another attitude [which] is to use our heads and learn those things which suit conditions in our country.' In the light of more recent events these words take on a new force.

As will be obvious from what has been said earlier, Mao is in favour of student participation in the government of schools and colleges. One of the *Quotations* specifically mentions this. It is taken from an article written in 1943 in which Mao outlines 'methods of leadership' for the CC CCP, especially the relationship between a leading group and the masses. Referring to, in this case, party schools, he says: 'a school of a hundred people certainly cannot be run well if it does not have a leading group of several people, or a dozen or more, which is formed in accordance with the actual circumstances . . . and is composed of the most active, upright and alert of the teachers, the other staff and the students.' At the same time a quotation from an earlier document on the same page states: 'For a military school, the most important question is the selection of a director and instructors, and the adoption of an educational policy.' (Mao, 1966a, pp. 166–7).

Very important for the development of educational policy since 1949 has been Mao's attitude to the intelligentsia. His basic approach to the question was put in 1942 when he talked about 'half-intellectuals' who only had book learning. These could become full intellectuals only by taking part in practical work. (Compton, 1952, pp. 15–17). In 1957 Mao complained of slow progress in changing 'the world outlook' of the intelligentsia, and criticized Party members for being 'stiff with them, lack[ing] respect for their work, and interfer[ing] in scientific and cultural matters in a way that is uncalled for' (Mao, 1957, p. 42). He called for a mixture of patience and increased study of Marxism-Leninism. In the same year he called on propagandists to convince only by persuasion and not by constraint (Mao, 1966c, p. 25), a plea which appears to have fallen on somewhat deaf ears if these terms are to be understood in their normal sense.

Finally it is relevant to look at Mao's ideas on youth. Section 30 of the *Quotations* is devoted to this subject and begins with the words: 'The world is yours, as well as ours, but in the last analysis, it is yours' (Mao, 1966a, p. 288). Further on he describes youth's peculiarities. 'The young people are the most active and vital force in society. They are the most eager to learn and the least conservative in their thinking' (Mao, 1966a, p. 290). But he warns that while they should be given special treatment and help, 'of course, the young people should learn from the old and other adults, and should strive as much as possible to engage in all sorts of useful activities with their agreement' (Mao, 1966a, pp. 290–1). Years before, Mao has praised young people (Mao, 1965, vol. 2, p. 245) while at the same time praising the old for the experience they had to offer. In 1957 he also warned youth that China was still a very poor country, and would continue to be so for a long time. Hard work was required from old and young to change this state of affairs. 'Some of our young people think that everything ought to be perfect once a socialist society is established and that they should be able to enjoy a happy life, ready-made, without working for it', he said. 'This is unrealistic.' (Mao, 1966b, p. 110).

26

Finally let us briefly examine Marx's ideas on education. In the first volume of *Capital* he spoke of 'the education of the future, an education that will, in the case of every child over a given age, combine productive labour with instruction and gymnastics, not only as one of the methods of adding to the efficiency of production, but as the only method of producing fully developed human beings.' (Marx, 1965, vol. i, pp. 529–30). In *The Critique of the Gotha Programme* Marx again stressed the importance of productive work. '. . . with a strict regulation of the working time according to the different age groups and other safety measures for the protection of children, an early combination of productive labour with education is one of the most potent means for the transformation of present-day society.' (Marx, 1966a, p. 33). In the same work he commented that productive labour was the 'sole means of betterment' of prisoners (ibid, p. 34). Mao is thus firmly within the European Marxist tradition on this question.

Educational policies, 1949–1966

Mao's ideas on education had been developed well before the Communists swept into power in 1949, but it was impossible to implement them immediately. The rapid collapse of the Guomindang armies had brought an unexpectedly early victory, and the new government took over an educational system which had been trying for some fifty years to get to grips with the twentieth century and find itself an ethos and identity. Old traditions struggled with foreign ideas, and both largely failed in the face of the poverty and political confusion of the country. A majority of the leading educators had been educated abroad and brought back with them the ideas of their host country. John Dewey had himself spent just over two years in China during the important May 4th Movement period (Chow, 1960, p. 192), and had many students and followers in China.

Thus the predominant aims of the system which the Communists inherited were those of the West: a selective system, aiming eventually to be universal, led by experts to train experts at the higher levels. Its ethos was liberal, academic, and scholastic, and its products were in the main isolated from the life of the ordinary people, and had a deep dislike of getting their hands dirty. There were, of course, exceptions to this, but they did not alter the general picture.

The Communists brought with them a different conception of education, worked out in the Red Armies and at Yan'an (Yenan) (Snow, part 6, 5). The aims were limited, practical, and as closely related to ordinary life and the need of the moment as possible. Michael Lindsay gives the aims of Yan'an 'University' as follows:

> This school will carry on education combined with production, in order, through organized labour, to cultivate the students' constructive spirit, their habit of labour, and their labour viewpoint. The foundation of teaching in this school shall be self-study and collective mutual help. Teachers and students should join in study to secure the interpenetration of book learning and practical experience. At the same time, democracy in teaching should be developed in order to encourage the spirit of asking questions in difficulties and of keenness in discussion. The object is to cultivate the ability of independent thought and criticism. (Fraser, 1965, p. 79).

The Common Programme and the Constitution

In order to prepare the way for a formal system of government the CCP had proposed, on 1 May 1948, the setting up of a Political Consultative Conference. By 15 June 1949 they were able to announce the establishment of a preparatory committee, with 134 delegates from various small anti-Guomindang political parties and other groups. Representatives of the national minorities and various prominent individuals were included. (*Guide to New China*, 1952, pp. 7–16).

On 21 September 1949, 662 delegates to the first plenary session of the Chinese People's Political Consultative Conference met and adopted the Common Programme. This was a pro tem constitution which was not superseded until the formal constitution was adopted in 1954. A careful reading of the chapter on education and culture reveals all the important aspects of Mao's thinking on the subject. Emphasis is placed on the practical, on serving national construction work (art. 41, 43, and 47). Culture and education are to serve the people (art. 41 and 45). The 'public spirit' to be promoted is patriotic and labour loving (art. 42). And Mao's first publicly declared interest, physical culture, gets a mention in article 48.

By comparison with this detailed statement of aims, the Constitution adopted by the First National People's Congress five years later, on 20 September 1954 is a very vague document, only guaranteeing citizens the right to education of an unspecified kind in a gradually expanding system of 'schools of various types'. (Constitution, p. 41). In view of the difficulties which have been encountered in putting this programme into practice, and the clarity with which its aims were expressed, it is worth quoting the relevant articles from the Common Programme in full.

Chapter V.

Article 41. The culture and education of the People's Republic of China are new democratic, that is, national, scientific, and popular. The main tasks for raising the cultural level of the people are: training of personnel for national construction work; liquidating of feudal, comprador, Fascist ideology; and developing of the ideology of serving the people.

Article 42. Love for the fatherland and the people, love of labour, love of science, and the taking care of public property shall be promoted as the public spirit of all nationals of the People's Republic of China.

Article 43. Efforts shall be made to develop the natural sciences to place them at the service of industrial, agricultural, and national defence construction. Scientific discoveries and inventions shall be encouraged and rewarded, and scientific knowledge shall be popularized.

Article 44. The application of a scientific, historical viewpoint to the study and interpretation of history, economics, politics, culture, and international affairs shall be promoted. Outstanding works of social science shall be encouraged and rewarded.

Article 45. Literature and the arts shall be promoted to serve the people, to enlighten the political consciousness of the people, and to encourage the labour enthusiasm of the people. Outstanding works of literature and the arts shall be encouraged and rewarded. The people's drama and cinema shall be developed.

Article 46. The method of education of the People's Government shall reform the old educational system, subject matter, and teaching methods systematically according to plan.

Article 47. In order to meet the widespread needs of revolutionary work and national construction work, universal education shall be carried out. Middle [i.e. secondary] and higher education shall be strengthened; technical education shall be stressed; the education of workers during their spare time and the education of cadres who are at their posts shall be strengthened; and revolutionary political education shall be accorded to young intellectuals and old-style intellectuals in a planned and systematic manner.

Article 48. National sports shall be promoted. Public health and medical work shall be extended, and attention shall be paid to safeguarding the health of mothers, infants, and children.

Article 49. Freedom of reporting true news shall be safeguarded. The utilization of the press to slander, to undermine the interests of the State and the people, and to provoke world war is prohibited. The people's broadcasting work and the people's publication work shall be developed and attention paid to the publishing of popular books and newspapers beneficial to the people. (Fraser, pp. 83–4).

The last article, n. 49, brings up a problem which returns again and again as one studies the ideas of Mao Ze-dong. The intention is obviously one which a majority anywhere would consider right and good. But it is, one would have thought, equally obvious that criteria for the interpretation of key concepts like 'true news' and 'beneficial to the people' are highly subjective. The real problem begins where the truism ends, and it is here that bureaucratic hesitations can triumph.

Early conferences and plans

During 1949, 1950 and 1951 the new Chinese government held a whole series of national conferences on different aspects of education in order to try and put the recommendations of the Common Programme into practice. The first was held in December 1949, only two months after the Ministry of Education was set up. Finally, on 1 October 1951 the Government Administration Council of the Central People's Government issued the 'Decisions Concerning the Reform of the Educational System'.

The immediate task was to educate the vast number of administrators and technical people required to run the country. For the new rulers of China this meant much more than professional competence. Liu Shi, writing in People's China (Fraser, p. 129) said that secondary and higher education should be 'closely related to the construction needs of defence and production. They must train the personnel to carry out the tasks of national construction with a clear understanding of Marxism-Leninism and the teachings of Mao Ze-dong and of the various branches of knowledge.' Short courses were to be set up to provide secondary school education for ex-PLA men who formed the backbone of the new administrators. In 1950 the Chinese People's University was set up in Peking to train workers and peasants to be administrators. At the same time plans were made to reorganize higher education by 1952, to increase the number of engineering faculties, agricultural, teacher-training, and technical schools, to bring about a better distribution of these throughout the country.

Alongside this attempt to educate a new intelligentsia from the ranks of the workers and peasants, a movement was launched to re-educate the old intelligentsia. This was seen to be necessary before any radical alterations could be made in the educational system. Mao Ze-dong stressed its wider significance: 'Ideological reform—first of all the ideological reform of intellectuals—is one of the important conditions for our country's all-out complete democratic reform and gradual industrialization.' (Fraser, p. 122). Qian Zhun-rui, then Vice-Minister of Education, revealed another aspect when he talked of the intellectuals' subservience to Anglo-American culture, and their lack of faith in the 'creative and inventive power of the Chinese people' (Fraser, p. 123). Some idea of what this movement hoped to achieve can be gathered from this somewhat optimistic description given by the first Minister of Education, Ma Xu-lun, in a report he made in 1952:

'All teachers, wishing to contribute their best to the labouring people, in keeping with education in the Mao Ze-dong era, responded to Chairman Mao's call for ideological remoulding through self-education. They studied the new theory, examined the new method and viewpoint of education, and criticized their old ideology, viewpoint, and method. They learned to seek for truth, to correct errors by mutual- and self-criticism, to draw a clear demarcation between enemies and friends, and to define the ideological boundary between the working class and the bourgeoisie. Through this movement, the teachers' ranks were purified, and teachers now display much greater enthusiasm in their work.' (Fraser, pp. 133–4).

Zhou En-lai attempted a numerical assessment at a Communist Party meeting on intellectuals in 1956:

'. . . statistics show that among the higher intellectuals, about 45 per cent are progressive persons who actively support the Communist Party and the People's Government, actively support socialism, and actively serve the people. Another 40 per cent are the middle-of-the-road sort who support the Communist Party and the People's Government and generally can fulfil the tasks assigned them, but who are politically not sufficiently progressive. Together the above two groups constitute 80 per cent of all. Apart from them, a little over 10 per cent are backward persons who lack political consciousness or who ideologically oppose socialism.' (Fraser, p. 224).

The liquidation of private schools

The reorganization of higher educational institutions was accompanied by the taking over of the private schools and colleges by the Chinese government. This was the time of the Korean War, and the mass campaign in China 'to resist America; aid Korea'. Chinese funds abroad were frozen by the United States government, cutting off support from many foreign-run institutions. Thus the take-over became, according to the Vice-Minister of Education, 'not a simple administrative job, nor a matter of funds, but a most important political undertaking.' (Fraser, p. 102). It would lead Chinese youth, he said, 'to love their fatherland, love the people, support the Central People's Government, support Chairman Mao, eradicate their mistaken blind respect for Europe and America, rectify their sentiments of inferiority, establish their self-respect and self-confidence, and become active members for the reconstruction of New China' (Fraser, p. 101).

A number of prominent scholars, educated abroad like the Education Vice-Minister, Zeng Zhao-lun stood up and denounced 'imperialist cultural aggression'. Zhou Pei-yuan, Dean of Studies at Qinghua University, admitted to being 'deeply contaminated by the "above-politics" and "above-class" ideology of the bourgeoisie' (Fraser, p. 144), through his education abroad and long contact with foreigners. In theory a distinction was made between 'American imperialism and its agents' and 'the American people', possibly dupes, but potentially revolutionary. But in practice only a tiny handful of foreigners escaped criticism and fewer remained on to teach under the new system.

It was not only foreign-run schools which were taken over. Zhang Zung-lin describes others. '. . . about one hundred were schools under the monopolistic control of politicians paid by the reactionary government [the Guomindang] for their mutual struggle for privileges and profits and for their factional strife; and several dozens were "shop-style" [money-making] private universities.' (Fraser, p. 29).

By the end of 1952 it would appear that all private schools had been taken over, and many of the famous foreign universities had been combined and dismembered in the reorganization process. Descriptions of the last years and the parting of the ways, from the foreigners' points of view, are given in the series of college histories published by the United Board for Christian Colleges in China, and also by one who stayed on for a time, W. G. Sewell, in *I Stayed in China*.

What kind of universal education?

In the first six years after 1949 the emphasis was on short-term courses for officials and on technical education. Attempts were also made to tackle illiteracy. But so far as the school system was concerned little more than an attempt to unify and co-ordinate the existing system of primary and secondary schools, and increase their number, was attempted.

In July 1955, in a report on the first Five-Year Plan, Vice-Premier Li Fu-chun gave a number of indications of the developments to come. 'We are of the opinion', he said, 'that more ways should be found in order to satisfy adequately the cultural and educational demands of the people.' (NPC docs 6, p. 101). He spoke of a shortage of primary and secondary school places, and suggested that while the state would continue to expand the school system, the people themselves should take a hand and 'organize certain cultural and educational services such as primary schools, peasants' spare-time schools, amateur theatrical groups, etc.' He promised 'the state will give guidance to the work of such establishments, and wherever possible, assistance in personnel, funds and materials.' (ibid). This suggestion should be seen against section 8 of the report, which is entitled 'Practising Strict Economy'.

The economic limitations on extending education were to be mentioned by many others over the following decade. Lu Ding-yi, in April 1960, said:

> All students in our present senior middle [secondary] schools now are full manpower units. For this reason, we cannot afford to extend our present senior middle school education to too many persons. We are graduating only several hundred thousand students from senior middle schools each year. Even if greater efforts are exerted in this work, the best we can do will be to graduate a little over one million students from senior middle schools each year. Should we try to increase this number, we would take away too much manpower from production.

And he went on to speak in favour of a ten-year school system which would terminate at between sixteen and seventeen years of age (Hu, 1960, p. 140). Lu Ding-yi made the same point in 1958, when attacking 'the bourgeois pedagogues' and their opposition to schools run by non-specialists.

> The bourgeois pedagogues know that if education were run along these lines [only state-run and full-time] our country would find it very difficult to institute universal primary and secondary education and have no hope at all of instituting universal higher education, because the state has no way of carrying the huge burden of expenditures involved and, moreover, production would suffer serious losses. (Lu, 1958, p. 8).

But there is another aspect of this problem which is less frequently mentioned. While it is true that the demand for full-time education exceeded the supply, there was also an important group of people who did not see the value of the still academic education which was being provided. Lu Ding-yi admitted it implicitly when he argued in favour of new-type, part-work schools: 'To combine education with labour, *so that education will be warmly welcomed by the workers and peasants* (my emphasis), is an important way of arousing mass initiative in the setting up of schools.' (Lu, p. 24). As the part-work schools developed in the following years the comment that they 'paved the way for the popularization of education' was repeatedly made (cf. SCMP, 3481, 1965, national conference on rural part-work schools). The full-time system was often criticized by implication in such remarks as: 'They understand that study is not prompted by personal interests and a desire to glorify one's ancestors' (SCMP, 3538, 1965); or 'the old idea or habit regarding "a scholastic endeavour as the only most supreme career of all other careers in the world" is on the way out' (SCMP, 3332, 1964).

In 1958 the CC CCP and the State Council issued a directive in which they stated that 'education must fulfil its political role, must serve the cause of the proletariat, must be combined with productive labour, and finally it must be carried out under the leadership of the Party' (Hu, p. 148).

From that time onwards much more emphasis was placed on productive labour, both in the part-work schools which began to develop, and also in the full-time school system. Speakers on education spelled out the aims of education in terms of 'training new men with a Communist outlook' (Fraser, p. 311). Lu Ding-yi quoted Mao Ze-dong and then went on to expand the definition:

'Our educational policy must enable everyone who gets an education to develop morally, intellectually and physically and become a cultured, socialist-minded worker'. This is our educational principle of all-round development. 'A cultured, socialist-minded worker' is a man who is both politically conscious and educated. He is able to undertake both mental and manual work. He is what we regard as developed in an all-round way, both 'red' and 'expert'. He is a worker-intellectual and an intellectual-worker. (Lu, pp. 16-17).

Lu Ding-yi devotes a lot of his essay, *Education Must be Combined with Productive Labour* to a criticism of 'bourgeois educationists'. According to him 'most bourgeois pedagogues hold that only book knowledge is knowledge and that practical experience cannot be regarded as knowledge'; 'greater, faster, better and more economical results cannot obtain in education'; 'laymen cannot lead experts'; 'the Party does not understand education'; 'students must not criticize teachers'; 'according to the bourgeois educational principle of so-called "all-round development", education can only be led by experts; it does not need the leadership of the Communist Party, as the Communist Party is "a layman"'. Unfortunately only during the short '100 Flowers' period did the 'bourgeois educationists' get a chance to speak out for themselves. Then it was certainly true that they attacked the Party officials for being inexpert. For example, Zhu Ming-bi, Principal of Hubei Medical College said: 'Many problems that exist in the institutions of higher learning today are attributable to the inappropriateness of the Party committee system. The Party committee monopolizes everything, insisting on having a finger in every pie and yet knows very little about the business of teaching . . .' (MacFarquhar, 1960, p. 962). Chen Ming-shu said he 'hoped that unqualified Party members would be removed from their present positions in institutions of higher education'.

How much the attack on 'bourgeois educationists' is determined by principle, and how much by economic necessity it is impossible to say, but certainly the enormous extension of elementary education could not take place if professional standards and methods were relied on.

Minister of Education, Yang Xiu-feng, speaking to the second session of the second National People's Congress in April 1960, criticized the old system and put forward a list of recommendations for future implementation. In contrast to the slogan of the 'general line' he commented on 'the problems in our school system and pedagogical methods which cause our general educational programme to achieve smaller, slower, poorer, and less economical results.' He cited the 'unnecessarily long period of schooling—twelve years'; too many subjects and a lack of emphasis on the more important ones; and within the subjects themselves, poor selection of content. For example, the mathematics, physics and chemistry taught in the secondary school was out-of-date, and 'in no way represents the science and technology of today'. (Hu, p. 103). He referred to various experiments in different places in China, and went on to make the following suggestions: to cut the length of the school course to perhaps a five-year primary school course, or a ten-year primary-secondary course; to improve standards by transferring material then taught at higher institutions down to the secondary school; merging some subjects (e.g. history, geography and natural science in the primary school); and reforming the syllabuses of others; improving the teaching methods, especially by providing more time for independent work and discussion with the teacher outside formal classes; and making sure that a proper foundation in mathematics and languages was given first as these formed the basis of other subjects.

Speaking at the same Congress, Lu Ding-yi said:

> We stand for the necessity of discussion and experimentation in all new tasks. We hold that we should spend from ten to twenty years on the reform of the middle and elementary [secondary and primary] educational system, phase by phase, and stage by stage, without trying to achieve success in a hurry . . . We are not in a hurry to issue decrees governing the new schooling system to be adopted throughout our country. Even in the future when the new schooling system is adopted, a period will be granted for the people to implement it on a trial basis.

Yang Xiu-feng here voices a number of criticisms which were made during the Cultural Revolution of 1966, but many of his suggestions for syllabus reform would today probably be regarded as 'academic' and 'bourgeois'. Lu Ding-yi's position at the Congress was clearly that of the technical-managerial-minded.

While the slogans did not change during the next few years the emphasis on productive work and the development of part-work schools was played down. In December 1962 a system of privileged schools was established which were to be criticized in the Cultural Revolution as 'little treasure pagodas'. As a counter-thrust a number of articles appeared in 1964 on the problem of finding 'successors' who would guarantee that China would not change its 'political colour' (NPC docs, 6). But it would seem that, politically, events had reached a stage when the 'expert' and 'maoist' lines could no longer continue in partnership.

These, then, were the main arguments about policies and the major decisions taken since 1949. It is now necessary to consider in what way traditional ideas are an obstacle to education reform, and their relation to the ideas of Mao Ze-dong described in this chapter.

2

The Chinese tradition—
background to Mao's thoughts

The current struggle between Mao's group with its strong anti-authoritarian attitudes and his technical-managerial-minded opponents cannot be properly understood without some knowledge of China's history and traditional ideas. The present chapter will attempt to show to what extent Mao can be considered as firmly within the Chinese tradition, and to what extent traditional ideas may be obstacles to the realization of his aims. At the same time it is necessary to take account of the effect of China's contacts with the outside world during the past 130 years, including the relation of Mao's ideas to European Marxism.

China's history

This is not the place to go into detail about the long history of civilization in China, peculiar because of its continuity, great stability, and its ability to absorb a series of foreign conquerors. Rather, attention will be drawn to those events which seem to the writer to be particularly relevant to the present.

Chinese civilization developed in and spread out from the fertile valley of the Yellow River (Huang He) some three thousand years ago. The south was not really conquered before the first great unification under Chin Shi Huang Di in 246 B.C., and even then the control over the numerous tribal peoples who occupied these areas remained tenuous for a long time. Some of them remained obstinately outside the dominant Han culture right down to present times, but the Yangzi valley, and the region south to Canton has been firmly held from Han times.

At its greatest extent, under the Qing dynasty between 1760 and 1842, sovereignty was exerted over Korea and the area east of Manchuria to the coast opposite the island of Sakhalin in the north, and over Burma and much of Indo-China in the South. Tibet was included in the empires of Kublai Khan (Yuan dynasty), and in the Qing (Manchu) dynasty, but at other times it assumed a more or less independent status. In the north, China built and maintained the Great Wall to keep out the 'barbarian' horsemen. For many centuries Chinese ships sailed far into the Indian Ocean, and a few went much farther afield. But the typical Chinese attitude was perhaps reflected in the closing of the big shipyards and the prohibition of ships with more than three masts in the first two decades of the sixteenth century (Needham, quoted in Davidson, 1959, pp. 155-63). China, or the Middle Kingdom (*Zhong-guo*) as its inhabitants call it, was and remains today largely inturning. The great emigrations to S.E. Asia and America were largely forced, under the pressure of disasters and poverty, and were sometimes encouraged by direct foreign interference (cf. the English verb, to shanghai).

China's cultural stability was determined when a ruling scholarbureaucracy was set up in the Han. The Emperor's administrators, this class established an orthodox system of moral-political ideas, proficiency in which remained down the centuries the sole criterion for membership. Examinations, which in the nineteenth century inspired those of the British Civil Service (Dawson, 1964, p. 337), dominated intellectual life and inculcated a tradition of social advancement through academic success which is not dead even today.

While cultural continuity has been maintained, territorial unity has been repeatedly broken and re-established. Most recently, between the declaration of a republic in the revolution of 1911, and the unification of China under the Communists in 1949, great areas were under the control of different authorities. Nominally the country was governed by the Nationalists (Guomindang) under Jiang Jie-shi (Chiang Kai Shek) who held control of the south and west. Various warlords ruled in Peking, the north-east and north-west, except where they were replaced by the Japanese and their puppet governments. The Communists first held areas in the south, and then in the Long March of 1935, to Shǎnxi (Shensi) in the north-west.

Of tremendous importance in the shaping of contemporary China has been its traumatic contacts with the West, and with Japan.

China's defeat by Britain in the Opium War of 1840 is a convenient marker of the beginning of this period. It was followed by further military defeats involving Britain, France, and then Japan. It is significant that these new conquerors and invaders were not only militarily stronger, but also obviously culturally at least equal. This was in strong contrast to previous Chinese experience of invading horsemen, Mongol or Manchu, from the north. These humiliations, and the accompanying Taiping Rebellion and Boxer Uprising rent the fabric of Qing society. Some, like the reformer Kang Yu-wei, sought to strengthen the monarchy through combining Confucian morality with European military science, an approach which gave rise to the first modern schools in China (Teng and Fairbank, 1954; and Biggerstaff, 1961). But their efforts failed and the advocates of 'Mr. Science and Mr. Democracy' appeared who wanted to throw out Confucius and all that went with him. Grouped around such journals as the *New Youth* (*Xin Qingnian*), these men played a prominent part in education, and in the movement to bring literature and the spoken language together. The event which gave its name, the May 4th Movement, to this trend, was the student demonstration of 4 May 1919 against the government policy of subservience to Japan (Chow). Two prominent professors at Peking University, Chen Du-xiu and Li Da-zhao, respectively editor and contributor to *New Youth*, became founder members of the new Chinese Communist Party in 1921.

The years between 1927 and 1949 saw two periods of civil war between the Guomindang and the CCP, and the uneasy truce of 1936–45 when they formed a united front against the Japanese invader. The Guomindang suffered from incompetence and corruption which drove peasants, intellectuals and capitalists alike to accept the communists as the lesser evil. In October 1949 Mao Ze-dong proclaimed the People's Republic of China as a coalition of classes, a 'new democracy'.

Traditional philosophy

The ideas which will be examined in this chapter are those set down in writings which have been studied by the educated few during the past two and a half thousand years. In contrast to other parts of the world, they have been strongly secular, which characteristic also divides them from the ideas current among the common people. Something of the popular tradition can be learnt from a study of those novels whose tales have been the stock-in-trade of village story-tellers, novels like *Monkey*, *The Water Margin*, or *The Romance of the Three Kingdoms*. These and the myriad stories of spirits and ghosts, heroes and miracles, have always been frowned upon by the scholars and teachers, but they are well known to the most illiterate peasant. And while they contrast with the philosophy proper, they nevertheless contain much of its basic teaching.

At the core of the Chinese tradition are the writings which form the Confucian canon. They are usually grouped as the Five Classics (*Wu Jing*) and the Four Books (*Si Shu*). Tradition ascribes the authorship or editorship of most of them to Confucius, but in fact they are a collection of writings from widely different times. The Five Classics are the *Book of Changes* (*Yi Jing*), the *Book of History* (*Shu Jing*), the *Book of Poetry* or *Odes* (*Shi Jing*), the *Ritual*, especially the *Book of Rites* (*Li Ji*), and another historical work, the *Spring and Autumn Annals* (*Chun Qiu*). The Four Books include two chapters from the *Book of Rites*, 'The Great Learning' (*Da Xue*) and 'The Mean' (*Zhong Yong*), the *Analects* (*Lun Yu*) and the *Mencius* (*Mengzi*). The last two consist of sayings by Confucius and Mencius, recorded by their students. The Four Books were grouped together by the Song scholar, Zhu Xi, and were for six centuries (A.D. 1313–1905) used as school primers, to be recited and memorized, and as the basis of the civil service examinations which selected the bureaucracy (De Bary, 1960, p. 113).

Against these books, and the numerous commentaries and explanations which grew up around them, were other important philosophical works which did not feature in the official education. These included the Daoist works, the *Laozi* (*Dao De Jing*), and the *Zhuangzi*, and that of another early opponent of the Confucians, the *Mozi*. The Daoists, whose great contribution to the tradition lay in their concern with understanding Nature (Needham, vol. 2, p. 33), together with the Buddhist writings which began to appear in China in the first century A.D., paved the way for the great synthetic school in the Song, the Neo-Confucians (*Dao-xue-jia*). The ideas of this school, and especially of Zhu Xi, exerted a profound influence right down into the present century.

The discussion here will be confined to those topics which

particularly relate to education, or to Mao Ze-dong's ideas, and to those ideas which 'because of their frequent appearance in widely separated times and contexts, may fairly be regarded as basic in Chinese philosophical thinking' (Bodde in A. F. Wright, p. 19).

The nature of man

Like the European, the Chinese tradition has always been interested in the problem of the relationship of nature and nurture. As in Europe, it has been divided on the question of whether man is by nature good or bad, but the majority of Chinese thinkers have come down in favour of his being rather more good than bad.

Confucius said: 'by nature, men are nearly alike, by practice, they get to be wide apart' (*Analects*, 17.2). At the same time he classified people according to their nature and attitude to study:

> Those who are born with the possession of knowledge are the highest class of men. Those who learn, and so, readily, get possession of knowledge, are the next. Those who are dull and stupid, and yet compass the learning, are another class next to these. As to those who are dull and stupid and yet do not learn—they are the lowest of the people (*Analects*, 16.9).

Mencius is more explicit: man is by nature good. The question is discussed at length in Book 6. 'From the feelings proper to it, it is constituted for the practice of what is good. This is what I mean in saying that the nature is good' says Mencius. 'If men do what is not good, the blame cannot be imputed to their natural powers.' And later he adds: 'In good years the children of the people are most of them good, while in bad years the most of them abandon themselves to evil. It is not owing to any difference of their natural powers conferred by Heaven that they are thus different. The abandonment is owing to the circumstances through which they allow their minds to be ensnared and drowned in evil.' (*Mencius*, 6.1.7).

Xun Zi expressed very strongly the opposite point of view:

> Man's nature is evil; goodness is the result of conscious activity . . . any man who follows his nature and indulges his emotions will inevitably become involved in wrangling and strife, will violate the forms and rules of society, and will end as a criminal.

Therefore, man must first be transformed by the instructions of a teacher and guided by ritual principles . . . (*Xunzi*, p. 157).

In the Han, Dong Zheng-shu claimed that man was by nature both good and evil, while others believed that some are born good, others evil, and yet others a mixture of the two (e.g. Xun Yue and Wang Cheng). Except for Wang Cheng, so strong a believer in man's predetermination that only the embryo might be accessible to instruction (Needham, vol. 2, p. 383), Chinese thinkers, optimistic or pessimistic about man's natural goodness, all believed in the efficacy of education.

A marked feature of Chinese morals is its prescriptive, rather than descriptive emphasis. From early times to the Cultural Revolution of 1966 there have been models of the ideal man: *junzi; zhen-ren; sheng* or sage; or revolutionary. Their qualities have been listed and the assumption seems to have been that prescription is at least a step in the direction of practice.

Confucius profoundly influenced all subsequent thinking on this question. He took the old term *junzi*, which had meant 'son of the ruler', and redefined it in terms of moral superiority which could be acquired by all men. The character of the *junzi* was the possession of *ren*, a virtue in which the individual and the society were harmonized. 'The man of perfect virtue (*ren-zhe*), wishing to be established himself, seeks also to establish others; wishing to be enlarged himself, he seeks also to enlarge others' (*Analects*, 6.28.2). *Ren* is further defined in terms of conscientiousness (*zhong*) and altruism (*shu*). Altruism is the well-known precept: 'What you do not want done to yourself, do not to others' (*Analects*, 15.23).

The *Analects* and the *Mencius* contain numerous references to the qualities of the *junzi*. 'The *junzi* in everything considers righteousness to be essential. He performs it according to the rules of propriety. He brings it forth in humility. He completes it with sincerity' (*Analects*, 15.17). 'In his conduct of himself, he was humble; in serving his superiors, he was respectful; in nourishing the people, he was kind; in ordering the people, he was just' (ibid, 5.15) 'The faults of the *junzi* are like the eclipses of the sun and moon. He has his faults, and all men see them; he changes again, and all men look up to him' (ibid, 19.21). 'To take example from others to practise virtue, is to help them in the same practice. Therefore, there is no attribute of the *junzi* greater than his helping men to practise virtue' (*Mencius*, 2.1.8). While the state is naturally conceived in authoritarian terms, the ruler is expected to be humane, and always considerate of the people's interests. One example of this comes in the *Mencius*, which discusses the territorial claims of the state of Lu. 'If it were merely taking the place from the one State to give it to the other, a benevolent man would not do it; how much less will he do so, when the end is to be sought by the slaughter of men!' (ibid, 6.2.8). Confucius emphasized the importance of uprightness. 'Man is born for uprightness. If a man lose his uprightness (*zhi*) and yet live, his escape from death is the effect of mere good fortune' (*Analects*, 6.17). Mencius emphasized a similar quality, sincerity (*cheng*). 'Sincerity is the way of Heaven . . . Never has there been one possessed of complete sincerity, who did not move others. Never has there been one who had not sincerity who was able to move others' (*Mencius*, 4.1.12).

For the Daoists, who turned their backs on the struggle for office, the *zhen-ren* was a man in harmony with the Dao—the Way. 'He who knows what it is that Heaven does, and knows what it is that man does, has reached the peak' says the *Zhuangzi* (p. 73). And it goes on: 'The *zhen-ren* of ancient times did not rebel against want, did not grow proud in plenty, and did not plan his affairs. Being like this, he could commit an error and not regret it, could meet with success and not make a show . . . His knowledge was able to climb all the way up to the Way like this.' (ibid). Commenting on the *Laozi*, Fung Yu-lan says:

> One should know the laws of nature and conduct one's activities in accordance with them. . . . The man who lives prudently must be meek, humble and easily content. To be meek is the way to preserve your strength and so be strong. Humility is the direct opposite of arrogance, so that if arrogance is a sign that a man's advancement has reached its extreme limit, humility is a contrary sign that the limit is far from reached. And to be content safeguards one from going too far, and therefore from reaching the extreme. *Laozi* says: 'To know how to be content is to avoid humiliation; to know where to stop is to avoid injury' (Fung, 1948, pp. 99–100).

Wing-Tsit Chan draws attention to a passage in the *Zhuangzi* in which the qualities of tranquillity and activity are equally stressed, and the value of the Daoist qualities to a ruler are asserted. 'Vacuity, tranquillity, mellowness, quietness, and taking no action are the root of all things. To understand them and to rule with them was how Yao was an emperor, and to understand them and to serve with them was how Shun was a minister. These are the virtues of rulers and emperors when they manage things above . . . In tranquillity he [a person] becomes a sage, and in activity he becomes a king.' (Chan, 1963, pp. 208–9).

The Buddhists, with the emphasis on the avoiding of inevitable sorrow through the abandonment of desires, shared a great many attitudes with the Daoists. A famous Mahayanist text prescribes: 'Renounce absolutely the good things of this world; bear difficulties with patience; always have the desire to devote yourselves to the good of others; aim always at the most perfect—with others, be gentle, compassionate, disinterested, generous . . .' (Wieger, 1927, p. 429). But always with the Buddhists the aim was spiritual salvation, and the emphasis was on the other-worldly, whereas the main stream of Chinese thought was concerned with the rules of conduct in and for the world of men.

The Neo-Confucians of the Song returned to the same themes on a new basis. For them the sage (*sheng*) was one who acted in accordance with the universal pattern, with *li*, or principle. Zhou Dun-yi wrote: 'The sages ordered their lives by the Mean, by the Correct, by Love and Righteousness . . . Thus it was that "the virtue of the sages was in harmony with that of heaven and earth". . .' (Needham, vol. 12, p. 462, cf. Chan, 1967, p. 6). Cheng Hao wrote: 'The constant principle of the sage is that his feelings are in accord with all creation . . .' (Chan, 1967, p. 40). When the Neo-Confucians developed their ideas about the qualities which the sage should possess they stressed the two which Mao Ze-dong stresses: unselfishness and devotion to the people's welfare. The *Jin Si Lu* has many passages stating how selfishness prevents a person from acting in accordance with principle. 'Basically there should be no selfish desires but only accordance with principle' (Chan, 1967, p. 128). Zhu Xi wrote: 'Whenever one can reach the point of completely eliminating his selfish desires so that the Principle of Nature will operate, there is humanity' (ibid, p. 139). Selfishness was linked with

E   45

having desires, but Zhu Xi commented that this meant those of the wrong kind. 'Having few desires refers to those desires that are improper, such as selfish desires. As to the desire for food when hungry and the desire for drink when thirsty, how can one be without them?' (ibid, p. 155). Mao, calling for abstinence and hard work, raises similar problems about the exact definition of 'selfish'.

'The purpose of setting up a ruler of the people', states the *Jin Si Lu*, 'is for him to support and maintain them' (Chan, 1967, p. 210). 'The king must be like a parent, loving the people like his own children' (ibid, p. 216). And again the ancient Confucian principle, still to be found today in Mao's teachings, that the ruler should set an example to his people, is strongly emphasized. 'If the ruler is humane, all will be humane' (ibid, p. 215).

Finally one should note that the sage was not conceived as the almost unrealizable exception, the man born to be king. With the right education anyone could be a sage. 'The essential training should be the way of choosing the good and cultivating the self until the whole world is transformed and brought to perfection so that all the people from the ordinary person up can become Sages' (ibid, p. 219).

This profound belief in the perfectibility of the common man which is so characteristic of the Chinese tradition, leads us to consider what Fung Yu-lan believes to be China's great contribution to world philosophy: methods of self-cultivation (Fung, 1937, p. 3). It is first set out in the *Da Xue* or *Great Learning*, where its social setting will be noted.

The ancients who wished to illustrate illustrious virtue throughout the kingdom, first ordered well their own states. Wishing to order well their states, they first regulated their families. Wishing to regulate their families, they first cultivated their persons. Wishing to cultivate their persons, they first rectified their hearts. Wishing to rectify their hearts, they first sought to be sincere in their thoughts. Wishing to be sincere in their thoughts, they first extended to the utmost their knowledge. Such extensions of knowledge lay in the investigation of things. (*Da Xue*, 4).

While differing sharply from the Confucians in aims and methods, the Daoists were also concerned with self-cultivation, or 'self-transformation' as Wing-Tsit Chan calls it (Chan, 1963, p. 178).

The *Laozi* deals at length with the qualities of those who understand the Dao, men of superior virtue, and sages, and (ch. 37) suggest that by power of example rulers will be able to transform the people: '. . . if kings and barons can keep it, all things will transform spontaneously' (Chan, 1963, p. 158). The *Laozi* also has the same chain, from individual through the family to the wider world, as the *Da Xue*. Virtue cultivated at each link has a greater extension, (ch. 54). But the explicit dependence of one stage on another is missing. The emphasis seems to be more on allowing each to follow its own nature.

The *Zhuangzi* has a number of passages which deal with self-cultivation, among them the supposed conversation between Yan Hui and Confucius, (*Zhuangzi*, pp. 86–7). Yan Hui describes how his is 'improving' by forgetting benevolence, righteousness, rites and music, categories beloved by the Confucians. He ends by saying: 'I smash up my limbs and body, drive out perception and intellect, cast off form, do away with understanding, and make myself identical with the Great Thoroughfare. This is what I mean by sitting down and forgetting everything.' The *Huai Nan Zi* discusses perfecting human nature by controlling the emotions, 'in imitation of the Principle' (Wieger, p. 294). Wang Bi, a neo-Daoist, emphasizing the universality of the Dao, says: 'one may know the world without going out of doors or looking through the windows . . . If we know the general principle of things, we can know through thinking even if we do not travel.' (Chan, 1963, p. 324). While yet another Daoist, Guo Xiang, commenting on the *Zhuangzi* in the first half of the third century A.D., says of 'the fundamentals for the cultivation of life' that 'if one attains the Mean and intuitively realizes the proper limit, everything can be done. The cultivation of life does not seek to exceed one's lot but to preserve the principle of things and to live out one's allotted span of life' (De Bary, vol. 1, p. 245).

The Buddhists went even further than the more mystical of the Daoists, and their form of self-cultivation consisted of an attempt to kill desire in order to escape from an endless cycle of birth and death. Techniques varied from one school to another but usually consisted of meditation and inward soul-searching uncharacteristic of the main streams of Chinese thought.

The Neo-Confucians took up and greatly developed the idea of self-cultivation. Their approach to this question is one of the factors dividing them into the two wings, the rationalistic school of Principle, and the idealistic school of Mind, though many ideas were common. Lu Xiang-shan, in the latter school, believed with Cheng Yi, in an innate knowledge of good, and that the way to wisdom was through examination of one's own self (Chan, 1963, p. 548). Zhu Xi, the great rationalist, developed the idea of investigating things and extending knowledge. He devoted great attention to the relation between knowledge and action (ibid, pp. 609–11). 'There is no other way to investigate principle to the utmost than to pay attention to everything in our daily reading of books *and handling of affairs* (my emphasis). He goes on: 'To investigate principle to the utmost means to seek to know the reason for which things and affairs are as they are and the reason according to which they should be, that is all. If we know why they are as they are, our will will not be perplexed, and if we know what they should be, our action will not be wrong' (ibid, p. 611). Particularly interesting is his remark: 'As one knows more clearly, he acts more earnestly, and as he acts more earnestly, he knows more clearly' (ibid, p. 609). But action must be directed by previous knowledge, and 'extensive study, accurate inquiry, careful thinking, clear sifting and vigorous practice' are all equally important. (Chan, 1963, p. 609, cf. The Doctrine of the Mean, ch. 20).

We have seen above (p. 10) that the Chinese Communists have used several terms with underlying meanings similar to those just discussed: rectification (*zhengfeng*); ideological self-cultivation (*sixiang gaizao*); and remoulding (*gaizao*). During the Cultural Revolution Liu Shao-qi's book, *How to be a Good Communist*, was strongly criticized on the grounds that he was advocating a selfish form of self-cultivation. According to some criticisms he was supposed to have advocated self-examination in isolation from revolutionary practice, and to have really defended self-interest and careerism (e.g. NCNA, 7 April 1967). Mao prefers the terms rectification and remoulding, and always emphasizes the social nature of the activity.

What has been new to China, and anti-traditional, has been the emphasis on public heart-searching involving a painful loss of 'face'. Traditionally self-criticism was expected, but only in a way which would carefully preserve the dignity of all concerned. Present self-criticism, especially in its more violent form of 'struggle meetings', robs all who participate of their dignity, and opens the way for insincerity and other vices condemned in words, by traditional philosophers, and Mao Ze-dong alike.

The nature of Society

Needham (vol. 2, p. 270) draws attention to a statement by Granet, that 'Chinese thought refused to separate Man from Nature, or individual man from social man'. Earlier he quotes Xun-zi, who distinguishes man from other animals thus: 'Man is able to form social organizations and they are not', a quality he thinks possible because of man's possession of justice and righteousness (Needham, vol. 2, p. 23).

The traditional view of society is dominated by the Confucian concept of filial piety. 'A youth, when at home should be filial, and, abroad, respectful to his elders' (*Analects*, 1.6). 'Filial piety and fraternal submission—are they not the root of all benevolent actions?' (ibid, 1.2). 'While a man's father is alive, look at the bent of his will; when his father is dead, look at his conduct. If for three years he does not alter from the way of his father, he may be called filial' (ibid, 1.11). Government, self-cultivation and education were all linked with filial piety:

Hence the sovereign may not neglect the cultivation of his own character. Wishing to cultivate his character, he may not neglect to serve his parents. In order to serve his parents, he may not neglect to acquire a knowledge of men. In order to know men he may not dispense with a knowledge of Heaven. The duties of universal obligation are five, and the virtues wherewith they are practised are three. The duties are those between sovereign and minister, between father and son, between husband and wife, between elder brother and younger, and those belonging to the intercourse of friends. Those five are the duties of universal obligation. Knowledge, magnanimity, and energy, these three, are the virtues universally binding (Doctrine of the Mean, 20.7 and 8).

The aged and the male are exalted; the duty of the young and the female is to serve.

This patriarchal view of society was strongly developed by the Legalists, a group whose ideas assisted the first unification of China in 221 B.C. They advocated clearly written laws to be enforced by severe punishments and mutual spying and denouncing by groups of five families (Wieger, p. 240). Some Chinese have wryly commented that while such extreme ideas have been denounced by subsequent thinkers, governments have often practised Legalism while publicly preaching the milder doctrines of Confucianism.

An important corollary of these principles was the idea sloganized during the recent Cultural Revolution as: 'To rebel is justified'. Perhaps the most famous expression of this idea is in the *Mencius* (1.2.8), where the killing of the tyrannical Shang king, Zhou, is excused on the grounds that his behaviour had reduced him to the rank of an ordinary man. 'I have heard of the cutting off of the fellow Zhou, but I have not heard of the putting a sovereign to death, in his case'. Similar views were expressed earlier. The *Guo Yu* discusses the killing of Duke Li by the people of Jin. 'The Duke said: "When a subject has killed his ruler, whose is the blame?" None of the great officials made reply, but Li Guo said: "It is the fault of the ruler . . . If with evilness he supervises the people, he will fall and be unable to get up. And if he is unwilling to employ the virtuous exclusively, he will find himself unable to employ anyone. When such (a ruler) comes to his doom there is no one to mourn for him, and of what good then is he?"' (Fung, 1937, p. 41).

Similarly in the *Zuo Zhuan*:

> Zhao Jian-zi asked the historian Mo, saying: 'The head of the Ji family expelled his ruler, yet the people submitted to him and the feudal lords assented to what he had done . . .' Mo replied: . . . 'The rulers of Lu have, one after another, followed their mistakes, and the heads of the Ji family have, one after another, diligently improved their position. The people have forgotten their ruler, so that, though he has died abroad, who pities him? The altars of the grain and soil are not always maintained (by the same ruler), and the positions of rulers and ministers are not ever unchanging . . .' (Fung, 1937, pp. 41–2).

The theme of the righteous rising against their unrighteous rulers has been the subject of much popular fiction, including *The Water Margin*. (Needham, vol. 2, pp. 130–1).

An important Chinese political concept is that of *wu-wei*, which literally means 'without action'. This is fundamentally a Daoist term, but the concept has been accepted by Confucians and even Legalists. Wing-Tsit Chan draws attention to two passages in Confucius where the idea of good government being a state in which the ruler does not have to act occurs. Both are from the *Analects*.

> Book 2, chapter 1. Confucius said, 'A ruler who governs his state by virtue is like the north polar star, which remains in its place while all the other stars revolve around it.'
> Book 15, chapter 4. Confucius said, 'To have taken no (unnatural) action and yet have the empire well governed, Sun was the man! What did he do? All he did was to make himself reverent and correctly faced south (in his royal seat as the ruler).' (Chan, 1963, pp. 22 and 43).

In the latter passage the word *wu-wei* is used.

Describing the Daoist attitude, the editors of *Sources of Chinese Tradition* point out that 'the sage is not one who withdraws into the life of a hermit, but a man of social and political achievements, although these achievements must be brought about through *wu-wei*, 'non-action' or 'taking no (unnatural) action'. (De Bary, vol. 1, p. 240). Needham (vol. 2, p. 68) argues against previous translators who have translated *wu-wei* simply as 'non-action' or 'inactivity' and himself prefers 'refraining from activity contrary to Nature'. He quotes from the *Huai Nan Zi* in support of this:

> What is meant, therefore, in my view, by *wu-wei*, is that no personal prejudice (or private will) interferes with the universal Dao, and that no desires and obsessions lead the true course of techniques astray. Reason must guide action, in order that power may be exercised according to the intrinsic properties and natural trends of things. (Needham, vol. 2, pp. 68–9).

Later (Needham, vol. 2, p. 576) Needham joins Wang Cheng (Chan, 1963, pp. 298) in recounting the famous story from the *Mencius* of the man of Song who pulled his corn to help it grow long, only to find it lying dead next morning. Needham suggests 'the conception of *wu-wei* [is] deeply congruent with peasant life'. The present writer is reminded of the Hegelian-Marxist idea of the relationship between freedom and necessity discussed by Engels in chapter 11 of *Anti-Duhring*: freedom as the consciousness of necessity, and the Marxist emphasis on the need to study the world 'free from pre-conceived idealist fancies' (Engels, 1936, p. 451) in order to be able to change it.

Finally, let us look at an alternative interpretation of some of the Daoist writings. These have always been regarded as highly mystical, with an emphasis on withdrawal which grew stronger with time. Zhu Xi commented on this when he said: 'Laozi still wanted to do something. But Zhuangzi did not want to do anything at all. He even said that he knew what to do but just did not want to do it' (Chan, 1963, p. 178).

Needham (vol. 2, pp. 104–21) suggests that rather than being mystical, many of these passages should be interpreted as political opposition to a class-divided society, and a harping back to a more homogeneous, collective society, such as there had been in the distant, tribal past, and was still among the 'barbarian' surrounding peoples.

The difficulty here is the common one of translation: to know what the writer is talking about! Needham admits (ibid, p. 109, footnote) that some of the translations he uses here 'may easily be considered rather "forced"', but argues for the need to redress a balance. Certainly in the light of modern Marxism these passages are tempting.

But whatever the original meaning of these passages was, they have not been traditionally regarded in this proto-Marxist way, and can have played no part in preparing the Chinese for Marxism. Communist protest has grown out of the conditions of the past century, and has been inspired by the history of peasant revolts, so often in the past Daoist-led.

The nature of knowledge

The discussions of epistemology and logic familiar to students of European philosophy were confined in China to such groups as the Moists, Logicians, and the Buddhists (Fung, 1937, p. 3). While their ideas are extremely interesting, they are not so central to the theme of this book as to warrant description here. Those interested should consult such works as Needham (vol. 2, pp. 165–204) or an early book on the subject by Hu Shih.

In the long history of Chinese thought the dominant Confucian trend has concerned itself with knowledge as knowledge of human society, of moral and political problems. Within this sphere there has been an almost equal emphasis on knowledge and action (Chan, 1963, p. 19), but with action considered as an end of knowledge rather than its source. With the exception of certain outstanding thinkers, the result has been an over-dependence on book-learning, and on observation and reflection, rather than active experiment (Chan, 1963, p. 611).

In the *Mencius* the essential knowledge, of love for parents and one's elder brother, is regarded as intuitive: 'The ability possessed by men without having been acquired by learning is intuitive ability, and the knowledge possessed by them without the exercise of thought is their intuitive knowledge' (*Mencius*, 7.1.15). Confucius sought such knowledge among the ancients: 'The Master said, "I am not one who was born in the possession of knowledge: I am one who is fond of antiquity, and earnest in seeking it there"' (*Analects*, 7.19).

To this knowledge of 'the distinctions between princes and grooms' (Needham, vol. 2, p. 87) the Daoists opposed the true knowledge of the Dao, and of Nature. Chapter 65 of the *Dao De Jing* is one of a number of passages which Needham uses to illustrate their attitude:

> In olden times the best practisers of the Dao
> Did not use it to awaken the people to 'knowledge',
> But to restore them to 'simplicity'.
> People with much 'knowledge' are difficult to govern,
> So to increase the people's 'knowledge' is to destroy the country.

. . . In spite of promising beginnings the Daoists did not pursue the path of the development of natural science, but became side-tracked into religious mysticism (Needham, vol. 2, p. 162).

Much of the discussion in China about the nature of knowledge has centered around a sentence in the *Da Xue*: 'such extension of knowledge lay in the investigation of things' (*Da Xue*, text, paragraph 4). As many as seventy-two different interpretations of the key term, *ge-wu*, have been put forward since the Han, all of them ethical, and almost all of them stressing that knowledge is to be achieved by the mind without the aid of external things (Chan, 1963, p. 562). Cheng Yi and Zhu Xi, while retaining the ethical approach, turned to the investigation of principle (*li*) in 'everything in our daily reading of books and handling of affairs' (Chan, 1963, p. 610). Zhu Xi explained: 'To investigate principle to the utmost means to seek to know the reason for which things and affairs are as they are and the reason according to which they should be, that is all' (Chan, 1963, p. 611). Needham notes the flowering of the pure and applied sciences which accompanied this kind of thinking in the Song (Needham, vol. 2, pp. 494–5).

Zhu Xi clearly stated the importance of practice. 'Knowledge and action always require each other . . . With respect to order, knowledge comes first, and with respect to importance, action is more important' (Chan, 1963, p. 609). He also pointed out: 'As one knows more clearly, he acts more earnestly, and as he acts more earnestly, he knows more clearly' (ibid, p. 609). Still clearer is: 'When one knows something but has not yet acted on it, his knowledge is still shallow. After he has experienced it, his knowledge will be increasingly clear, and its character will be different from what it was before' (ibid). This point was taken up by Wang Yang-ming, who warned that knowledge and action could be separated by selfish desires. He said that people 'must have actually practised filial piety and brotherly respect before they can be said to know them . . . Or take one's knowledge of pain. Only after one has experienced pain can one know pain' (ibid, p. 669). Mao makes the same point, using the old example of tasting the pear (Mao, 1966*b*, p. 8). Yan Yuan, attacking the scholastic degeneration of the Neo-Confucians of the Ming, makes the same point again. 'Even if he reads a book on the rules of propriety hundreds of times . . . he cannot be considered to know them at all. He simply has to kneel down, bow, . . . and go through all these himself before he knows what the rules of propriety really are. Those who know propriety in this way know them perfectly' (ibid, p. 708).

An aspect of the subject which is treated in the tradition, but which Mao perhaps somewhat neglects is the effect of various kinds of prejudice. In the *Da Xue* this is mentioned in chapters 7 and 8 in connection with cultivating the person and rectifying the mind. The emotions, such as passion, terror, or family love are seen as causes of prejudice. Another interesting comment on the problem is quoted by Needham, from a work by the Song scholar, Lin Jing Xi. It refers to the Daoist concept of 'the empty mind' (*xu xin*):

Scholars of old time said that the mind is originally empty, and only because of this can it respond to natural things without prejudices. Only the empty mind can respond to the things of Nature. Though everything resonates with the mind, the mind should be as if it has never resonated, and things should not remain in it. But once the mind has received (impressions of) natural things, they tend to remain and not to disappear, thus leaving traces in the mind. It should be like a river gorge with swans flying overhead; the river has no desire to retain the swan, yet the swan's passage is traced out by its shadow without any omission. (Needham, vol. 2, p. 89).

Finally it is important to note that in linking knowledge and action the Chinese have always considered, as Mao does today, that the latter is a necessary consequence of the former. As Wang Yang-ming clearly put it: 'There have never been people who know but do not act. Those who are supposed to know but do not act simply do not yet know.' (Chan, 1963, p. 669).

Dialectics

Here we must turn our attention to the important question of the widely noted similarities between certain very ancient and recurring Chinese ideas and the idea of dialectics found in modern Marxism. Mao Ze-dong himself makes a number of references to it. In *On Contradiction* he comments that 'the dialectical world outlook emerged in ancient times both in China and Europe . . . [but] was not yet able to form a theoretical system . . .' (Mao, 1966*b*, p. 29). In the same essay he refers to examples in the novel, *The Water Margin*, in the military writings of Sun Wu-zi, and in other popular works. Holubnychy comments: 'The importance of all this lies in the fact that Mao is able to find a source for his dialectics even in the comparatively simple and popular products of the Chinese thought and culture, so much are they really dialectical.' (Holubnychy, p. 15). Mao's only reference to dialectics in the classical philosophical literature is to the *Laozi*, when in *On the Correct Handling of Contradictions Among the People* he discusses 'can bad things be turned into good things', and quotes: 'Good fortune lieth within bad, bad fortune lurketh within good' (*Laozi*, ch. 58).

There is wide agreement among writers that traditional philosophy contains many examples of the kind of relative thinking used by Marx and described by Engels. Needham, comparing the

Zhuangzi and Hegel, says that 'both would have subscribed to the view of change as eternal, and reality as process' (Needham, vol. 2, p. 77). Zhang Dong-sun remarks that Chinese logic is not based on the law of identity, but emphasizes the relational quality between opposites. He calls it 'correlation-logic' or the 'logic of correlative duality', or to 'be in vogue', 'dialectical logic' (Chang Tung-sun, 1939). Needham quotes Whitehead on the negative value of Aristotelian logic and goes on:

> . . . it provided the natural sciences with an inadequate tool for the handling of the greatest fact of Nature, so well appreciated by the Daoists, Change. The so-called laws of identity, contradiction, and the excluded middle, according to which X must be either A or not-A, and either B or not-B, were constantly being flouted by the fact that A was palpably turning into not-A as one watched, or else showed an infinite number of gradations between A and not-A, or else indeed was A from some points of view and not-A from others. The natural sciences were always in the position of having to say 'it is and yet it isn't'. Hence in due course the dialectical and many-valued logics of the post-Hegelian world. Hence the extraordinary interest of the traces of dialectical or dynamic logic in the ancient Chinese thinkers, including the Moists . . . (Needham, vol. 2, p. 201).

In describing this type of thinking as 'a philosophy of organism' Needham (vol. 2, p. 458) is not alone. Derk Bodde sums up the Chinese view using the same term: '. . . the universe, in Chinese eyes, is a harmonious organism; that its pattern of movement is inherent and not imposed from without; and that the world of man, being a part of the universe, follows a similar pattern' (Wright, 1953, p. 36). Professor Schwartz seems to concur in general terms, but objects to a comparison with Whitehead's system 'with its enormous pluralistic emphasis on the reality and value of particular "actual entities"' (Schwartz, 1964, p. 53).

Within this relational thinking there is a strong emphasis on opposites. The Neo-Confucian, Cheng Hao wrote: 'According to the Principle (*li*) of Heaven and Earth and all things, nothing exists in isolation but everything necessarily has its opposite. All this is naturally so and is not arranged or manipulated. I often think of this at midnight and feel as happy as if I were dancing with my hands and feet' (Chan, 1967, p. 22). Zhu Xi goes on to comment: 'As there is the high, there is the low, and as there is the large, there is the small. This is true because of principle. In the things produced by Heaven, there cannot be *yin* alone; there must also be *yang* . . . There must be opposition. In this opposition it is not principle that opposes, but according to principle there should be opposition like this' (ibid). Earlier Zhang Zai had written: 'As it [material force— *qi*] is acted upon, it engenders the two fundamental elements of *yin* and *yang*, and through integration gives rise to forms. As there are forms, there are their opposites. These opposites necessarily stand in opposition to what they do. Opposition leads to conflict, which will necessarily be reconciled and resolved' (Chan, 1963, p. 506).

Not only is there this assertion that the contradiction of opposites is universal, but there is also a hint of the mutually determined nature of each pair. Zhang Zai wrote:

'According to principle nothing exists alone. Unless there are similarity and difference, contraction and expansion, and begin-ning and end among things to make it stand out, it is not really a thing, although it seems to be. To become complete (to attain individuality), a thing must have a beginning and an end. But completion cannot be achieved unless there is mutual influence between similarity and difference (change) and between being and non-being (becoming).' (ibid, p. 515).

This extract finds its echo in Lenin's comment on Hegel's *Science of Logic*: 'The dialectical moment . . . demands the demonstration of difference, connection, transition. Without that the simple positive assertion is incomplete, lifeless, dead' (Lenin, 1961, p. 227).

The following quotation, from chapter 25 of the *Zhuangzi*, will give something of the flavour of the earlier, Daoist, 'dialectical' writings.

Little Knowledge said, 'Within the four cardinal points and the six boundaries of space, how did the myriad things take their rise?' Tai-gong Tiao replied, 'The Yin and Yang reflected on each other, covered each other and brought one another to an end. Likings and dislikings, avoiding of this and movements towards that then arose in all their distinctness, hence came the separation and union of male and female. Then were seen now safety, now danger, in mutual change; misery and happiness produced each other; slow processes and quick jostled each other; and the motions of collection (or condensation) and dispersion (or rarefaction, scattering) were established. These names and processes can be examined, and however minute, can be rewarded. The principles determining the order in which they follow one another, their mutual influences, now acting directly, now revolving; how, when they are exhausted, they revive; and how they come to an end only to begin all over again—these are the properties belonging to things. Words can describe them and knowledge can reach them—but not beyond the extreme limit of the natural world. Those who study the Dao (know that) they cannot follow these changes to the ultimate end, nor search out their first beginnings —this is the place at which discussion has to stop.' (Needham, vol. 2, pp. 39–40).

A closer study of these writings soon convinces one that Marx and Mao would not jar the traditionally trained with their concept of development determined by the interplay of opposites. At the same time, this is not to suggest any too detailed a similarity in the concept. Bodde stresses that 'Chinese philosophy is filled with dualisms in which, however, their two component elements are usually regarded as complementary and mutually necessary rather than as hostile and incompatible' (Wright, p. 54). The Marxian-Maoist concept is one of opposition and 'struggle' of opposites. D. C. Lau, examining the 'treatment of opposites in *Laozi*' comments on 'the similarity between the theory of change in *Laozi* and the dialectical process' but goes on to say: 'an attempt to press this similarity by offering a detailed interpretation of the theory in *Laozi* corresponding to a detailed account of the dialectical process is unwarranted' (Lau, 1958). Needham sometimes makes a claim for a closer similarity, for example: 'The dialectical reconciliation of contradictions in a higher synthesis, which is so often seen in science, appears with much clarity in the Daoist writings, especially in the second chapter of the *Zhuangzi*' (Needham, vol. 2, pp. 76–7). But to others the 'higher synthesis' is not so clear. Fung Yu-lan certainly sees no such idea in the Daoists. Commenting on the *Laozi*'s use of the term 'reverting' (*fan*) he says: 'The idea is that if anything develops certain extreme qualities, those qualities invariably revert to become their opposites', which is a turning-back to a former state, rather than going forward to a 'higher synthesis'. (Fung, 1948, p. 97). D. C. Lau prefers the model of the children's slide with the slow upward climb and then the sharp slide back to the ground again (Lau, 1958, p. 354).

Education

Because of its position in society, it was the Confucian school which from ancient times concerned itself with education. Early Confucian writings contain discussions of the aims of education, and of systems which may have been practised in the Western Zhou. As Galt comments, what is important is not whether these systems actually existed, but that for two thousand years they were accepted by Chinese scholars both as having existed, and as being norms which subsequent societies should follow. (Galt, 1951, p. 69).

In all these writings, whether of the ancient period, or those of the Neo-Confucians of the Song, the aim of education was clearly stated as moral-political. In the *Li Ji* it is written that when the ruler wishes 'to transform the people and to perfect their manners and customs, must he not start from the lessons of the school? . . . On this account the ancient kings, when establishing states and governing the people, made instruction and schools a primary object' (*Li Ji*, 2, p. 82). A passage from the *Mozi* emphasizes the connection between successful rule and education. The emperor is able to govern successfully 'only because he can unify all ideas of the whole realm' (Galt, p. 114). 'And the rule of the realm depends on all minds being unified with that of the emperor, and so in harmony with heaven also.' The moral-political nature of the teaching is brought out in the description of the duties of the minister of instruction. He 'prepared the six rites to restrain the nature of the people. He made clear the seven teachings in order to stimulate the virtue of the people. He arranged the eight regulations of government in order to maintain order among the people. He unified the doctrines of morality in order to secure common customs' (Galt, p. 102, cf. *Li Ji*, 1, p. 230). Galt emphasizes that first the emperor was himself carefully educated, and then he became the official head of the educational system, participating in its administration and inspection (Galt, p. 115).

Two quotations will suffice to show the importance attached to passing on moral-political education to the common people. Again it should be borne in mind that these statements may not record what actually took place, but rather an ideal towards which Chinese society approached at different times. The first is from the *Zhou Li*: 'The county magistrate controlled the education and government in his own county. On the first day of the first month he assembled the people of the county, read the laws to them, inquired into their conduct, and exhorted them' (Galt, 1951, p. 144).

The second is from the *Li Ji*: 'The township teacher controlled the regulations and government in his own township. On the first day of every month he assembled the people, read the laws of the kingdom, and made a record of the people who had progressed in learning filiality, fraternity, friendliness, and family affection' (Galt, p. 144).

Teaching by example is one of the methods which Chinese thinkers have constantly stressed. The *Li Ji* records how at the university they used 'the good influence of example to parties observing one another' (*Li Ji*, p. 86, cf. Galt, p. 137). Writing about a thousand years later, the Neo-Confucians quoted the same idea. 'Discussion and study among friends is not as effective and beneficial as to observe each other and emulate each other's goodness' (Chan, 1967, p. 51). Zhang Zai comments: 'In one's words there should be something to teach others. In one's activities there should be something to serve as a model for others' (ibid, p. 76). At the same time the need to learn, even from one's inferiors is stressed. 'Many people think they are mature and experienced and therefore are not willing to learn from their inferiors. Consequently they remain ignorant all their lives' (ibid, p. 84).

Another idea which finds its echo in the practice of contemporary China, with its hymns to Mao Ze-dong and quotations set to music, is the role of music in traditional education. Confucius said: 'It is by the *Odes* that the mind is aroused . . . It is from music that the finish is received' (*Analects*, p. 211). Cheng Hao complained that the *Odes* were obscure and not understood by the people of his day. He said: 'I want to write some poems generally instructing boys to attend to the duties of sprinkling, sweeping, answering questions, and serving elders, and let them sing these morning and evening. This should be of some help' (Chan, 1967, p. 263). Cheng Yi emphasized the importance of early training. 'When a person is young, he is not master of his own knowledge or thought. Proverbs and sound doctrines should be spread before him every day. Although he does not yet understand, let their fragrance and sound surround him so his ears and mind can be filled with them. In time he will get used to them as if he had originally had them' (ibid, p. 261).

The *Jin Si Lu* contains numerous passages on the need to do more than take on trust, or accumulate information. Cheng Yi wrote: 'A student should think deeply and accumulate his thoughts, and cultivate himself leisurely so he may find things out for himself' (ibid, p. 264). The approach to the classics reminds one of Lin Biao's instruction on reading Mao's works: 'One's accumulation becomes great through learning. It depends on knowing much about the words and deeds of former sages and worthies. One must inquire into their deeds to see their application and examine their words to find out what was in their minds' (ibid, p. 45). There is also the same emphasis on 'little but essential' (*shao er jing*) which was advanced recently by Mao. Chen Zhi wrote: 'merely to memorize what one has recited and to have extensive information, but not to understand the principle or to teach the point of thorough understanding and penetration, is to chase after what is small and to forget what is great' (ibid, p. 52).

Finally, from early times the Confucians expressed an idea which is very much part of the current educational scene. 'Dong Zhongshu said: "Rectify moral principles and do not seek profit. Illuminate the Way and do not calculate on results"' (ibid, p. 57). Cheng Yi commented on a saying in the *Analects:* 'In ancient times men learned for their own sake, that is, their own improvement. Nowadays men learn for the sake of others, that is, in order to become recognized by others' (ibid, p. 47). Bearing in mind that self-cultivation was cultivation for others, these attacks on seeking profit are basically the same as those made during the Cultural Revolution of 1966, and the education advocated was fundamentally one of an attitude of service to the people.

Religion

Turning now to the role of religions in China, we enter the world of the common people. It is important to understand that religions have not played the same official, state role as in Europe, and that no one religion has ever dominated in the same way. Also the various elements which make up religion in the European sense have been differently distributed. Morals, both personal, and the theory of good government, have been independent studies, particularly of Confucian philosophy. Ritual has been highly developed at both state and family level, both as a secular art, and in connection with the ancient ancestor cult, and the various religions.

The indigenous folk religion is a confused mixture drawn from many sources, a system of village superstition and magic practices. The oldest and most widespread form is that of the ancestor cult, with its belief in survival after death in another realm, and the possibility of mutual communication and influence between living and dead. On top of this there is a host of ghosts and spirits, dragons and demons, all of them potential sources of evil, requiring propitiation. Mahayana Buddhism contributed the Bodhisattvas, superhuman beings who are popularly believed to be able to relieve suffering. Numerous other gods are connected with Daoism in the religious form which it assumed after AD 143. This vast pantheon is organized into a heavenly bureaucracy which parallels the earthly one. It contains a Jade Emperor, his family, including the Queen Mother Wang, and a host of Ministers and minor figures. The various posts in the heavenly bureaucracy are filled with figures mythical and historical, and posts change hands both in time and regionally. *Larousse Encyclopedia of Mythology* gives a description of many of these figures, while not attempting to bring order into the confusion which exists.

The ritual connected with the ancestor cult is linked with another set of mystical beliefs called *feng-shui* (wind and water, or geomancy). Freedman regards this as a more sophisticated art lying 'largely outside the framework of folk religion' (Freedman, 1966, p. 124). Needham quotes its definition by Chatley as 'the art of adapting the residences of the living and the dead so as to co-operate and harmonize with the local currents of the cosmic breath' (Needham, vol. 2, p. 359). A wrongly placed building or grave could bring misfortune to a family, while correct positioning could bring wealth and power. The *feng-shui* master, armed with his magnetic compass, his knowledge of the stars, and of the ancient classic book, the *Yi Jing*, is, claims Freedman, 'held in an esteem not shared by other religious practitioners. They are gentlemen and attract the curiosity of gentlemen' (Freedman, 1966, p. 124). A peculiarity of Chinese thought is that such pseudo-sciences share with the secular, rationalistic philosophies a belief in the essential unity of man and nature, a peculiarity which perhaps dulls the edges between the mystical and the rational-scientific in China, and which has prevented the 'typical schizophrenia of Europe' which Needham comments on—the dichotomy between mechanical materialism on the one hand and theological spiritualism on the other. (Needham, vol. 2, p. 154).

Another peculiarity of China is the remarkable tolerance of belief which has existed. Organized religions have always been under some degree of state control (Hu, 1960), perhaps because with the exception of Daoism they have been of foreign origin. But the ordinary Chinese family has employed both Buddhist and Daoist priests to organize ceremonies for their dead, while practising Christians have turned to the shamans, Buddhists and others in times of sickness or great distress, and have been uncomprehending when the Christian clergy objected.

A number of foreign religions have been brought to China, but only Buddhism made any deep impression. Judaism, Nestorianism, Manichaeism and Mazdaism came, only to die out. When the writer visited Kaifeng in early 1966 the handful of Jews registered as a National Minority remembered only that their ancestors had come from the far west, and a few customs practised by their grandparents. Islam came to stay, and W. T. Chan reports (Chan, 1953) the Koran being studied in Chinese, and the use of modern European-style dress, like that used by other sections of the Chinese population. In the border provinces, particularly Xinjiang (Sinkiang), Islam is still very strong.

Christianity entered China on several occasions, first as Nestorianism in the Tang. Roman Catholicism (*Tianzhujiao*) came in the sixteenth century, when the learning of such great figures as Matteo Ricci made a favourable impression on the Chinese scholar-bureaucrats. Protestantism (*Jidujiao*) forced open the door in the nineteenth century. Both religions made a big contribution in the educational field but both suffered from the association with other features of foreign intervention in China. By 1951 all foreign Christian institutions had been taken over by Chinese authorities, and Christianity was completely separated from education. During the Cultural Revolution of 1966 a number of foreign cemeteries were wrecked and churches spoiled, and the group of eight foreign nuns of the Franciscan Mission who had kept open a school for children of the diplomatic missions were expelled from China.

The exact date of the entry of Buddhism into China is unknown. It probably entered along the Silk Routes from central Asia during the first century A.D. Between the end of the Han (A.D. 220) and the beginning of the Song (A.D. 960) it flourished, producing many translations and religious writings, and numerous fine works of art. At a lower level, it fused with the Daoist religion to produce 'a mongrel religion which in innumerable local variations maintained itself in the lower strata of society till modern times' (Zurcher, p. 66). Buddhism survived the great persecution at the end of the Tang dynasty in A.D. 845, but 'in the totality of Chinese culture, has always been a more or less marginal phenomenon' (ibid, p. 58). Today its temples have been stripped of their idols and in their place stand political slogans and quotations from Mao Ze-dong.

It is difficult to make any accurate numerical estimate of the strength of the various religions. Figures for the late forties show about 20 million Muslims; 600,000 Buddhist monks and nuns, and between 3 and 4 million Buddhist lay devotees; several hundred thousand Daoist priests and 'vegetarian women'; 3.3 million Roman Catholics and about 600,000 Protestants. This gives a total of only about 4 per cent of the present population, assuming no great change has taken place in the number of the religious. But if those who might better be classified as superstitious are taken, a figure of nearer 90 per cent might be more accurate. For the majority of the people the old saying is no doubt still true: they 'wear a Confucian crown, a Daoist robe, and a pair of Buddhist sandals' (De Bary, vol. 2, p. 286).

While we are considering religions we should, perhaps, look for a moment at anti-religion in China. There have been isolated examples of persecution and oppression in the past, but very few compared with Europe. In recent times Christianity has come under particularly heavy criticism as a result of its foreign connections. In 1922 an Anti-Christian Society was formed.

Mao Ze-dong's attitude to anti-religious actions is to be found in his *Investigation of the Peasant Movement in Hunan*, written in March 1927 (Mao, 1965, vol. 1, pp. 44-7). Mao lists 'the supernatural system (religious authority)' as one of the three systems of authority which a Chinese was subjected to, one of the 'four thick ropes binding the Chinese people'. (The others are political, clan, and, especially for women, male authority.) He describes how the peasants took over temples as offices, sweeping the idols into a corner, or actually smashing them up in some places. While obviously approving this sentiment, Mao warns that this is not the main issue and that 'if too much of an effort is made, arbitrarily and prematurely, to abolish these things', it will only enable the 'local tyrants and evil gentry' to stage a counter-attack. He advocates a policy of 'draw the bow without shooting, just indicate the motions' for the Communist Party. 'It is the peasants who made the idols, and when the time comes they will cast the idols aside with their own hands; there is no need for anyone else to do it for them prematurely.' He then quotes from a speech he had made attacking *feng-shui* and gods, in which he had argued that peasant committees were more efficacious.

Turning to the recent anti-religious actions, during the Cultural Revolution of 1966, it would seem that Mao Ze-dong has not altered his fundamental attitude of drawing the bow without shooting. In the Sixteen Points drawn up by the CC CCP in August 1966 there is no specific mention of religions. The aim is set out as an attack on the four olds: old ideas; old culture; old customs; and old habits. Education, literature and art, and 'all other parts of the superstructure not in correspondence with the socialist economic base' are to be transformed. Writing *In Praise of the Red Guards* in September 1966, *Red Flag*, the CP theoretical journal, never mentions religion. It speaks only of attacking the 'remaining viruses of feudalism, . . . capitalism . . . [and] the evil roots of revisionism'. While the attacks on religion were not opposed, they do not seem to have been officially encouraged. Central propaganda has been against more solid 'ghosts and monsters' within the earthly bureaucracy, and in favour of increasing material production. And considerable efforts have been made to preserve those religious objects which represented genuine cultural treasures.

In the field of publishing there seems also to have been little serious anti-religious effort. In 1961 a collection of *Stories About Not Being Afraid of Ghosts* was published with an introduction by the Director of the Institute of Literature of the Chinese Academy of Sciences. (English translation, Foreign Languages Press, 1961).

The preface opens with an optimistic statement: 'There are no ghosts. Belief in ghosts is a backward idea, a superstition and a sign of cowardice. This is a matter of common sense today among the people.' How optimistic this is may be judged by two stories told to the writer in 1966. The first concerned a woman teacher who had recently returned from a remote village where she had been engaged in the Socialist Education Movement. She was very happy one evening to find her class all agreed that spirits and ghosts did not exist, and that putting paper on the graves was a useless superstition. But the following morning her happiness was disturbed by the sight of fresh white paper fluttering on the mounds of earth in the nearby fields.

The second story was told by a young PLA man, recently demobbed and sent to work in a Peking institution. He told how one night he and two fellow-soldiers had been disturbed by a mysterious noise and the shaking of their beds. One of the others suggested ghostly origins. But the speaker reassured him. Three PLA men were quite powerful enough to overcome any ghosts! When one remembers how intensive political education is in the PLA, this story is the more revealing.

Finally, mention must be made of the *Village Practical Handbook*, of which some 660,000 copies had been published in Shanghai by 1966. Together with information about farming techniques, making clothes, first aid, writing letters, the calender, and much else, there is a section entitled 'Abolish Superstitions'. Occupying eight pages out of a total of 504, it deals with twenty-eight superstitions. They include such items as: 'Dead people can't change into ghosts'; 'Those possessed by spirits are people who have lost the ability of self-mastery'; 'Physiognomy has absolutely no scientific basis'; and 'Ghost winds are whirlwinds'.

Mao Ze-dong and the tradition

Mao Ze-dong's ideas are thus clearly in harmony with the Chinese tradition in three main areas. First, his dialectical materialist philosophy, which sees man as central, both shaping and being shaped by his human and non-human environment. Second, his concept of education as fundamentally moral-political, and as something which goes on throughout life and involves all that man does. Third, his concept of good government as dependent on the moral qualities of the rulers, in this case the revolutionary activists at all levels.

In other areas Mao's ideas conflict with those of the tradition. Class struggle and his form of grass-roots democracy cannot be reconciled with ideas of social harmony and the traditional hierarchy of power from father to emperor. On another level, popular superstitions are an obstacle to rational-scientific education, and a prop to older social mores. At this stage it is too early to estimate which ideas will prove the stronger.

3

Obstacles to educational reform

This chapter will examine some of the non-educational factors which must be taken into account in any attempts to develop or change the educational system. They include the size and diversity of the country and its peoples and the relatively backward state of the economy in 1949. The pre-1949 school system will also be briefly examined, together with those direct foreign influences which have set up internal obstacles to the developments which Mao Ze-dong is attempting to bring about.

Geographical and demographic factors

The area of the People's Republic of China is some 3.5 million square miles (9.6 million square kilometres), which is a little larger than the United States of America. Both these countries also lie roughly within the same latitudes. But China has about half as much arable land as the U.S.A. 62.1 per cent of China's land area is classified as 'waste, city and other', compared with only 10 per cent in the U.S.A. Large areas of the country are mountainous, or desert, and these can only be cultivated, if at all, at too high a cost at the present time.

China's climate varies from hot deserts in Mongolia and Xinjiang, to cold desert on the high Tibetan plateau, and from continental climates in the loess region and Manchuria in the north, to semi-tropical and tropical in the south. Dust storms are common in much of the north, where it is generally very dry. In the Yangzi basin and to the south it is very humid during the summer, and much of the surface is occupied by standing water in the form of canals and streams, or paddy-fields.

A number of factors make a division of the country into north and south along the Qinling Fu Niu Shan line a useful one. In the north temperatures are extreme; it is dry with inadequate rainfall; and there is a short growing season. To the south it is temperate to tropical; there is much more rain; and the longer growing season allows for two and sometimes three crops a year. The main cereal in the north is wheat; in the south, rice. There is even a distinction in the inhabitants. In the north there are only two important minorities: the Mongols, and the Turki (Uighur) Moslems. The Manchus have been scattered and absorbed and Manchuria is mainly settled by Han Chinese. In the south there are many minorities, and the Chinese inhabitants of Guangdong and Guangxi are to some extent both culturally and physically different from their northern relatives, and style themselves the Tang Ren. The names Han and Tang are, of course, taken from the names of the famous dynasties.

It is probably not an exaggeration to say that the life of the Chinese has been dominated by water. The majority of Chinese live along the main river valleys: the Huang He (Yellow River); the Yangzi Jiang; the Huai He; and the Xi Jiang (West River) and the Zhu Jiang (Pearl River) which join to form the delta to the south of Canton. As well as being a source of life, these rivers have been a major cause of death, breaking their banks and flooding huge areas. On the other hand, life has been taken by the absence of water, by drought. The sun has dried up the paddy fields in the south; the rains have not come in the north; and the crops have withered and died. And if that were not enough, freak storms of rain or hail suddenly batter down the crops and tear holes in terraces and roads in the north, or typhoon winds of over a hundred miles an hour strike the coastal provinces of the south.

China's enormous population is proverbial and is often referred to with pride by her present leaders. The only accurate census which has ever been taken was in 1953 and the following figures are based upon it. Figures for other years are estimates from various sources. The total population of mainland China was 582,603,000 in 1953. American estimates of present numbers and future trends suggest a 1965 figure of between 715 million and 875 million, and a 1975 figure of between 696 million and 1,063 million (EPMC, p. 363). This population is largely rural, probably to the extent of over 85 per cent. It has been calculated that the overall population density, per square kilometre of cultivated land, is between 1,800 and 2,200 (1967). Actual population densities in different parts of the country vary widely. In some parts of the north China plain they may reach 1,000 per square mile, while in parts of Xinjiang and Inner Mongolia they may be less than 1 per square mile.

The population is a relatively young one. In 1953 36 per cent of the population was below 15 years of age; 53 to 56 per cent was below 25; and 86 per cent was below 50. This compares with U.S.A. figures of 21 per cent below the age of 14, and 85 per cent below the age of 60. This pattern is likely to continue in China until at least 1985.

The overall ratio of males to females in 1953 was 107.6 males to 100 females. This figure is expected to drop to perhaps as low as 101 males in 1985.

In considering the problem of providing education for such a big population it is important to know what numbers to expect in the different age groups. In the present state of Chinese statistics only broad guesses can be made. The estimates in the following table are from an American study (EPMC, pp. 367–8). The size of the labour force is included, as its relative size and productivity is an important factor determining the possibility of providing school places. According to one estimate it takes three peasants to support one student at a full-time school under present conditions.

	Number of people in millions		
	1953	1965	1985
Primary school age (7–12 years)	75–90	110–140	125–190
Primary+secondary school age	145–175	200–250	180–350
Labour force (men: 18–60 years women: 18–55 years)	290–340	330–400	450–650

The annual increment in the primary school population was 1 to 2 million in 1953: 1.6 to 3.0 million in 1965: and will be about 3.5 million in 1985 on the most optimistic assumptions (EPMC, p. 368).

It is these figures of population which must be borne in mind when considering the factors affecting the development of part-work schooling.

Language problems

The ubiquity of the Chinese characters has obscured the language problems with which China is beset. First there are a number of quite different peoples, some of them descendants of aboriginal tribal inhabitants, within the national boundaries. Secondly, within the Han people itself there are serious dialectal differences. And on top of these speech problems comes the problem of writing, and the enormous illiteracy with which the government was faced in 1949.

When the census was taken in 1953 33 different peoples were listed as National Minorities, with a total population of 35,320,360, or about 6 per cent of the total population of China. The largest groups included:

Minority	Region in which found	Population
Zhuang	West Guangxi Province	6,611,455
Uighur	Xinjiang Uighur Autonomous Region	3,640,125
Hui (Moslems)	Gansu and Qinghai	3,559,350
Yi	Sichuan-Yunnan borders	3,254,269
Tibetan	Tibet, Chamdo (Sichuan) & Qinghai	2,775,622
Miao	Guizhou & West Hunan	2,511,339
Manchu	Widely distributed	2,418,931
Mongolian	Inner Mongolian Antonomous Region	1,462,956
Puyi	South-west Guizhou	1,247,883
Korean	Yanpian Korean Autonomous *Zhou* in Jilin province	1,120,405

From: T. R. Tregear, *Geography of China*, London, 1965, p. 103.

The exact relationships of the different languages spoken in and around China are still a matter of dispute. Few of them have been studied with the tools of the modern linguist (Carroll, 1963, pp. 55–6). Chinese is usually placed with a group of languages commonly called the Sino-Tibetan languages. This includes Tibeto-Burman (Tibetan, Burmese, Lo-lo in China, and others); Miao-Yao (tribal languages in Indochina, N. Burma, and S.W. China); and Kam-Thai (spoken in Siam, Laos, the Shan areas of Burma and parts of S. China). These are very different from Mongol, Tungus (the original Manchu language) and the Turkish languages spoken by Uighurs and others in Western China, all of which languages are grouped together in the Ural-Altaic family.

Chinese is itself divided into a number of dialects, some of which are mutually unintelligible. Whether they should be described as different languages involves historical-political considerations which are outside the province of linguistics. Readers are referred to the discussion in Kratochvil (1968, pp. 14–15). While the complete pattern is far from known, present knowledge admits the following divisions:

(1) Northern Chinese or Mandarin dialects—divided into northern, north-western, south-western and river dialects. c. 387 million speakers.
(2) Wu dialects around Shanghai, in Jiangsu, Anhui and Zhejiang. c. 46 million speakers.
(3) Xiang or Hunanese dialects. c. 26 million speakers.
(4) Gan or Jiangxi. c. 13 million speakers.
(5) Kejia or Hakka dialects, spoken in parts of Guangxi and Guangdong. c. 20 million speakers.
(6) Yue or Cantonese dialects, spoken in Guangxi and Guangdong. c. 27 million speakers.
(7) Min or Fukienese, divided into northern and southern Min dialects, and spoken in Fujian, south Zhejiang, N.E. Guangdong, and in Hainan and Taiwan (Formosa) islands. c. 22 million speakers. (Kratochvil, p. 16–17).

From the foregoing it will be seen that for the purposes of maintaining and developing the unity of the country, and for education, the development of a national language is of some importance. From the fifteenth century onwards officials communicated orally by means of an educated variant of the Peking dialect, known as *guanhua* (official speech, or Mandarin). After 1911 the need for a national language became more widely recognized, and the term *guoyu* (national language) was borrowed from the Japanese, whose efforts in the same direction had impressed Chinese students studying in Japan. In 1916 a National Language Research Committee was set up with the aim of assisting the development of a standard, national language.

Modern Chinese shares with other members of its language family three main features. It has a high proportion of monosyllabic words. It distinguishes words of different meaning, but similar sound, by the tone in which they are uttered. And it employs special words called measure words, or classifiers, between numerals or demonstratives and nouns.

In the northern dialects there is today a paucity of phonetic difference, especially of final consonants. In all there are some 412 syllables which can be spoken in one or more of four tones, to give a total of only 1,280 possible monosyllables. Compared with European language this is small, and makes the identification of isolated fragments of speech very difficult, if not impossible. It also provides a rich basis for punning, which is very popular. As an example of this phenomenon we will take three entries from the *Xinhua Zidian*, a small Chinese dictionary published in Peking in 1965. For the sound *ji* there are 100 entries, 32 of them to be pronounced in the first tone, and thus phonetically indistinguishable. This is an extreme example. There are only 13 entries for the sound *ming*, and 4 for the sound *pen*. It should be noted that in modern speech a large number of bi-syllabic words are employed which makes confusion less likely.

Contrary to popular misconceptions, the Chinese script is based upon the sounds of the language, and any pictorial remnants which it possesses are of interest only to the scholar. It differs from the more familiar alphabetic systems in being based on rather larger elements of sound. Kratochvil used the term a morphemic script (p. 157), as the element involved in a minimal meaningful unit of the language, known technically as a morpheme. The system has a number of advantages: it is more stable over long periods of time than a system which is based on phonemes (consonants and vowels); it can be understood by a wider group of related dialect-users, who would read the symbols as quite different sounds; and it is very compact. The second advantage is the one usually advanced for the retention of the system, as it is supposed to unify China in space and time. But here again the popular view is greatly exaggerated. Without special training no modern Chinese can easily read his classics, any more than the Englishman can read *Beowulf* (Kratochvil, p. 161), and the greater the difference between the dialect used and the standard language, the more difficult it is to understand the modern written language.

While it has the advantages mentioned above, the system suffers from grave practical disadvantages, the most important being the enormous number of the basic elements. Compared with some 25 to 35 letters of a European alphabet, it is necessary to learn several thousand characters if one is to read a newspaper or simple book. Frequency counts during the past forty years have suggested a basic vocabulary of about 2,000, but 3,000 is probably a more useful number to acquire, and the writer's university-trained colleagues in Peking claimed to know between 6,000 and 8,000. The famous *Kang Xi* dictionary of 1716, still reprinted in 1958, contains over 40,000 characters, but probably about 34,000 of these are redundant.

Each character is composed of a number of strokes, ranging from one to thirty-six. In the handwritten forms these are run together, which increases speed, but does not add to the clarity. The complexity and number of the characters places a very heavy burden on the educational system, ensuring that a high proportion of time is spent on the form, rather than the content of the written matter.

Another disadvantage of the system is that mechanical reproduction is a specialist's job. No ordinary Chinese could operate a Chinese typewriter, which picks up separate pieces of type and strikes them against a movable carriage before dropping them back among their 2,000 bed-fellows. And type-setting for printing is a formidable job too, with plenty of chances for mistakes to be made.

There are really two major language problems: the development of a standard spoken form; and the reform of the writing system. These problems are connected, and attempts to solve them have involved both. Around the period of the May 4th Movement (4 May 1919) a number of writers began to reject the old system of writing in the artificial classical style known as *wenyan*. Instead they adopted a form based on the vernacular which they called *xin biahua* (new plain speech) similar to that used in the great medieval novels.

In spite of influential support, the movement towards adoption of a standard speech remains slow. Most educated Chinese probably recognize the need for such a thing, and regard *guoyu*, or *putonghua* (common speech) as it is called in People's China today, as a form which should at least be understood. But few make serious efforts to actually speak it.

Efforts to develop a phonemic alphabet began with the Italian Jesuit, Matteo Ricci, who used the Latin alphabet to write Chinese in 1605. The widely-used Wade-Giles system was invented by Thomas F. Wade, an Englishman, in 1867, and popularized in a modified form in H. A. Giles's *Chinese-English Dictionary* in 1912. More than eight schemes, using already existing and newly invented alphabets, were put forward during the *qie yin zi yundong*, (movement for a phonetic alphabet) between 1892 and 1908. In 1918 a *zhuyin zimu* (pronunciation alphabet) was invented, and this was

74

officially adopted in 1920 and used in schools to facilitate learning the characters and to help in standardizing the spoken language. In 1928 another official system was adopted, *guoyu luomazi* (national romanization, or *Gwoyeu Romatzyh*), based on the Latin alphabet.

In 1952 the new Chinese government set up the Research Committee for Reforming the Chinese Written Language, and by 1956 its work bore fruit in two directions. On the one hand a number of the more complex characters were simplified; and on the other, yet another alphabet was published. But this time the reforms were not only passed by the State Council, and finally approved by the National People's Congress, in February 1958. They were immediately introduced into the schools, and the simplified characters began to be used in newspapers, journals and popular books.

Zhou En-lai, introducing the reforms in a speech to the National Committee of the Chinese People's Political Consultative Conference in 1958, pointed out that the aim was to make it easier for people to learn to read the characters. It was not intended to replace them. The new alphabet was a teaching aid which would help in learning to read, and could be used as a basis for the development of alphabets for the various national minority languages which had not so far acquired one. Finally it was hoped that the use of *hanyu pinyin*, as the alphabet was called, would help to popularize the national language.

It is difficult to estimate the support for, and the effect of the introduction of these measures. Most vocal have been the opponents, though criticism has been more on the detail than the principle. The use of the alphabet has been limited and half-hearted. It has been used in dictionaries to show the pronunciation; under street and shop signs; and on the title pages of many publications. But material produced by the Foreign Languages Press, which is used by students of foreign languages in China, still uses a form of Wade-Giles romanization for Chinese names. To add to the difficulty, the form they use does not distinguish related sounds, like *ch/zh*, *t/d*, or *p/b*, for which Wade-Giles employs a single form followed by a prime (*ch* is contrasted with *ch'*).

The simplification of the characters was also limited in scope, but basically the reform has been a great success. Some 2,300 characters in all have been changed. In a few cases an old simplified form was used. In other cases part or all of the character was changed to reduce the number of strokes. In a few cases the changes have been unfortunate as the form chosen suggests a different sound from the correct one, while in others simplification of part of a character has only been applied to a few of the possible cases. It should be realized that only occasionally has simplification made it necessary for a really literate person to reach for a dictionary of simplified characters. Not least in importance has been the change in arrangement of the characters from vertical files, read down from right to left across the page, to horizontal rows read from left to right. The latter arrangement, like European writings systems, is more suitable to the human eye, which is able to take in a wider field horizontally, and thus read faster than with vertically written scripts.

During the Cultural Revolution of 1966 posters appeared advocating a further reduction in the number of characters, so that one sound would be represented by only one character. This suggestion was supported by a quotation from unpublished remarks supposed to have been made by Mao Ze-dong to a visiting Nepalese delegation of teachers. Such a reform would destroy the advantages of the present system, while only reducing the time required to learn it. Mechanical reproduction would still be a specialist job. As more people devote long hours to learning and retaining the characters, it will become more and more difficult to abolish them. Certainly no voice was raised in favour of a more revolutionary change at a time when so much was being said about revolutionary changes elsewhere in Chinese affairs. But this is not so surprising when one saw the variety of careful and beautiful calligraphy displayed in town and village during the Cultural Revolution. One then realised that the characters were valued as the expression of a cultural heritage now within the grasp of all, and also as fulfilling a strong aesthetic need.

Administrative and social factors

From very ancient times, probably about the fifth century B.C., *min*, or common people of China have been divided into four occupational groups: the *shi, nong, gong* and *shang*, i.e., the scholar-gentry, the peasant-farmers, the artisans, and the merchants. This division expressed a scale of values rather than an institutional pattern, and it is remarkable that the military, so important a feature of other parts of the world, did not feature at all. The traditional view of the soldier is perhaps summed up in the old Chinese saying: 'You do not make good iron into a nail; you do not make a good man into a soldier'. The Communists have broken with the tradition by changing the order to *gong, nong, shi, shang*, and adding that peculiarly non-militaristic soldier, the PLA-man (People's Liberation Army), recently put forward as the new model hero.

The administrative pattern for some two thousand years was of a semi-divine monarch ruling, not through a hereditary aristocracy, but through a scholar-bureaucracy selected by merit from almost all classes of society. 'The viability of this system', comments R. Dawson, 'deeply depended on the skilful choice and handling of administrative personnel, and on the emperor's appreciation that the right of Confucian wisdom to govern was as inalienable as his own right to occupy the throne.' (Dawson, p. 365).

This system, which operated down to the county (*xian*) level and kept law and order, collected taxes and organized conscription, came to an end in 1911. The less formal administrative system which operated below the county level continued with little change throughout the warlord period, and in the areas under the control of the Nationalist (Guomindang or KMT) Government. Power was vested in the owners of property, in lineage organizations, religious bodies and secret societies. Criminal gangs, often linked with the secret societies, sometimes played an important role, as on 12 April 1927, when the Shanghai gang headed by Du Yue-sheng was used by Jiang Jie-Shi (Chiang Kai-shek) to massacre thousands of communists, and ensure Jiang's control of the Nationalist movement. In many places the traditional *bao-jia* system was also used by Jiang in the anti-communist struggle. This was a system of local political control involving spying and mutual surveillance, based on a hierarchy of families, which had been used on and off throughout Chinese history (Lee, 1960, and Barnett, 1967, p. 319).

In the villages power rested in the hands of the landlords, and especially in those who acted as money-lenders. Lineage organizations, far from easing the oppression, all too often tended to consolidate it. They were run by the wealthier families and were linked with the other local centres of power. (Freedman, 1961–2).

When the Communists came to power in 1949 the whole power

structure was rapidly changed, and the Communist Party became the most important centre of power at all levels of society. The old system was harshly swept away by the land reform in the villages, during which the landlords were 'eliminated as a class', and in many cases also physically. After public trials at which the peasants were encouraged to pour out their past sufferings, those landlords who were deemed to have been guilty of particularly severe oppression were executed. In one report over 400 people were executed in a single county: 80 per cent of the old village administrators (*xiang-zhang*), between 10 and 20 per cent of the Bao (*bao-jia* system) heads, and over 20 per cent of all landlords (Barnett, 1967, pp. 228-9).

During the land reform the practice began of classifying people according to the class analysis worked out by Mao Ze-dong and the CCP, and this system was later extended to the towns. As time has passed and more and more people have come to work in collectively-owned organizations, the system has become more a question of family origin than the actual economic status of the individual concerned. While current jobs, and more particularly attitudes, play an important part in such classification, family origin is very import-ant, and membership of a former landlord or capitalist family is a formidable obstacle to entry into all positions of authority. The ideal hero is always the son of a worker or poor peasant, with perhaps an emphasis on the latter.

Officially recognized social groups include landlords, rich pea-sants, middle peasants, poor peasants, and landless peasants in the village. In the towns there are workers, and various former owners of shops and factories. Sub-divisions of these groups exist, but the system would seem to have administrative and propaganda, rather than scientific value in its definition of many of its groups.

Some groups have received particular official attention. For a time the government ran an Office for the Reform of Private Entre-preneurs (*Siren Gaizao Bangongshi*) which carried out propaganda among the property owners in the cities. There is also an Oversea Chinese Affairs Section (*Huaqiao Shiwu Ke*), an agency of the county (*xian*) government which takes care of those families which have returned from abroad, or who have relatives overseas.

Another group which gets special treatment is the 'five (bad) elements' (*wu-lei fenzi*). It is not so much that this group poses any serious threat to the society, though there is always this possibility. But they have acted as living examples of the danger of opposing the policy of the CCP. (Barnett, pp. 231–3). The 'five (bad) elements' consist of landlords, rich peasants, counter-revolutionaries, people labelled as rightists during the 1957 movement, and various petty criminals collectively referred to as 'bad elements'. Unless under special sentence, these people take part in the normal work of their community, but they have no right to vote on any matter, or to be elected to any office. They have to report regularly to the public security personnel (police), and in many cases other members of the community are expected to keep a constant watch on their activities. This, it has been reported, leads not only to their being left very much alone, but also to a wide circle of their relatives being avoided for fear of contamination. In theory, after a sufficiently long period of good behaviour, a member of this category can ask the Party and public security authorities to change his class status (*gaibian jieji chengfen*), but this is probably seldom done. One of these former landlords told his story to Jan Myrdal (Myrdal, pp. 335–51).

The group which has probably received the most attention, and which is certainly decisive for the future development of China, is that heterogeneous group which has come to be known as the cadres (*ganbu*). Defined in the Shanghai *New Phrases Dictionary* for 1954 as 'persons who work in state institutions or a department of production, capable of unifying and leading the masses to carry out Party and Government policies and directives . . .' (Schurmann, 1966, p. 165), the group consists of leaders of widely different kinds. Schurmann discusses the evolution of the concept of the cadre from pre-1949 Yan'an (Yenan) days through to the 1950s and distinguishes cadres from traditional bureaucrats, modern bureaucrats, and managers (Schurmann, pp. 162–7 and 235–8). He points out that the cadre is supposed to be both an institutional and a personal leader, requiring both expertise and ideology (ibid, p. 172). He must be both 'red' and 'expert'.

Cadres have been recruited from the PLA, men with a record of struggle in the Anti-Japanese and Civil Wars; from the 'activists' among the working class; from the non-Party, but highly technically qualified members of the former administrative class, the old intelligentsia; and, increasingly, from among the students and graduates of the universities. In the main, cadres have been drawn from the poorer classes of the old society, and thus stand out in strong contrast to the administrators of the pre-1949 period.

Cadres are organized into a well-defined, but unpublished hierarchy, which includes distinctions between Party and non-Party cadres, and between Party members of long standing and those who joined after 1949. There is a wage differential which does not necessarily comply strictly with job distinction, or other distinctions of status (Barnett, pp. 38–48). Many cadres live in furnished accommodation provided by their place of work, and they eat in institution canteens. Transfer from job to job is frequent for all but the highest cadres, and this often means that husband and wife are separated for long periods. Upward mobility is very slow, while, on the contrary, with the years there has been increasing pressure to move cadres from town to village, and from the coastal belt into the interior.

The cadres, more than any other group, are under constant pressure to live up to the mores of the new China. Compared with previous Chinese administrative groups their behaviour has been exemplary. But at the same time they have developed certain group interests and behaviour patterns which set them against the rest of society. There has also been some development of a division of interest between the old Party 'generalists' and the newer, often non-Party technical personnel and specialists. These divisions were certainly factors in the Cultural Revolution of 1966.

In present-day China everybody is expected to take an active part in the life of some small group. This may be a workshop group, the Party branch, school class, subject-teachers' group, or a street committee. Many people belong to several different groups at the same time.

Describing the early days of the new government, at a university in Sichuan, W. G. Sewell says: 'The small groups, seemingly so spontaneous and informal, were in fact organized most cleverly. At the heart was a meeting of the *ganbu* or cadres, the official workers of the Communist Party and the Government. They were responsible for introducing ideas into each district and seeing that official plans were carried out.' One of the cadres explained the system to Mr. Sewell, contrasting communist and Christian methods:

You Christians are not very clever, . . . You set before people an ideal which they cannot possibly reach. They very soon grow discouraged, and then no real progress can be made . . . We, on the other hand, never suggest through the chairman any thought too advanced for the groups to grasp, or any action too difficult for them to take. Then, having successfully taken one step, they have confidence and are ready for the next one. Time is no object as long as even the smallest movement takes place and the direction is right. (Sewell, 1933, pp. 97–8).

The pattern of groups set up about the same time in Peking University was described by Maria Yen. Academic classes were divided into 'mutual-aid groups' of five to ten students. Above them there was a class organization, responsible for all students of the same year studying one subject. Each class had an administrative manager and assistant, a study manager, welfare manager, and a business manager. These got their orders from the departmental council, formed from four classes in a particular subject. The mutual-aid groups always included one Party member, and/or a Youth League member. In addition to these groups, students belonged to another system of groups for political classes, and yet a third tier of 'living-circles' based on the dormitories where the students lived. All of these groups had regular meetings. (Yen, 1954, p. 125).

The same type of hierarchical group system exists in the People's Liberation Army. In fact it was experience of these groups during the long period of the anti-Japanese and civil wars which led to their introduction into the wider society after 1949. A. L. George describes their structure and functioning as seen through the eyes of a group of prisoners taken in Korea in *The Chinese Communist Army in Action*. He notes that at the lowest level the different squads of a company were subdivided into three or four groups, each of three or four men. Each such group had a leader who was, ideally, a Party member (George, 1967, p. 51).

It will be seen that the groups are mainly based on the place of work and directly related to a member's immediate work. The subjects discussed by the groups range widely from the international political scene (the Korean War; Vietnam; Indonesia) through theoretical studies of Mao's works, or the history of the Chinese Communist Party, to ways of implementing the latest big campaign (1951—against corruption, waste and bureaucracy; 1958—against waste and conservatism; 1966—the Cultural Revolution). In addition to reading together and talking about actions to be taken, the groups take part in the much more powerful 'criticism and self-criticism' technique. Maria Yen voices the general opinion when she comments: 'The criticism meetings are perhaps the most important single part of the whole pattern of supervision . . .' (Yen, p. 157). As one would expect, opinion on these criticism sessions varies widely through the spectrum from total support to total opposition. W. G. Sewell's discussion of them, as a sympathetic outsider, is particularly interesting. Commenting on the atmosphere after the 1951 'three antis' campaign he says: 'They were passing through an experience which preachers of an earlier age might have described as being "washed in the blood". It was only partly true to talk of political studies and political awareness; this was an overwhelming religious revival that was sweeping the land. A religion that demanded his all from every man.' (Sewell, p. 194). He gives examples of the feeling of guilt engendered which made people confess to private misdemeanours. Other people give a less optimistic account of the system's success. Two of the prisoners in the study by A. L. George comment: 'Such meetings were useful to some extent . . . however, the same errors were repeated without regard to such meetings . . . The man who was criticized was careful not to commit the fault any more, but the other men who were present in the meeting forgot the lesson two or three days afterwards . . .' (George, p. 104). An important factor contributing to the efficacy of criticism meetings would seem to be the Chinese attitude to loss of 'face' (George, p. 105). 'Face' might be roughly translated as 'social prestige', and traditional Chinese behaviour patterns were designed to maintain the maximum of 'face' of all concerned. Making someone else lose 'face' was itself a 'face'-losing action.

Family loyalties

The traditional Chinese family, which still largely persists today, is an extended family with three generations under the same roof. Its ethic down the centuries has been that of Confucian filial piety (*xiao*) which we discussed above. Obedience to parents and elders was the basis of the social order. 'Filial piety at the outset consists in service to one's parents, in the middle of one's path in service to one's sovereign, in the end in establishing one's self', says the *Classic of Filial Piety*, (*Xiao Jing*, Hughes, 1942, p. 113). And all schoolchildren, who memorized the *Three-character Classic* (*San Zi Jing*) recited: '. . . a child should know how to obey his parents . . . children must respect their elders . . . first comes the duty to parents and superiors . . .' (*San Zi Jing*, ch. 3). It was only in this century that the principle became seriously disputed. An early opponent was Hu Shih. He wrote: 'All the much-idealized virtues of filial piety simply could not exist, and in those rare cases where they were consciously cultivated, the price paid for them was nothing short of intense suppression, resulting in mental and physical agony.' Fung Yu-lan, another noted philosopher, took the opposite point of view. He wrote:

'It is by becoming a father or a son, a husband or a wife, that an individual enlists himself as a member of society, and it is by this enlistment that a man differentiates himself from the beasts. In serving his father and sovereign a man has not given up his personality. On the contrary, it is only in these services that his personality has its fullest development.' (Lifton, 1961, pp. 417–8).

The concept was strongly attacked by Chen Du-xiu and others associated with the early socialist and communist movements (Chow pp. 304–7).

Mao Ze-dong has touched on the problem at various times, and has made clear that he regards mutual respect between young and old to be desirable, with both parties giving their major loyalties to the wider social group. The 'little red book' extols young people as 'the most active and vital force in society . . . the most eager to learn and the least conservative' (p. 290), but goes on: 'Of course, the young people should learn from the old and other adults, and should strive as much as possible to engage in all sorts of useful activities *with their agreement*' (p. 291, the author's emphasis). The Marriage Law, promulgated on 1 May 1950, lays down quite clearly in article 13: 'Parents have a duty to rear and to educate their children; the children have a duty to support and to assist their parents. Neither the parents nor the children shall maltreat or desert one another.' (The Marriage Law, p. 4).

Filial piety was closely linked with ancestor-ritual. Dawson notes 'the supreme filial duty of ensuring that there were sons to carry on the sacrifices', and the connection of this with 'the low status accorded to girl children because ultimately they could play no part in securing the family line' (Dawson, p. 366). Changing social beliefs and practices have already begun to affect the male/female ratio in the population, and will ultimately have their effect on education as girls' status improves and there is a demand for a higher education for them. The traumatic experience of getting rid of girl children, often by exposing them to the elements, which poor families frequently had to resort to is a thing of the past. But it is a long way from that to full sex equality.

In the past rich families aimed at gathering four generations under a single roof, or rather, under a number of roofs within a high-walled compound. One such family is described in the novel by Ba Jin, written in the 1930s (Ba Jin, 1964). Around such families were organized the interlinked groups of families bearing the same surname, which in English have been called clans or lineages. Lineage loyalties were in many cases very strong, leading in some cases to armed conflict. Lineage groups, seeking power through government office, would often support the education of a poor but promising child.

Next to immediate family, and then lineage loyalties, Chinese have always had a strong attachment to their home village or town. Even after five hundred years in a new home, families are still referred to by their neighbours as 'strangers' or 'foreigners', while people will tell you that they are really from another province, their grandfather having moved as a result of flood or famine. This attitude is described in the old expression: *an-tu-zhong-qian*, which means: to be content in one's native place and consider moving a serious affair.

Economic factors

Agriculture

China has always been, and still is, an agricultural country. Some 80 per cent of her population are engaged in agriculture, and in 1957 its product amounted to some 50 per cent of the national income. In 1965 almost 70 per cent of China's exports were directly or indirectly agricultural (EPMC, pp. 252–3). It is an agriculture which depends on the careful control of water, and it is highly labour-intensive. The fields are meticulously cultivated by crowds of peasants using simple hand-tools. Earth is broken with heavy hoes; mud from nearby streams and ponds is carried in round wicker baskets slung from the ends of a carrying-pole, and then spread by hoe to fertilize the fields. Wooden pails may be used to carry the carefully treated mixture of human and animal excrement to the fields. Trenches are dug each autumn in the fields around Peking to plant vegetables, protected by screens of *gaoliang* (sorghum) stalks from the biting winds. Huge earth houses are built to store the cabbages, only to be knocked down the following spring so the land can be planted again. Enormous areas of the northern plains are divided up by low ridges and gullies to guide the irrigating water. In the paddy-fields of the south thousands of girls bend their backs under the sun, planting and transplanting the rice, or harvesting it with their short sickles. Needham aptly called it 'garden-agriculture'.

All this is not to say that machinery is not used. The Chinese can claim a number of important firsts in the invention and use of agricultural machinery (Needham, vol. 4, 2), and they have lost none of their ingenuity today. Standardized electric motors can be seen all over the country, being used to pump water, and work various machines. Small hand tractors are beginning to appear in greater numbers. But in the main modern machinery is confined to the state farms, and a number of tractor stations which serve the bigger communes. The *People's Daily* reported in April 1966 that there were then 2,263 mechanical stations in over 1,300 *xian* and municipalities, with about 135,000 tractors (in 15 horse-power units) (EPMC, p. 249). But these figures must be seen against official estimates of a need for some 1.2 million tractors, 300,000 to 350,000 combine harvesters, the same number of trucks, and 3.5 to 4 million power pumps (EPMC, p. 247).

The new government in 1949 took over a heavy burden. Agriculture was at a low ebb. Tregear suggests the country was facing an 'imminent danger of famine' (Tregear, 1968, p. 161). M. R. Larsen says: 'They found a country ravaged by civil war with insufficient food and raw products, inadequate transportation and communication, an outmoded and weak industrial base, and a population weary and discontent from struggle and deprivation' (EPMC, p. 200). Communist policy to cope with these problems evolved through a number of stages, beginning with land reform between 1950 and 1953.

According to the traditional inheritance pattern, land was sub-divided amongst the different heirs: a system which prevented the continuance of large estates and brought about a considerable downward mobility. Nevertheless, a landlord class existed which often brutally exploited the peasantry, and it was their land and goods which was distributed during the land reform. According to official figures about 115 million acres were distributed among more than 300 million peasants, together with some 3 million draught animals. The result was to leave people almost as poor as before (Hinton, 1966). Land belonging to one person was still divided into miserable little patches scattered about the village so that time was wasted in travelling, and a rational system of cropping was impossible. Individual need governed what was grown, rather than considerations of soil suitability and the wider interest. Division of landlord property so that a family owned 'one leg of a donkey' resulted in much quarrelling about whose turn it was to use the beast.

It was considerations of this kind which spurred the government on to measures of co-operation. At first the poorer peasants were encouraged to band together in Mutual-Aid Teams. These consisted of up to five households which shared labour, implements and draught animals and took compensation according to the work and materials contributed. While the Mutual-Aid Teams were often temporary, and always limited in scope, a number of more stable co-operatives were formed. The biggest of these, the higher-stage agricultural producers' co-operatives (APCs) embraced 30 to 40 households, and pooled their land for cultivation according to plans made by a central management. Compensation still involved an element according to the quantity of land contributed. The majority of these higher-stage APCs were formed between 1956 and 1958.

In 1956 the CC CCP ordered that co-operatives should be stabilized at an average of 100 households. By this time the more advanced had given up compensating members for land contributed, and draught animals and the larger farm implements were owned in common. Private plots, not exceeding 5 per cent of the average land per capita in the farm, were allowed, and families could raise poultry and hogs privately.

During the Great Leap Forward period, in 1958, APCs were grouped together in larger units, the People's Communes, which took over all the functions of local government, in addition to organizing agricultural and other forms of production and distribution. In the first few years these communes attempted all kinds of 'communist' practices: communal dining halls, free food, and various welfare facilities. This and the subsequent period of retrenchment is described for one commune in D. and I. Crook's *The First Years of Yangyi Commune*. The present situation seems to be that economic functions are now firmly in the hands of the production brigades, which correspond more or less to the original APCs, while the commune committee handles the more political administrative functions. From 1962 on production teams have been the 'basic accounting unit'. They must hand a proportion of the product to the brigade for management costs, welfare, and reserve funds, but the majority of their product they dispose of themselves. Production teams average some 20 to 40 households.

Before 1949 only a handful of people in a village could read and write, and these usually came from landlord families. Those families who could afford it did not always send their children to school, or only did so for a short time, because they did not see the value of academic education unless their children were to abandon the land and seek a living in the towns. Schooling was certainly not something which was regarded as beneficial to farming. On the other hand, lack of ability to read and write often had disastrous effects on individual peasants who could be tricked into putting their mark to documents which they could not understand. But apart from such matters, the nature of small-scale individual peasant farming did not demand literacy. Techniques were handed down from father to son by imitation and word of mouth.

With the beginning of mutual aid the situation began to change. Relations became more complex, requiring a more sophisticated system of records. The groups began to have more and more relations with bodies outside the village. They began to receive letters, and were required to write them. Difficulties could often be seen to stem from an inability to understand the written word. And so the organization of agriculture began to set up a demand for education, albeit of the most limited kind. As development proceeds and the communes begin to use more artificial fertilizers, pesticides, machinery and new methods, so the pressure for better education will increase, but it will be pressure for a limited, technical education, closely related to the life of the peasants.

The development of co-operative agriculture has given rise to a limited number of new jobs in the villages for which literacy and some degree of technical competence outside the traditional range are necessary. These include accountants; electricians to handle the pumps and motors; mechanics; and people to operate the network of local weather stations which has been set up.

Industry

Industrial development took place very late in China, and only on a limited scale. This was partly because of the nature of the Confucian society, with its contempt for trade, and partly because of the relations which developed with foreign powers during the years following the Opium Wars. Most investment took place in railways, mines and textile mills, and was located in or near the coast where the foreign powers had seized their concessions. Apart from coastal cities like Shanghai and Canton, the Japanese-occupied north-east was the most highly industrialized area, but this was stripped of an estimated \$2 billion worth of machinery and equipment by the Russians at the end of the anti-Japanese war in 1945-6.

In the seventeen years between 1949 and 1966 the situation changed considerably. Visitors to the Shanghai Industrial Exhibition, a permanent display of goods produced in that city, are dazzled by the range and quality of the materials, machines and consumer goods displayed. Friend and foe alike have had to recognize that rapid strides have been made in the development of nuclear weapons. But it is much more difficult to obtain an overall picture of the development of industry and to judge its rate of development, the more so since the Chinese authorities ceased to publish any kind of overall figures after 1959.

The years 1949-52 were years of rehabilitation when the wounds of war were healed. A. G. Ashbrook, Jr. lists the following successes of the new government: suppressing banditry; restoring the railways; repairing and extending the dikes; replacing the 'graft-ridden bureaucratic system of local government with apparently incorruptible Communist "cadres" '; introducing a stable currency and enforcing a nationwide tax system; starting a big programme of public health and sanitation; and ensuring a minimum and more even distribution of food and clothing (EPMC, p. 18).

88

Between 1953 and 1957 China embarked on her first Five-Year Plan. This was based on Soviet experience, and emphasized the development of capacity and output in heavy industry, in such commodities as steel, coal, electric power, petroleum and cement. Li Fu-chun, reporting on the Plan to the second session of the first National People's Congress in July 1955 said: '. . . the policy of giving priority to the development of heavy industry is the only correct policy to make our country strong and prosperous and to create happiness for our people. By carrying out this policy, we will lay a strong material basis for socialism in our country.' Commenting on the results of the plan, A. G. Ashbrook, Jr. said: 'In this period also, the Chinese Communist leadership should be graded high for its economic policy and its economic achievements at this stage of its development.' (EPMC, p. 25).

The period 1958–60 is known as The Great Leap Forward. Sober expert planning was suddenly replaced by efforts to tap mass enthusiasm under such slogans as: 'Politics must command economics', and 'Produce more, faster, better and more economically'. Perhaps those are right who say that the movement was devoted to social rather than economic ends, and success in this sphere compensated for losses elsewhere. The large reserves of under-employed peasants were organized to make bricks, gather fuel, run improvised railways, build dams, and dig irrigation ditches on a huge scale. And great numbers of peasants again swarmed into the cities, drawn by hopes of an easier life.

In July 1960 the Soviet technical advisors, who had been building the first batch of a promised 300 industrial plants, were withdrawn. They took their blueprints with them. Added to this, the Chinese were harassed by three disastrous harvests, in 1959, 1960 and 1961. The winter of 1960–1 saw the first real food shortage since the Communist government came to power. People were unable to work at the pace of the Great Leap and students spent much of their time resting in bed. The skating rink annually constructed at the First Foreign Language Institute in Peking was for once not made.

During the Great Leap inflated claims of production increases had been put forward, only to be officially scaled down in August 1959. The years since 1962 have been devoted to the long haul back in agricultural production under the slogan: 'agriculture as the foundation and industry as the leading factor' (NPC docs. 1, p. 19).

Emphasis has been placed on key sectors of industry, particularly the development of artificial fertilizers, small electric motors and pumps; and hand-tractors—commodities which will raise agricultural production without displacing people from the land and creating further problems of unemployment.

The position in 1966, at the start of the unpublished third Five-Year Plan, with China in the midst of the Great Proletarian Cultural Revolution, was that industrial output was probably 50 per cent greater than in 1957 (EPMC, p. 85). Development in such fields as petroleum, chemicals and nuclear weapons was far ahead of other fields.

As in agriculture, the period since 1949 has seen a steady development of socialist forms of ownership in industry. Large new industrial plants were set up from the start as state-owned entities under various central ministries. Enterprises belonging to 'war-criminals', 'collaborators', 'bureaucratic capitalists', the former (Guomindang) government, or foreign (especially Japan) powers were nationalized soon after 1949. This particularly affected the 'Four Big Families', Jiang (Chiang Kai-shek), Kong (H. H. Kung), Song (T. V. Soong) and Chen (the brothers Chen Li-fu and Chen Li-kuo). From about 1953 to 1956, large firms employing upwards of 500 workers, were taken into a state-private partnership. This was envisaged as being of limited duration, and it is doubtful whether any such partnerships continue at the present time (1969). The mass of small handicraftsmen so typical of the Chinese scene were organized into co-operatives between 1954 and 1956 (EPMC, pp. 426–9).

The great expansion of industry provided a large number of jobs for skilled and semi-skilled workers, and resulted in a great increase in technical education. The much slower rate of expansion following 1960 has not given rise to a commensurate decrease in technical education, perhaps because of the demand for yet higher qualifications for those already started on the training ladder. Some idea of the scale of these changes can be obtained by studying the detailed figures which are available for the period up to 1959. There was an increase in the number of non-agricultural workers from about 8 million (92.5 per cent male) in 1949 to 44 million (81.2 per cent male) in 1959 (EPMC, p. 433). Of these, 1.5 million were employed in state industries in 1949, compared with about 7.5 million in 1956.

At the end of this period the majority of new jobs were being created in heavy industry, the traditional preserve of male workers. Of the total of over 10 million new jobs created in heavy industry in 1958, 6.6 million were in coal, iron and steel, and metal processing (EPMC, p. 434). In the same year, 1958, in two sectors of light industry there were only 428,000 new jobs, in textiles and food processing—sectors employing about 70 per cent women workers. These figures should all be seen against the background of the total population, and the numbers of young people leaving school.

In considering the effect of industry on education it is necessary not only to know the total number of workers, but also the different grades of skill within the different sectors. Accurate assessment of this depends on the evaluation of training and experience used, and presently available data are far from satisfactory. But they do give some indication of the relative size of the problems involved, and are therefore given. The total number of engineers and technicians increased from 164,000 in 1952 to 618,000 in 1958. Of these, 58,000 worked in industry in 1952 and 259,000 in 1958. J. P. Emerson considers that about 10 per cent of these totals can be classed as fully qualified engineers; which means a rise of about 6,000 to about 26,000 engineers in industry during this period (figures from EPMC, p. 454).

It is these figures which we must bear in mind when we come to consider the employment prospects of school graduates and the repeated calls made by the Party for youth to go to the countryside.

Transport and the location of industry and schools

Industry, like the population, has always been concentrated in the eastern coastal areas of the country. In 1947 the Guomindang Ministry of the Economy published figures which showed that 50 per cent of the country's enterprises and factory workers were located in one city, Shanghai. With Tianjin, Qingdao (Tsingtao) and Guangzhou (Canton), 70 per cent of all enterprises and 69 per cent of workers were accounted for (EPMC, p. 663). Naturally, the best schools and colleges were also located in these areas. Many of these were foreign founded and supported, and various restrictions, Chinese imposed and other, limited the majority of them to cities on or near the coast.

Since 1949 the new Chinese Government has made vigorous efforts to alter this state of affairs. Their reasons are given by Zeng Wen-jing in *China's Socialist Industrialization* (quoted: EPMC, p. 663). They include bringing industry close to the source of raw materials and markets to cut transport costs; developing the backward areas of the country; attempting to bring about a balance between regional division of labour and regional self-sufficiency; an attempt to begin the elimination of the distinction between city and the village; and the dispersal of industry so as to make it less vulnerable in the event of war.

Much of the re-locating of colleges which took place during the early fifties took place within the coastal areas, but many new colleges sprang up then and since in new industrial areas further west. The setting-up of technical schools by factories and farms has greatly helped to rationalize their distribution. Nevertheless, there are still great inequalities in distribution of both industry and educational establishments which it will take a long period to solve.

Because of its relation to the siting of industry, it is convenient to consider transport here. Except for water transport, which is largely coastal or confined to the southern parts of the country, facilities were very poor before 1949. Since then the government has devoted considerable efforts to improving all forms of transport and comparatively great improvements have been made.

The railway network has been greatly extended so that 'with the exception of Tibet, railway lines now penetrate every province of China' (EPMC, p. 674). These railways only link the main cities and only a small part of them have so far been double-tracked, but the essential framework has been completed. Particularly impressive has been the bridging of the Yangzi at Wuhan, in 1957, at Chongqing (Chungking) in 1959, and at Nanjing (Nanking), where a huge new bridge was opened in 1968.

Road transport has not received so much attention as the railways, but improvements in both quantity and quality have been made. According to Tregear (p. 198) in 1960 just under half the total length of roads was surfaced, and therefore available to wheeled traffic throughout the whole year. While unsurfaced roads can be constructed fairly easily with local materials and labour, stone and particularly asphalt for surfaced roads are probably in short supply.

All kinds of vehicles are to be found on the roads of China. In the big cities there are trolley-buses, buses, trams, lorries carrying both goods and people, horse- and donkey-drawn carts, pedicabs and pedicarts—three-wheeled vehicles for the carriage of passengers or goods respectively, and propelled like a bicycle, bicycles and hand-carts. The handcart, with its modern, stout bicycle-type wheels, is especially common in the north-west and south, where it has to a great extent replaced the ancient carrying-pole. The writer vividly remembers his mixed feelings when he first saw it in Kaifeng in 1966, and heard it praised as economic, convenient and modern.

Transport between many small towns is by a network of buses, but most villages must be reached by cart or on foot. In the south boats can be used on the extensive network of canals and streams. Here there are large areas with no proper roads and land passage between villages is by narrow, slippery balks between the fields. The only vehicle possible in such an area is a single-wheeled handcart (wheelbarrow).

The most important inland water transport takes place along three great rivers, the Xi-jiang (West River) by Guangzhou (Canton); the Yangzi Jiang, which links Shanghai, Wuhan and Chongqing (Chungking); and the Songhua Jiang (Sungari) which passes through Ha'erbin (Harbin) in the north-east. 40,000 km of the 160,000 km of navigable waterways reported in 1959 were open to river-going steamers (Jen, 1964, p. 57). Large numbers of families live on the small boats which ply these inland waters, and the education of their children presents similar problems to the education of gipsy children in Europe. The most recent figure for the number of junk operatives was 1,156,000 in 1958 (EPMC, p. 446).

There is now a growing air service linking the main cities of China, and connecting with international airways through the USSR to the north and variously to the south. China's aircraft industry is very limited and the air services are used only for the more important purposes.

Transport can be viewed in relation to education as a source of employment requiring various degrees of skill. This will vary from the airline pilots and navigators at one extreme, through such skilled men as railway engine drivers, to the carters and boatmen whose skill requires little if any formal education, and whose conditions of work must be a great disincentive to study. The importance of a thorough training in the economics and administration of transport was early recognized in the setting-up of special transport universities, e.g. the Gangwan Xueyuan set up in Shanghai in the autumn of 1959 to train people to administer the inland waterways.

Transport, or rather its present limited nature, exercises a big influence on the conduct of secondary and tertiary education. Not only do the majority of such institutions have to provide boarding accommodation, but they have to continue these facilities for large numbers of the students during vacations. In the northern parts of the country many villages are inaccessible during the short winter vacations because of distance and lack of transport. Even during the long summer vacation, the distance, and hence the cost of transport, may deter a few of the students from going home every year. The full extent of this problem cannot be judged as no data are available, but the experience of the author and his friends during 1965-7 demonstrates its presence.

In view of the distribution and transport problems it would be interesting to know something of the pattern of home-background of students at higher educational institutions. The author was only able to record two of his own classes while in China, and while they show a very wide spread, no conclusions can be drawn as to whether such a distribution is typical.

Home city or province of two classes at the 2nd Foreign Language Institute, Peking, 1965-6

City	Number of students in class		Province	Number of students in class	
	1	2		1	2
Peking	3		Jiangsu	3	2
Shanghai	3	2	Hebei	1	2
Tianjin	1		Sichuan	2	2
Suzhou	1		Shandong	1	2
Fuzhou	1		Shanxi		1
Xiamen (Amoy)	2		Hunan		2
Nanjing	1		Fujian		4
Yangzhou		1			
Guangzhou (Canton)		1			
Totals: city:	12	4	village:	7	15

The influence of the pre-1949 school system and foreign education

The classical schools

During the long period from the Tang Dynasty (A.D. 618–906) to the late Qing Dynasty, in 1905, the ruling bureaucracy of China was selected by a state system of examinations. While the details varied from time to time, the content remained basically literary-philosophical. A thorough knowledge of the officially recognized Confucian classics was required, and from the Ming Dynasty onwards, the ability to write very formal, 'eight-legged' essays, which in recent times have been pilloried as exemplars of formalism (cf. Mao, 1965, vol. 3, pp. 53–68).

Hu Zhang-du points out that this was essentially a selection system, alongside which both state and private education systems developed to train candidates for office (Hu, p. 11). In theory the examinations were open to all but a few classes, such as entertainers and brothel-keepers, but in practice the sons of the wealthy, carefully trained by the best teachers in special family schools, with easy access to well-stocked private libraries, had the advantage.

While at its best the system produced educated thinkers of the highest quality, its general effect was rather to confine the mind and train the memory. Texts were committed to memory, with the aid of liberal physical encouragement and much noise. When successfully mastered they were recited by the individual student, back to his teacher, facing the class. The English pronunciation of the word used for this system of learning by heart, *bei*, or to 'back' a text, suggests well the sound of a busy classroom, with each pupil reciting at full voice his peculiar passage. That such traditional methods die slowly will be attested to by foreign teachers recently working in China.

Finally, it should be noted that the examinations were written ones, set up and supervised by an elaborate system of government officials. The first round was fought in the various *xian*. Successful candidates could then go on to the prefectural level, and then to the provincial. Those passing the provincial examinations could go on to attempt the metropolitan examination in the capital. A series of titles, or degrees, were awarded to the successful.

The modernization of schools

As has been noted above, the military defeats, beginning with the Opium War of 1841, and subsequent encroachments on her sovereignty, not only shook the declining Qing Dynasty to its foundations, but also made a profound impression on wide sections of the Chinese people. Reactions varied from attempts to return to a refurbished traditional way of life, through compromise attempts to select the best from east and west, to outright westernization. It was natural for the Chinese to see education as a main means of national salvation, and historians of the period find it hard to separate the political from the educational and cultural events (Wang, 1966, or Chow, 1960).

One of the first attempted solutions to China's difficulties was to send students abroad to learn foreign techniques. A group of 120 students was sent to the U.S.A. between 1872 and 1875, and the first group went to Europe in 1875. The intention was for them to concentrate on practical subjects in which China was weak, such as military science, navigation, ship-building and surveying (Wang, pp. 42–3). In 1896 the first Chinese students went to study in Japan (ibid, p. 59).

One of the early influential writers on education was the official, Zhang Zhi-dong. In 1898 he wrote: 'Knowledge alone can save us from destruction, and education is the path to knowledge. The literati ought to take the lead and then instruct the farmer, the workman, the merchant and the soldier . . . If we do not know the (Western) principles of government, we shall be unable to practise their technology.' He proposed sending students, particularly mature ones, abroad; the establishment of a modern school system in China; the translation of foreign books and the study of foreign newspapers (Wang, p. 52).

Wang Y. C. draws attention to the dominant role which the foreign-educated Chinese came to play in the reform of education at home (ibid, p. 362). Between 1906 and 1922 the influence was Japanese. The official aim of education in 1904 was: 'to foster loyalty to the emperor and veneration for Confucianism, and to promote public spirit, martial spirit, and practical learning'. In 1912 it changed to 'fostering moral education, and supplementing it with utilitarian, military and aesthetic education'. The words moral, military and utilitarian were an echo of Arinori Mori's programme for education in Japan (ibid, p. 363). Similarities in the two school systems included the length and curriculum of the primary school, the division of the secondary school into departments of arts and sciences, and the specialization of schools for academic, normal, vocational and technical education.

By 1922 the number and influence of those who had been educated in the U.S.A. began to preponderate. The official aim became 'to foster the formation of healthy character and to promote the democratic spirit'. Individual schools were given much more freedom, and single-faculty colleges were given the right to call themselves universities. Primary education became six years, and secondary education was divided into three years of junior and three years of senior high school. Four-year college courses were introduced. The American credit system was adopted, and the multi-track system was replaced by separate disciplines within the same school. In the high schools ethics and citizenship courses were combined in a new social studies course, and electives were introduced.

While the majority of teachers probably favoured the policy of learning from abroad, there were objections. The following extract from an article written by a student of Nankai University in December 1924 might almost have come out of the Cultural Revolution of 1966, if 'foreign' was substituted for 'American'. 'The university teachers teach American politics, American economy, American commerce, American railways, American this, American that. They praise the United States in the same way old scholars praised the sages Yao, Shun, Yu, Tang and the like.' (ibid, p. 371).

The foreign schools

During 1951 the Chinese government launched a campaign against the foreign-controlled schools and colleges, and by 1952 all of these had been nationalized. During the campaign numerous teachers denounced their past, and what they called 'American cultural aggression'. Accusations of political support for the Guomindang in its struggle against the insurgent Communist Party were mixed with complaints of fostering a Western-orientated cultural elite, isolated from the majority of Chinese and their problems.

It is difficult, if not impossible, to make an objective balance-sheet for the foreign schools. Many foreigners who worked in them will probably agree with the substance of the charges, if not with the way in which they were made. But these charges could almost all have been made against the Chinese-run institutions too. The League of Nations mission of experts in 1931 commented: 'A visitor who examines the plan of work in history, political science, or economics in some universities in China may be pardoned if he feels uncertain whether it is for Western students who are studying China, or for Chinese students who are studying the West. In the natural sciences, the exotic character of much of the teaching is even more noticeable.' (quoted: Wang, p. 372).

The number of missionary colleges in China was small, and few penetrated far into the interior. In 1916 there were about 12, compared with some 70 government colleges, and about 23 private, Chinese-run colleges. In 1947 the number of missionary colleges had only risen to about 18, while the government colleges had increased to about 120, and the private, Chinese-run colleges to over 60 (ibid, p. 368, calculated from table 9). But what they lacked in number they made up in the devotion of their staff, and the more stable financial support which they received from their foreign backers. They were thus able to provide relatively lavish accommodation, such as that at Yanjing University, now occupied by Peking University.

Any attempt to estimate the contribution made by foreign schools and colleges would have to take into account the number and quality of the students they trained, and the material legacy in the form of buildings and equipment which they handed over to the government in 1952. Not least in importance was the training of scientists and technicians, and such ancillary activities as stimulating local artisans to make apparatus, from simple laboratory glassware to precision chemical balances. Colleges also made apparatus for use in local schools, so raising the general standard of science teaching.

The oversea trained

During the period since 1872 a total of about 100,000 students studied abroad, in the U.S.A., Europe, and in Japan. Some went as private students. Others were sent on provincial or government scholarships. About half of them studied engineering, medicine, agriculture or the natural sciences. After 1932 no government students were sent to Japan. Some of the money used to provide scholarships to the U.S.A., and later to Britain, was money originally paid to these countries by China as the Boxer Indemnity, compensation which was exacted in 1901 after the Boxer uprising. Qinghua University, which sent all its graduates to study abroad, received funds from this source.

From the beginning the Chinese government attempted to supervise these students closely. From time to time regulations were laid down governing who should be allowed to study abroad, and how their qualifications should be rated on their return. The young students who went to the U.S.A. in the 1870s were given Chinese calendars containing details of traditional rituals which they were expected to follow, and they also took regular classes in Chinese at the Chinese Mission. In Europe both the students, and the Chinese commissioners appointed to supervise them, were expected to keep diaries which were later to be examined by the government for evidence of their diligence (Wang, p. 47). Official attempts to encourage the students to concentrate on their studies included a ban on marriage with foreign girls, first issued by the Board of Education in 1910, and reissued on at least two later occasions (ibid, pp. 58–9). The Guomindang in its turn attempted to make the best use of overseas studies, and first ruled that government students must be college graduates chosen by examination. It also tried to control private students. The 'Basic Policy of Education According to the Party Principles' of September 1931 laid down that self-supporting students must be graduates of secondary schools who had passed suitable tests. In April 1933 stricter regulations were passed, requiring all students to obtain authorization certificates from the Ministry of Education before applying for passports (Wang, p. 128). But as with previous regulations, enforcement was not strict, especially for private students.

It is important to try and assess the value to China of this huge expenditure on foreign study. Wang Y. C. gives details of the subjects studied, and what is known of the jobs taken by students on their return home (ibid, pp. 168–74). During the whole period engineering was the most popular subject. This was followed to an increasing amount by the natural sciences. Agriculture, ironically, was always the least popular field of all, attracting only 3.38 per cent of students who went to the U.S.A. between 1905 and 1953. Of the arts subjects, economics, political science and education were the most popular.

On their return to China the majority of students found employment in education. Between 1917 and 1934 this field accounted for between 32 and 40 per cent of jobs. Between 16 and 42 per cent of students went into government service. The most serious feature of the situation was that very few returned-students went into employment related to their field of study. Perhaps the only exception to this was the training scheme organized by the Ministry of Communications, established in 1906 and continuing through the 1940s (ibid, pp. 144–5).

In addition to this waste of talent through malemployment, and even unemployment, there was a serious change of ethos from that of traditional Chinese education. Wang Y. C. points out that the former goals of moral and academic excellence were replaced by technical efficiency, and he goes on:

> As a consequence, there was a steady weakening of the moral sense and an increasing dedication to professional achievement. While the international standing of Chinese scientists rose perceptibly, their attachment to the masses became increasingly more remote. As a number of them recently admitted (under Communist prodding but not necessarily insincerely), they had never even tried to further science or technology in China. Thus, scholars became experts in their own fields but paid almost no attention to national needs. (Wang, p. 500).

As a result of Western influence, the old ties with the rural areas were severed. The majority of the new intelligentsia came from a mercantile background and lived in the coastal cities.

> With the rise of industry and the professions they no longer had to seek employment in government service but were increasingly susceptible to the lure of high living so characteristic of modern industrialized society. As a consequence, material gain loomed large in life, and the old habit of hiding the urge to accumulate beneath a display of public virtue completely disappeared. (ibid, p. 502).

A further problem which has become more important since 1945 is the unrelatedness to Chinese conditions of much which was learnt abroad. This, coupled with the social attitudes acquired, must have severely limited the value of all but a few of the expensive foreign-trained.

Nevertheless, in the fields of engineering, science, and medicine those trained in the U.S.A., Europe and Japan still form a substantial group, especially at the higher levels. Zheng Zhu-yuan (Cheng Chu-yuan) estimates that in 1966 there were some 4,500 such graduates working in China, of whom 900 to 1,000 held Ph.D. degrees. They occupied a high proportion of places in the Academy of Sciences, and third level educational institutions (EPMC, p. 542). Top jobs in the Institute of Atomic Energy and in rocket research were held by graduates of European universities, and of Massachusetts Institute of Technology and California Institute of Technology (ibid, pp. 542–3).

Russian influences

Russian influence on Chinese education was strongest during the first ten years of the People's Republic. Before that there had been some influence on activities in the communist-held areas in the north, and a number of Chinese communists had gone to the Soviet Union to be educated. Wang Y. C. sees Russian influence in some of the measures introduced by the Guomindang after they came to power in 1927. These included the introduction of compulsory military training and courses in 'Party doctrine', the standardization of the curriculum, and abolition of the American-type electives system in secondary schools, and the curbing of single-faculty colleges (Wang, p. 363).

Immediately after the declaration of the People's Republic in 1949 the new Chinese government set up the USSR as a model of socialism to be widely studied and followed. Some, like Chen Bo-da, thought to learn the distilled wisdom of the West, much as an earlier generation had looked to Japan for the same service. Speaking to a research group of the Academy of Sciences in 1953 he said:

. . . when we advise studying the Soviet science, we do not mean to say that the works of British and American scientists may not be used as reference. They may and should be. However, generally speaking, the good things in British and American science have already been absorbed by the Soviet scientists; hence, the quickest and best way is to learn from the Soviet Union. (Fraser, p. 185).

Soviet influence was felt especially in the early reform of third level education, with its regrouping of faculties, and the formation of a number of big polytechnical institutes. Special institutions, like the People's University (Renmin Daxue), were strongly influenced in structure and content (Fraser, p. 89).

Russian influence was brought directly into the classroom by Russian teachers themselves. Between 1950 and 1958, 583 Russian teachers taught in Chinese universities and colleges, while between 1952 and 1958, a further 117 Russians taught in Chinese schools. Their length of stay varied from one to three years. While they lived separately from their Chinese colleagues at comparatively fabulous standards, their behaviour seems on the whole to have impressed the Chinese favourably. Speaking of the total of some 11,000 Soviet experts from whom workers and technicians, students and teachers had all learnt something, Yan Ji-ci, Director of the Technical Science Department of the Academy of Sciences, said in February 1960: 'Through our close contacts with Soviet scientists, their noble communism, their habits of enduring hardships, living a plain life, and studying persistently have given every one of us a very deep impression and a great lesson.' (Fraser, p. 347). The writer himself heard simpler, but similar tributes in 1965.

In addition to teaching students, the Russian teachers trained a number of Chinese teachers, especially in the field of political theory. Seven hundred young teachers were trained for the People's University, and a further 2,000 for other schools. Altogether, the China News Analysis claims, two-thirds of all political theory teachers in Chinese universities in the middle fifties were Russian-trained (C.N.A., no. 223).

Perhaps more widespread and long-lasting in its effect was the enormous volume of Russian written materials, either in translation or in the original language, which China received. From 1952 to 1956, 1,400 textbook titles were translated (C.N.A., no. 223). A further 2,746 literary works were translated between 1949 and 1956. In June 1955 Zhang Zhong-lin, Director of Planning of the Ministry of Higher Education, reported the translation of over 800 kinds of

Soviet teaching materials. The Swedish magazine, *Clarté*, reported that up to 1959 a total of 295 million books had been sold and translated (*Clarté*, vol. 1, 1967). Anyone visiting the bookshops in the Wang Fu-jing in Peking, even during the height of the Cultural Revolution in 1966, could testify to the enormous number of science books with telltale Cyrillic initials to the apparently Chinese authors' names.

Yet another source of Soviet influence was the large number of students who went to study in the Soviet Union. Up to 1959 a total of 36,000 students went, the majority to colleges and universities. Six hundred scientists and engineers went to study Soviet industry. After 1959, in spite of political coolness, a further 25,000 students were trained in the USSR, according to Soviet sources. This total of 61,000 may be compared with the figure of 35,931 students in the U.S.A. between 1905 and 1952 (Wang, p. 511). It should also be borne in mind that these students were more likely to use their speciality on their return to China, though no data have been published on this point.

Yan Ji-ci, in 1960, paid tribute to yet another important Soviet contribution, the establishment of whole new fields of research. These included nuclear energy, especially Soviet help in building the first Chinese nuclear reactor and cyclotron; and semi-conductors and electronic computers (Fraser, p. 346).

The pressure to learn from Soviet experience was very strong, and it is no wonder that the forms were often mechanical. Warnings like those of Lu Ding-yi, in May 1956, that 'our method of learning must not be doctrinaire, mechanical adoption, but must be adapted to the actual situation of our country' all too often went unheeded, or came too late. Zhang Zhong-lin complained in June 1955 about the difficulties of attempting to do in four years what Soviet students did in five or longer (Fraser, p. 213). Liu Bu-tong, a professor of the North Western University, described the 'three-copy teaching method' used in his university.

The teachers' lecture notes were copied from Soviet teaching materials, which were, without alteration of a single word, copied out on the blackboard by teachers at the classes, and then duly copied into their notebooks by the students. In the case of the student not understanding a point, the teacher would confront him with the stick, with the remark: 'this teaching material originates from the Soviet Union'... (MacFarquhar, 1960, p. 97).

The professor of education at East China Teachers' University complained: 'Up to the present, Chinese institutions of higher education are still using only Russian textbooks on education. No textbook on education has been written and published by ourselves to suit the actual conditions of China...' (ibid, p. 91).

While few tributes have been paid in recent years to Soviet help, there can be no doubt of the considerable net help which it has been, in spite of all the mistakes made. In an ideal world things might have been done better, but in the conditions of the fifties the Chinese obtained technical-professional help of high quality and in quantity. There is also no doubt that Soviet elitist ideas came to be seen as a threat to Mao Ze-dong's plans for 'training successors', and that this was one factor in the cooling off of relations between the two countries.

Foreign publications

Another source of foreign influence, now carefully controlled, is the circulation of foreign publications. Their import is a monopoly of the International Bookshop (Guoji Shudian). Publications are then distributed by it, or by the New China Bookshop (Xinhua Shudian), or the Post Office.

Another way in which China is able to obtain foreign material is by the exchange of materials with foreign institutes through the National Library in Peking, and by the Institute of Scientific and Technical Information of China of the Academy of Sciences. The National Library increased its activities considerably between 1949 and 1961. The number of countries and areas with which it exchanged materials increased from 18 to 160, while its receipts of books and periodicals rose from 30,000 in 1954 to 110,000 in 1961 (Nunn, p. 4).

The Institute of Scientific and Technical Information is the main body responsible for abstracting foreign scientific periodicals, and it publishes a number of journals of abstracts, including *Science News* (*Kexue Xinwen*), with abstracts of Chinese as well as foreign sources, and a special *Abstracts of Articles Published in Japanese Scientific and Technical Periodicals*, begun in 1963.

Some idea of the balance of subjects translated can be obtained from the following table.

Books translated from the Russian and other languages in 1964 (Nunn, p. 10)

Subject area	Russian	Other
Works of Marx, Engels, Lenin and Stalin	22	14
International Communist Movement	2	10
Communist movement, party, party construction	2	4
Philosophy	4	8
History	2	4
Economics	8	—
Politics and social life	2	4
Culture and education	—	2
Language	—	2
Literature	4	6
Arts	4	16
Religion and atheism	—	2
Science	40	38
Geology and geography	10	2
Biology	8	10
Medicine	10	2
Agriculture	—	4
	118	128
Industry—	—	4
standards	6	—
power machinery	4	10
electrical machinery, radio, automation	72	32
mining	10	4
metallurgy, mechanical engineering	74	14
light industry, handicrafts	8	4
chemical engineering	22	8
construction	24	2
highway engineering	30	2
	250	80
Grand totals:	368	208

Nunn gives an interesting table of the percentage of books published which had been translated from Russian and other languages (Nunn, p. 9). From 1954 to 1957 Russian books accounted for between 45 per cent and 38 per cent of all titles, and then fell sharply to between 11 per cent and 7 per cent in 1964. Books translated from other foreign languages remained fairly steady throughout the period, ranging from 6 per cent to 3 per cent. Nunn notes that after Russian, English is the next largest language, with some 1 to 1.5 per cent of titles. American books predominate over those of British origin.

Another avenue by which certain institutions and individuals can obtain copies of material which originated from abroad is the official 'pirating' service by which foreign publications are copied. In those books on the English language which the author's students used, the copying was perfect. Title and author were given, but the original publisher's name was omitted. This practice dates from long before 1949, and is also used in other poor countries. While it arouses the anger of many foreigners, a number of factors should be borne in mind. The need for good teaching materials is very great. At present there is no other way in which foreign materials could be distributed on the necessary scale. When China is richer she will certainly give up the practice as uneconomic, compared with buying in the more normal manner. In the meantime publishers can console themselves that a potential demand is being developed.

Educational change

The internal factors which have here been discussed all tend to favour the more conservative elements within the CCP. The school system has traditionally been authoritarian and academic, and recent Soviet influence, while it has brought about changes, has strengthened this pattern rather than weakened it. Because of the difficulty of the written language, courses of study have always tended to be rather long, and the introduction of weighty Soviet syllabuses in many subjects has reinforced this.

The external factors make all forms of development difficult, but on balance probably also favour conservative solutions. Social changes have created new managerial, technical and cadre groups, but these to a great extent continue to hold traditional values and prefer a hierarchical school system run on conventional lines. Economic development has been insufficient to provide the school buildings, furniture and books needed by the growing population with its high proportion of youth, while many peasant families are still too poor to release their children from work to attend school. All this has tended to preserve the old system, though at the same time it has also stimulated the search for an alternative pattern. The shortage of industrial and commercial jobs for urban school-leavers has underlined the irrelevance of much of the present education. But Mao and his supporters have so far not translated their general proposals into the detailed alternatives which might inspire confidence in their success. The part-work principle may turn out to be the key to change, but it can as easily be incorporated into the conventional pattern of education which Mao wishes to overthrow.

4

The full-time schools

In this chapter the full-time first, second and third level schools will be described. These have until now formed the backbone of the educational system. It is important to remember that, up to the present, school attendance is not compulsory at any level. Nevertheless, especially in the cities, demand for school places is greater than the supply.

The special foreign language institutions will be discussed here at greater length than their role in Chinese education would justify because their employment of foreign teachers has made available the detailed information which brings many of China's more general educational problems to life.

First level schools

Primary education was divided into pre-school kindergartens (*you'er yuan*), and a junior school (*xiao xue*) which was usually divided into a lower school (*chuji xiaoxue*) and an upper school (*gaoji xiaoxue*).

Crèches and kindergartens

For convenience, and because in practice they were often found together, crèches (*tuo'er suo*) and kindergartens will be considered together. They were run by various local organizations. Some were run by local People's Councils, while the majority were run by rural Communes, and urban factories, offices and other institutions. All of them had to be run according to regulations set out from time to time by the central Ministry of Education.

Kindergartens normally catered for the age range 3 to 7, crèches started at different ages. In the Tian Shan estate in Shanghai the writer was told that children were admitted at the age of one year.

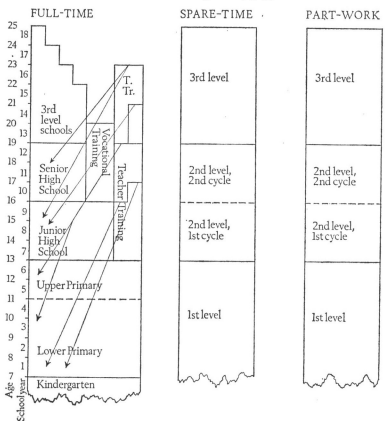

China's School System (1965)

The length of time during which these institutions were kept open varied considerably. The main trend was towards day-schools which keep open for some 8 to 10 hours a day. Some schools only operated a half-day, four-hour system. Some were boarding schools, with the children going home only at weekend. At the Railway Workers' Estate in Taiyuan, which the writer visited in August 1966, 78 out of the total of 210 children were boarders. In yet other cases the kindergarten was a temporary affair, set up during such events as the harvest. Small fees were charged which helped to offset the cost of meals provided.

The full-time schools

The buildings and equipment varied according to the wealth of the organization to which the institution belonged, and according to the imagination of the teachers concerned. Sometimes the kindergarten was housed in its own building. Sometimes it occupied a few rooms in the junior school. Classrooms varied from small rooms crowded with tiny desks, as in a building in Shanghai whose wooden floors and stairs appeared to the writer to be a considerable fire hazard, to a tall, barn-like former landlord's house in a tea-growing village near Hangzhou, where the circle of children on tiny stools was dwarfed. Where possible, sleeping accommodation was provided for an after-dinner nap, or for more extended periods for the younger children. In the northern villages the rows of glossy black heads sticking out of colourful quilted bundles resembled dolls as they lay in rows on the matting-covered *kangs* (warmed brick platforms on which people sleep). In the south, and in the cities, rows of tiny beds were provided.

The furniture was always carefully made to measure. In one classroom in a commune near Peking, in a not particularly rich village, the writer remembers rows of benches, each row a little higher than the one in front. The ubiquitous towel-and-basin stand was also low. Only the flower-painted enamel basins and hot-water vacuum flasks were adult-size.

The curriculum, laid down by the Ministry of Education, included physical education, language arts and general knowledge. Physical education was supposed to include health habits, free play, gymnastics, and dance. Language arts were verbal skills: conversation and story telling. Reading was not normally taught at this stage. But in some cities academic pressure began to act in the final year. Two textbooks produced in Jinan, Shandong province, in 1960-1, aimed to teach 332 characters in order to pave the way for work in the primary school! General knowledge included knowledge of the natural and social environment, together with some drawing, singing and number work. The extent to which this curriculum could be carried out depended on the wealth of the community, and the educational level of the teachers.

The foreign visitor was normally entertained by an exhibition of singing and dancing. A class might be conducted by one of its older members, who sang the first line and then firmly called out: *yi, er,* . . . (one, two, . . .). The songs tended to be the currently popular adult political ones. Small groups of children might perform a dance, or recite, again on political themes. The shy solemnity and competence displayed were always endearing.

To western educationists, trained in infant teaching, the children's surroundings seemed very bare, and lacking in the kind of teacher-pupil-made apparatus which one would expect a society stressing self-reliance to produce. The small collections of factory-made model animals (15 in one class of a Peking rural commune), or elaborate tricycles (8 in the Taiyuan Railway Workers' Kindergarten) seemed at the same time too much and too little. But such criticism is expecting too much at this stage and misunderstands the main purpose of the crèches and kindergartens which is socialization, rather than the development of individual capabilities. It also overlooks the fact that many of the activities so essential in the nature-starved urban communities of Euro-America are part of the everyday out-of-school experience of Chinese children.

The junior school

Full-time junior schools were of three types: government, voluntary and private. Voluntary schools were set up on a resolution of the local People's Council, with the approval of the *xian* education authority. The local People's Council was then responsible directly, or through a specially appointed committee, for the organization, finance and maintenance of the school. Funds were collected from fees, and either by a special local tax, or voluntary contributions. Teachers were either obtained from the *xian*, or recruited locally. Private schools were allowed in the towns, with the approval of the *xian* educational bureau. They could be set up by individuals, or by factories, offices and other institutions. If the schools were judged satisfactory, they might receive a subsidy of up to 50 per cent of their budget should they be in financial difficulties.

All three types of school had to comply with Ministry of Education directives on administration, organization, curriculum, textbooks, and methodology. These were passed on to them through provincial, municipal, *xian* and *xiang* education offices.

Organization

Except for very small schools, every junior school had a head-teacher (*xiaozhang*). Usually he was assisted by a deputy-head (*fu-xiao-zhang*), and perhaps a director of studies (*jiaowu zhuren*). Big schools had a clerk.

Schools were normally run by a small council. The head was the chairman, and other members included the deputy-head, the director of studies, and a representative of the other teachers. Both educational and administrative problems were discussed. But decisions appear to have been taken only after a decision had been reached at a full staff meeting, which was attended not only by the teaching staff, but also by all other workers in the establishment, such as cooks and cleaners. Recommendations from the staff meetings were sent to the local education authority for further action.

Another administrative body was the school council. In the rural areas this was composed of representatives of the different commune labour brigades from which the school received pupils. In the towns members represented the factories and other organizations where the parents of the children worked, and perhaps the street committees in the area. The school head was the chairman. This council concerned itself with questions of general administration, and the maintenance of buildings and provision of materials. On such matters as the making of new desks or blackboards it was probably usually able to act independently, but other matters had to be referred to the local education authority.

Finally there was the parents' committee. Parents elected representatives according to local conditions, perhaps one for each village from which the school drew pupils. Again the head was chairman. The committee had only advisory powers, and was concerned with personal problems rather than administration. Recommendations from the parents went to the head-teacher's council, who then decided what action should be taken.

The teaching unit was the class, which was mixed, and was not to be larger than 45 pupils. According to the UNESCO Survey of 1958 there were on average one and three-quarters to one and a half teachers per class. Normally there was a class teacher who moved up each year with his class. This was thought to be desirable in order to foster a close relationship between teacher and pupil. At the same time, the class teacher did not teach all subjects to his class. Teachers specialized to a certain extent. Myrdal gives the example of Ji

Zhong-zhou, class teacher of class 5, then class 6. Mr Ji taught Chinese language in the sixth class, nature study in the fifth class and drawing in the fourth, fifth and sixth. Formerly he had taught music and singing in the fifth and sixth classes (Myrdal, p. 384).

Each class elected a leader whose job it was to help the teacher maintain discipline. With two elected assistants the leader supervised such things as cleaning the classroom, work in the school garden, group private study, and class excursions and sports.

The school year consisted of 2 terms, the first beginning on 1 September. There was a holiday in January-February, at the time of the lunar New Year, and the second term ended in July. The total time was some 34 weeks, each of 6 days. The day began at 8 a.m. and went on to 12 midday. Afternoon work began at 2 p.m. and went on to 5 p.m. Each period lasted from 40 to 45 minutes with a break of 10 to 15 minutes between each. Where demand for school places exceeded the possibility of supply the school day could be reduced and classes alternate between morning and afternoon schooling only. Two schools reported from Hebei in 1965 operated a 4 hour, 40 minute day and a 6 hour, 30 minute day respectively (SCMP 3431, 1965). In Anhui, in 1964, after a careful study of peasant difficulties and the rural calendar, the education authorities instituted a 3-term year. In this way they were able to avoid the busy seasons when children were needed, especially by the poorer peasants, to help with farm work. The first term ran from mid-September to the end of January. The second, from mid-February to the end of May (some $3\frac{1}{2}$ months). The third term was from the beginning of July to the beginning of August. In all, this made a total of $8\frac{1}{2}$ months. There was a winter vacation of 21 days, a summer vacation of 40 days, and an autumn vacation of about 50 days. New students were admitted each term, and school was held on Sundays. The only rest days during term were the first and fifteenth days of the lunar month. The *People's Daily* report (SCMP 3369, 1964) claimed a large increase in the number of pupils enrolled, and in those who stayed the course as a result of these changes. It seems highly likely that a similar year will become general, at least in the rural areas, when education settles down again after the Cultural Revolution.

One of the big problems which faces children, particularly in rural areas, is the distance between home and school. The lower primary school may involve a walk of between three and four kilometres. To get to an upper primary school may be even longer. In 1958 the teacher in Niufangkou village, Zhingerkou Commune, Hebei (Hopei), set out to overcome this problem by converting his school from a lower primary school into a new, mixed-type school. He began by taking correspondence classes and getting help from other schools to improve his own qualifications, to enable him to teach to the higher level required in an upper primary school. At the same time he began persuading the local education authorities and the parents that such a school was desirable. By 1961 there were 35 schools in the province with 42 combined senior and junior classes, and by 1964 the number of schools had risen to 92 (SCMP 3431, 1965). There appear to have been some differences in the way the classes were handled, but basically it seems that classes contained pupils from various grades of both the lower and upper primary school.

Except for army dependents, the children of revolutionary martyrs, and such very poor people as the boat people, parents were normally expected to pay school fees and provide their children with pencils and notebooks, and what textbooks were available. Basil Davidson (1953) was given some figures for Guangzhou (Canton) schools which showed a reduction by one-fifth in fees compared with pre-1949, to a figure which was equivalent to about 7 English shillings at that time. Current reports suggest a figure of about 5 yuan per year, or 15 shillings in current exchange rates. Such figures need to be seen against incomes if they are to make any sense. Most writers on China have ignored this question and the impression seems current that education in China is free.

Buildings and equipment

Buildings varied from the makeshift ex-temple or landlord's house, to excellently constructed modern schools. And it was not always the towns which had the latter. The most impressive school building the writer visited was in the rich tea village near Hangzhou to which foreign visitors were often taken. This had six classrooms on two floors, and a large assembly hall. Like all Chinese schools, it struck the visitor as very bare. But it was light and very clean. Too many schools had drab, dirty walls, and were quite devoid of colour, other than the children's clothes which were often very gay.

Furniture varied considerably, from neat modern desks and chairs to grim, old-fashioned twin-desks with fixed seats. Blackboards were sometimes fixed to the wall, and sometimes on easels, and varied considerably in size and texture. The teacher was usually supplied with a tall version of the child's desk from which he could read from notes when standing.

Some classrooms had a stand with a wash-bowl, soap and towel. But more important was the spittoon, placed perilously near to the teacher's desk. Its regular use was part of the pupil's education in hygiene. Heating in the north might be provided by a stove, removed in summer. But many schools were probably not heated for most of the time, the pupils being protected by thickly padded clothing, hats and gloves.

Most schools managed to have a library, if only of paperback children's books. Myrdal reports a library of 300 such volumes for the village of Liu Ling (Myrdal, p. 379), together with 300 others borrowed from the labour brigade, and each class had up to 60 volumes in addition. Big city schools, like the Peking primary school visited by Sundarlal (1952) had libraries of 20,000 volumes, and additional luxuries like music rooms and even a small zoo.

Curriculum

The timetable was laid down by the Ministry of Education, which specified subjects and time to be devoted to each. In the lower primary school half the time was devoted to language work, while a quarter was occupied by arithmetic. Two hours a week were spent on physical education, and a further hour a week on manual labour. Singing, drawing, and a weekly assembly devoted to moral-political education took one hour each. The whole programme was limited and strictly practical. Efforts were constantly being made in different areas to relate the content more closely to the life and needs of the local community. This appears to have resulted in increased attendance and better results in a number of cases.

One example of an attempt to raise standards was reported in the *Liaoning Ribao* in April 1960 (SCMP 2270, 1960). The local CCP Committee, the Education Committee, and experts from the Institute of Psychology of the Chinese Academy of Sciences got together and prepared new teaching materials which they tried out in two second-year classes in Beiguan Primary School. The aim was to enable the pupils to 'acquire knowledge systematically and make them think'. At the same time work was done on character recognition and writing in the first year. While other schools did no essay writing till the third year, the experimental classes successfully managed to write short essays and poems, and to keep a diary in their first year. The second-year arithmetic class, which in other local schools only handled numbers below 100, successfully coped with numbers up to 100,000, and used multipliers of two digits, a feat normally reserved for the fourth year. When class 2A was tested against 4D in another district, they proved better at identification of characters, dictation, reading, explaining the meaning of phrases, and composition. In arithmetic the results were:

	2A (experimental)	4D
Mean mark	96.6	90.2
Pupils scoring 100% ...	54.4%	38.1%
Pupils failing test	0.0%	not known

It was also reported that all 2A pupils 'loved the Party and Chairman Mao', and 'loved the people's communes and labour fervently'. Proof of this appeared to be 'incomplete data' of '442 good characters and good deeds in one term', attendance of 98 per cent, and the fact that after studying a lesson on 'fervent love for the people's commune' 21 pupils organized themselves without prompting to go out and weed the fields. Homework during the test period took only 20 minutes per day.

In the upper primary, classes 5 and 6, the time devoted to language work was reduced by 2 or 3 hours, and the length of day extended to add 3 or 4 subjects to the curriculum. Natural science, geography and history each occupied 2 hours a week, while since 1957 an hour of agricultural science has been laid down for rural schools. According to the timetable reproduced by Chen (p. 100) this would seem to replace the time devoted to manual labour.

The lower primary Chinese language course

The following account of the Chinese language course in the lower primary school is mainly derived from a study of a selection of the

The Primary School Timetable

Subjects	Weekly hours by year						Total hours for 6-year period
	1	2	3	4	5	6	
Language	12	12	12	12	10	10	
				*	9	9	2,244
Arithmetic	6	6	6	6	6	6	
				* 7	6	5	1,224
History					2	2	136
Geography					2	2	136
Natural science					2	2	
				*	2	3	170
Agricultural knowledge					1	1	68
Manual labour	1	1	1	1			136
Physical education	2	2	2	2	2	2	408
Singing	1	1	1	1	1	1	204
	* 2	2	2				306
Drawing	1	1	1	1	1	1	204
Weekly assembly	1	1	1	1	1	1	204
TOTAL HOURS	24	24	24	24	28	28	5,032†

*alternative hours given in UNESCO *World Survey of Education*, 1, Primary Education, 1958.
†total given in the World Survey, which does not include agricultural knowledge or the weekly assembly.
Other figures taken from the table in Chen (*China Quarterly*, no. 10), which quotes Ministry of Education figures for 1957–8, taken from the *Jiao-shi Bao*, 12 July 1957.

textbooks available to the writer, supplemented by descriptions by Chinese who have been both pupils and teachers during the past twenty years. The textbooks are very revealing, especially as they include detailed instructions as to what is to be memorized, read aloud, or used for dictation. But unfortunately very few copies are available, as they cannot be bought freely by the general public. It is also important to remember that frequent revisions have taken place, and that different books have been used in different parts of China. There are eight textbooks in all, one for each term of the four-year course.

The main object of the course is to teach the pupils to read and write. Another object is to teach standard pronunciation, and to assist with this much attention is given in the early part of the course to phonetic work, and to learning transcriptions. Before 1958 the system known as *bopomofo* was used, but with the introduction of *hanyu pinyin* in the autumn of 1958 this was discontinued. The number of characters taught is:

Book	Number of new characters	Cumulative total
1	337	337
2	451	788
3	455	1,243
4	431	1,674
5	309	1,983
6	298	2,281
7	281	2,562
8	189	2,751

The first twenty-three pages of Book 1 are devoted to phonetic work, using *pinyin* only. The first page shows the vowels *a*, *o*, and *e* with four tone markings, while a coloured picture on the previous frontispiece shows the teacher holding up a card with an *a* on it for the children to recognize. Pictures give meaning to the sounds, and by page 5 the *pinyin* word is given below the pictures which are used to illustrate the consonants. On pages 9–13 the idea of initials and finals is introduced and then three more pages are used on finals with *–n* and *–ng*.

The first characters to appear, on page 24 of the textbook, are those which are obvious pictographs. They are accompanied by drawings of the five basic brush strokes, and ruled squares to show the proportions of the written characters. Such ruled squares are used with new characters throughout the first four books, and then more rarely in the later books. For example, in Book 6 only six characters are shown in this way, in exercise 11.5, where the pupil is instructed to copy the characters, paying attention to the stroke form, stroke order and structure of the whole.

The basic teaching method is the familiar one of look-and-say. A character is presented, on the blackboard, on a flash-card, or in the textbook, and the pupils repeat the sound while looking at the shape.

Yu wen—language primer, book 1, page 22

This page comes two pages before the introduction of the first characters. It illustrates certain two-syllable words (garden, moon, magpie, etc.); the division of monosyllables into initials and finals; the word for two; and the four tone markings.

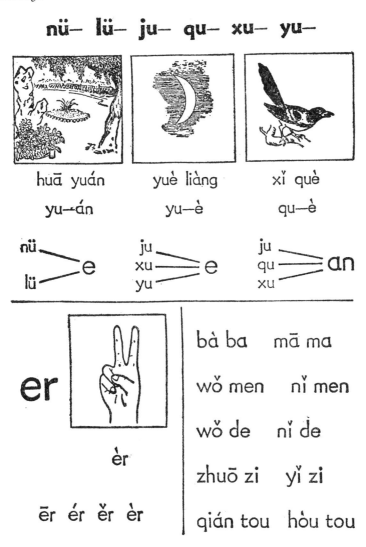

nü– lü– ju– qu– xu– yu–

huā yuán   yuè liàng   xǐ què

yu–án   yu–è   qu–è

nü
lü   e

ju
xu   e
yu

ju
qu   an
xu

er

èr

ēr ér ěr èr

bà ba   mā ma

wǒ men   nǐ men

wǒ de   nǐ de

zhuō zi   yǐ zi

qián tou   hòu tou

Yu wen—language primer, book 3, page 24.

The four pictures are an exercise. Pupils must make up one sentence to illustrate each, giving it first orally and then writing it down.

At the foot of the page is the typical layout by which the correct proportions of the characters are taught.

缺少　　缺点　　缺席　　缺课　　经手　　经过

集体　　集中　　半天　　半边　　半劳动力

二　认一认下面的偏旁，写一写括号里的字。

　　岳（缺）止（此）卩（印）戈（战）鱼（鲁）

三　看图说话，说完写句子，每幅图写一句。

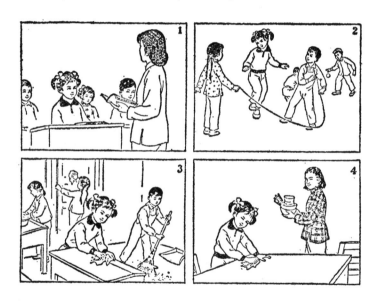

四　写下面的字，要写得左右匀称。

助　此　印　所　粒　鼓　缺　醒

120

After repetition of the sound some ten to twelve times in unison, the teacher then draws the character stroke by stroke and the pupils call out the strokes: dot, transverse, vertical, and so on. In this way a character can be described in terms of its stroke order, and verbal aid is given to the memorizing process in another way.

Writing is practised with a pencil, and in the higher classes with ball-pens or fountain pens where these are common. The *maobi*, or writing-brush, is used for the special calligraphy lessons which take place three times a week in years 1 and 2, and twice a week in years 3 and 4. The general standard of writing reached appears to be very high compared with Europe, where calligraphy is not held in such high regard.

From the first introduction of complex characters, attention is drawn to their separate parts, especially to radicals under which they are to be found in many dictionaries. Already in the first revision list (Book 1, p. 44) grouping by both sound and radical is used.

From page 35 of the first book onwards sentences, and then longer passages of text are used. Exercises at the end of each text indicate whether the passage is to be memorized or not. The proportion to be memorized falls steeply after Book 4, though in practice the habit is probably continued with material for which no instruction is given. Western readers who might condemn such methods would do well to consider the problem of learning to read a script which gives only slight aid, and then to the highly initiated only, as to how it is pronounced.

Book	Number of passages to be memorized	Total number of passages
1	13	15
2	32	40
3	26	40
4	28	39
5	6	34
6	4	38
7	7	31
8	8	29

Exercises are given at the end of each text, and in special sections between every three or four lessons. Many of the exercises concern the detailed study of characters. Transcriptions are to be copied.

Lists of characters are to be read. Similar characters are to be compared. Or a list of characters has to be read out, stroke by stroke. In the more advanced books phrases and sentences are given with blanks to be filled from given alternative characters. Oral comprehension is introduced by exercises in which pupils have to give sentences to describe each of four pictures which tell a simple story. By Book 3 these sentences have to be written after they have been given orally. Comprehension questions are also given with the texts.

The content of the textbooks is serious and moral, with almost no reference, in those books studied, to play of any kind. Pleasure is to be found in hard work and in helping other people. Happy children sit up straight in class and co-operate with the teacher in their studies; wash their clothes and help in the house; or join in the work of harvesting the crops. Next to earnest work, the message of thinking of the public good is put over. Little Brother is firmly told by his elder sister that the flowers in the park are not to be picked because they are 'for everyone to look at' (Book 1, lesson 35). Wang Xin helps an old lady who has fallen down in the street, in spite of her being a complete stranger (Book 2, lesson 5). The power of example is shown in picture form when two tree-destroying youngsters are converted into tree-protectors (Book 4, p. 27).

Directly political material mainly takes the form of stories about heroic deeds performed during the anti-Japanese or civil wars, or a small number of stories in which life before and after 1949 are contrasted. The main message is the importance of the Communist Party, without which the improvements would have been impossible. Mao Ze-dong is seldom mentioned, and then as a modest, approachable leader, sharing the life and work of others, and constantly thinking of their welfare. When persuaded to sit in the front seat at the theatre in Yan'an (Yenan), Mao takes a little girl on to his knee and chats with her during the interval (Book 3, lesson 11). Also in Yan'an, in 1939, Mao finds time to work in the fields alongside his soldiers (Book 6, lesson 1).

Most of the volumes contain one or more traditional tales, usually strongly moral. The resourcefulness of Si Ma Guang, when a child, in saving the life of a friend contrasts with the boy who cried wolf once too often (Book 2, lessons 35 and 36). Versions of Aesop's fables include the grasshopper and the ant (Book 3, lesson 36).

Another type of text describes simple scientific and technical matters. The majority are biological: organs of the human body (Book 4, lesson 34); the silkworm (Book 4, lesson 15); or how seeds grow (Book 6, lessons 14 and 15). Finally there are a number of practical lessons on how to write messages (Book 3, lesson 22); or notices (Book 3, lesson 34); or how to write letters and address envelopes (Book 6, lessons 17 and 18).

The world outside China only appears briefly, and then as the story either of great men, or as American imperialism threatening China. Lenin and James Watt both appear in one volume (Book 3, lessons 22 and 28).

The upper primary Chinese language course

The four textbooks on which the following account is based were first published in 1957 or 1958 and were reprinted in 1963 and 1964. They can be taken as representative of the kind of course following in the majority of upper primary schools during this period.

The lessons are printed in the type of script which seems to be reserved for adults and the more literate learners, and they are considerably longer than those in the lower primary school. While the majority of texts continue to be specially written, a few are taken from other works, and there are even a number of classical poems.

The emphasis has shifted from the forms of the characters to their meaning. Incomplete sentences have to be completed. Similar words have to be distinguished, usually by choosing the correct one to complete a sentence. And idioms are given which have to be explained. In a few cases pupils are instructed to consult a dictionary.

Hanyu pinyin occurs in the exercises in all four books when attention is being directed to phonetic problems. In most cases the pupils are instructed to pay attention to initials or finals which are confused in some dialects, such as *zh-* and *z-*, or *sh-* and *s-*.

As in the case of the lower primary school books, the texts are almost all essentially moral-political in content. Eleven texts, or about 8 per cent, are devoted to scientific and technical subjects, which include spraying crops from the air; how the Russian horticulturist, Michurin, grew pears and apples; the production of salt; the life of a spider; the underwater world; and the work of the famous Chinese railway engineer, Zhan Tian-you. Four texts, or less than 3 per cent, are devoted to practical advice on writing letters and notices of various kinds, and making work agreements. Four of Mao Ze-dong's prose writings are included, and two of his poems. The six fables include some from Aesop, and the 'Emperor's New Clothes' and the 'Little Match Seller' by Hans Andersen. The legend of Antaeus is described as a prelude to a homily on the need for the Communist Party to remain in contact with the people. The world outside China is again only dimly glimpsed. There are short accounts of Marx (Books 2, lesson 1 and Book 3, lesson 4), Engels (Book 3, lesson 4), Lenin (Book 3, lesson 5), Spartacus (Book 3, lesson 27), Galileo (Book 2, lesson 11), and Maxim Gorky (Book 4, lesson 3), but these mainly deal with the moral-political qualities which these men displayed, rather than the society in which they lived. An exception is the story about the exploitations of Africans on a rubber plantation (Book 2, lesson 30), where the emphasis is on social relations.

Arithmetic

Available information on the arithmetic course gives no indication that mathematics is one of the subjects for which Chinese scholarship is famous. The aims are limited and practical, and the methods appear to be slow and thorough.

A division is made between numbers up to 100, and those above. In the first year only addition, subtraction and multiplication of numbers less than 100 are undertaken. In the second year division of these numbers is taught, and addition and subtraction are practised with numbers larger than 100. Only in year 3 are multiplication and division of large numbers tried.

According to Myrdal (pp. 370–3) time is introduced in the third year and calculations involving time come in the fourth year. Chinese and metric scales are introduced in the fourth year, and there is a special course on the use of the abacus for addition, subtraction, multiplication and division. But in a 1964 edition of the fourth volume of the textbook, i.e. in year two, there are pictures of clock-faces and simple exercises in time-telling and calculation, while units of weight and length are introduced in Book 3.

Years 5 and 6 are occupied with more practical exercises, including simple book-keeping and calculation of cubic content. Decimals, fractions and simple statistical tables are all reserved for year 6. The abacus is used as an aid during the final two years.

A number of familiar aids are pictured in the textbooks. Bundles of sticks, in 10s and later in 100s; pictures of rabbits, bowls of apples; dots and ducks; table-tennis bats and aeroplanes; all are enlisted to bring the numerical symbols to life. On the cover of Book 2 the teacher is holding up a flash card showing two numbers to be added. Book 3's cover shows a vertically mounted abacus on the teacher's desk.

History

According to the official timetable, history is taught for 2 hours a week during both years of the upper primary school. But according to Myrdal (p. 373) it was confined to the final, sixth year. Nor is it clear how many textbooks are used, as the two which the writer has examined appear to cover the whole course which Myrdal indicates.

In order to give some idea of both the range and balance of the subject-matter covered, and the approach, the titles of the various lessons in these books is given.

Upper primary school textbook—History, volume 1

1   The non-exploiting, classless primitive society.
2   Struggle between slaves and slave-owners.
3   The ancient educator, Confucius.
4   The beginning of feudal society in our country.
5   The establishment of a centralized feudal state.
6   The first great peasant uprising—209 B.C., Chen Sheng and Wu Guang.
7   Economic and cultural exchanges with Central Asia.
8   Revolt of the Yellow Turbans.
9   Settlement south of the Yangzi and the development of agriculture in the north.
10 The Grand Canal connects the south and the north.
11 Strength and prosperity in the Tang dynasty.
12 Songzan Gambo (Tibetan unifier) and Princess Wen Cheng (of Tang).
13 Yue Fei—national hero (A.D. 1140, fought the Jin).

14 Four great inventions in ancient China (paper, printing, the magnetic compass, and gunpowder).

15 The beginning of sailing on the distant oceans (c. 1405).

16 The peasant revolt led by Li Zi-cheng (1636 to end of Ming dynasty).

17 The struggle led by Zheng Cheng-gong to retake and settle Taiwan (1661, Dutch defeated).

18 Friendly relations between different races during the Qing dynasty.

19 The struggle against aggression by the people of San Yuan Li, Guangdong. (Opium War—battle with British under Captain Elliot on 30 May 1841).

20 Proletarian revolutionary leaders, Marx and Engels.

21 Taiping Tianguo revolution.

22 Struggle against Japanese imperialist aggression against China (1894).

23 Yihetuan struggle against imperialism (The Boxers).

24 The capitalist democratic revolution led by Sun Yat-sen.

25 The birth and growth of the Chinese proletariat.

Upper primary school textbook—History, volume 2

26 The great workers' leader, Lenin, and the October socialist revolution.

27 The anti-imperialist, anti-feudal May 4th Movement.

28 The first period of Comrade Mao Ze-dong's revolutionary activities.

29 The birth of the Chinese Communist Party.

30 The great strike of 7 February (1923).

31 The anti-imperialist movement of 30 May (1924).

32 The Northern Expedition (1926–7).

33 The peak of the worker-peasant revolution.

34 Jiang Jie-shi (Chiang Kai-shek) is a traitor to the revolution.

35 The establishment of a revolutionary base on Jinggangshan (Mao Ze-dong and Zhu De, 1927–8).

36 The struggle of the Chinese people against Japanese aggression in the north-east (Manchuria).

37 The Long March (October 1934 to October 1935).

38 The 9 December anti-Japanese patriotic movement (1935).

39 The beginning of the anti-Japanese war.

40 The heroic struggle of the soldiers and people of the anti-Japanese base areas.
41 The people's struggle in the Guomindang-governed areas.
42 Victory in the anti-Japanese war.
43 The beginning of the war of liberation.
44 Land reform in the liberated areas.
45 The people's democratic movement.
46 Decisive victory.
47 The birth of the People's Republic of China (1 October 1949).

Both textbooks end with a list of important dates. Each lesson is followed by two or three short comprehension questions. (Note: explanatory notes added in parenthesis above).

Other subjects

Geography, for which unfortunately no textbooks have been available for study, is apparently confined to the geography of China. Drawing is largely copying objects in pencil, with water-colour reserved for the fifth and sixth years. Music consists mainly of choral singing. More modern, creative work in the last two subjects appears to be confined to out-of-school clubs. One interesting feature of the singing teaching is the successful use of a form of tonic solfa which enables large numbers of young people quickly to learn new songs published in the newspapers or on cheap newssheets.

Second level schools

Secondary schools, under the People's Government, have continued to operate on basically the same pattern as before 1949. The aim has been to provide a general, fundamentally bookish education, and the number and distribution of the schools has severely limited the number of peasant children who have been able to obtain a secondary education. The old, American-influenced division of the schools into two stages of three years each has continued, and the number of senior high schools has remained even more restricted. The pre-1949 distinction into general academic schools, teacher-training schools, and vocational schools has continued, though it would appear that the majority of the vocational schools operate on a part-work principle, rather than being full-time schools. A number of schools restricted their entry to the children of the higher cadres, while after 1958 certain schools were designated for the training of 'specialized personnel of higher quality' to fill important technical and administrative posts (Zhou En-lai, April 1959, in Fraser, p. 311). Such schools received special treatment in relation to staffing and equipment.

The private schools, particularly the three hundred odd religious schools, were gradually brought under State control, and finally by 1956, state ownership. But the management of secondary schools, like that of primary, is still very varied. The majority of full-time general secondary schools are run by the various state bodies; provincial, municipal, and local education authorities.

Full-time secondary schools have always been located in the urban areas. L. A. Orleans comments: 'Until 1958, for all practical purposes, there were no middle schools (i.e. secondary schools) in the Chinese countryside' (EPMC, p. 508). While there have been some efforts to remedy this since, e.g. the report from Jilin (Kirin) Province in the *Guangming Ribao* of 16 January 1962 that they were 'trying to move full-time secondary schools deep into the country-side' where some 38 per cent of the population lived, the main trend has been rather to set up quite different, part-work schools. These, the agricultural secondary schools (see chapter 5) have enabled the Chinese press to report remarkable strides in the provision of secondary education. For example, the Shuining Region of Sichuan (Szechwan) reported that nearly every *xiang* had, by May 1958, one secondary school, following the setting up of 758 agricultural secondary schools (SCMP 1785, 1958). In the same period the *People's Daily* reported from Henan (Honan) that private secondary schools had been set up, presumably by communes, so that there was one in every *xiang* (SCMP 1788, 1958).

No figures are available for the number of schools of different types, and figures available for students' enrolment have to be interpreted with caution because of the wide discrepancy in standards between the different schools. The last global data published, in 1959–60, gave figures of 8 to 10 million students in secondary schools, which speakers claimed to be nearly six times as many as in the pre-1949 highest year (1946). (Yang Xiu-feng in Fraser, pp. 304 and 323; and Lin Feng in Fraser, p. 378). Technical education was reported to occupy some 1.47 million of these students, or some 2.8 times the previous peak figure (Yang Xiu-feng in Fraser, p. 304).

During the past nineteen years considerable efforts have been made to develop secondary education for the various minority peoples. Here we shall give only a few examples which have been reported. In Jilin (Kirin) Province a private Manchu secondary school was set up in August 1957. Eighteen of the 33 teachers and over 500 of the 1,400 students were Manchu. (SCMP 1634, 1957). In October 1958 the NCNA reported that 1,000 new secondary schools had been set up in Inner Mongolia with a total enrolment of 140,000 students. While it did not say so, it is probable that the majority, if not all of these, were part-work schools. In the Gueiyang area of Gueizhou (Kweichow), where there are some 17 million minority peoples, including Miao, Tung, Shui and Yi, the NCNA reported that by 1959 there was a senior high school in every *xian* and a junior high school in every commune (*xiang*) (SCMP 2084, 1959). Finally, in Xinjiang (Sinkiang) in 1963 the *Guangming Ribao* reported that there were then 300 secondary schools compared with only 9 before 1949 (SCMP 3124, 1963).

School organization

The school was presided over by a head-teacher (*zhong xiaozhang*), assisted by a deputy-head and director of studies. Administrative work was done by an Office of General Affairs (*Zongwu Chu*) and an Office of Studies (*Jiaowu Chu*). There was a school council, chaired by the head-teacher, with representatives of both students and workers, which had the right to discuss general matters affecting the running of the school. But in practice the power probably rested with the head-teacher and the Party secretary. Parents' committees may have played a role where the school was a local one, but most parents probably lived too far away from the secondary school to make participation practicable.

The extent to which the Communist Party was organized in secondary schools varied, but from the late fifties increasing attention was paid to this problem. In 1959 Fujian (Fukien) Province reported that there were CCP branches in all its secondary schools, and that 10 per cent of its teachers were Party members (SCMP 2174, 1959). A *People's Daily* editorial, on 21 December 1959, referring to successes in Fujian (Fukien), spoke of the importance of Party leadership in education, saying that it should 'take charge of the teaching business' (SCMP 2174, 1959). This and other articles have suggested that the higher party cadres should take part in classroom teaching so as to really familiarize themselves with the problems. Yang Xiu-feng made the general position quite clear in 1960 when he said: 'Strengthening of Party leadership and insisting on placing politics in command is a basic guarantee for carrying out teaching-reform successfully . . . All educational workers should accept Party leadership, subordinate themselves to Party leadership, and resolutely follow the Party's policy on teaching-reform' (Fraser, p. 371).

Teaching was on a class basis, and one teacher was assigned as a special class-teacher to each class. He bore the main responsibility for discipline. The December 1959 *People's Daily* editorial stressed the importance of all teachers as models politically, professionally, and in their daily life, and added that the position of the class-teacher should be strengthened (SCMP 2174, 1959).

The shortage of school buildings was so acute that many schools were only able to meet for half a day, either in the mornings or in the afternoons. Yang Xiu-feng, in June 1960, spoke of the need 'gradually and by separate groups' to change 'schools which operate morning and afternoon sessions into schools of full-day sessions and then into boarding schools' (Fraser, p. 373). How far this process has gone it is impossible to say.

In those schools which had a full, two-session day, E. I. Monoszon comments on how those subjects which were 'comparatively easier to assimilate', such as drawing and singing, were generally reserved for the afternoon session (Monoszon, 1957, p. 114).

As in other parts of the educational system, there have been complaints about the pressure of school work and meetings on students and teachers. In October 1965 the *Guangming Ribao* reported how Yucai Secondary School in Shanghai had attempted to solve this problem. They organized the timetable so that 'students could do most of their work in class', during the compulsory 8-hour classroom day. This was divided into two sessions with a 2-hour break at noon, and a further short break at 4.30 p.m. Students were free before school in the morning, and there were no meetings on Sundays. In the evenings students could do private study, or take part in voluntary cultural and recreational activities. Only the weekly school or class meetings were compulsory for everyone. League meetings were for members only. Not more than 10 hours per week, or some 1½ hours per day were to be devoted to meetings, productive labour and militia training. Politics, militia training and physical training were each allotted 2 hours per week. The point was stressed that student leaders were students first, and that it was important for their health that they should not do more than 4 hours a week administrative work.

This article was obviously published in order to encourage other schools to cut down on the number of compulsory meetings and extra-curricular activity. It is probable that the load was so heavy as to occupy almost the whole waking day in many cases.

Because of the shortage of secondary school places competition was keen, and regulations were strict. Entrants to junior high school had to be not less than 12 years old and to senior high school not less than 15 years old. They had to have completed primary school before entering the junior high school, and junior high school before going on to senior, or be able to show that they had reached an equivalent standard. In addition to this they had to pass entrance examinations to the particular school they wished to study at. An account of this painful struggle in the late fifties is given by Dong Ji-bing. At that time a number of private schools still existed, and the aspiring students would go from one to another, trying to pass the entry examinations (Tung and Evans, 1967, p. 33).

The great majority of secondary schools were boarding schools. This was necessary because of the size of the area from which their students were drawn. Monoszon draws attention to the state grants available to help parents, which in many cases completely covered the cost of food, and also clothing (Monoszon, p. 114). He also notes that the boarding system allowed teachers, and the Pioneer and Youth League organizations to continue education after school by various forms of extra-class activity. It should be noted that boarding schools were not a new institution, set up after 1949, but go back at least to the early days of educational reform under the Republic.

Buildings and equipment

Buildings were plain and functional, and equipment in the majority of cases was very limited. But variations were very wide and some of the schools in the big cities had well-equipped laboratories and other specialized rooms, similar to those in European schools. Dormitory accommodation was provided for boarders. Self-help was the rule, and so standards depended to a great extent on the wealth and energy of the local community and the authority responsible for the school.

The curriculum

The curriculum only varied in detail from what one finds in academic secondary schools everywhere, and in the subjects and allocation of time was still very similar to that under the Guomindang government of 1946 (Morrison, 1952). Guomindang politics had been replaced by Communist politics, and scouting had been abolished (Arens, 1952, pp. 153-4). A number of detailed curricula are available: Monoszon for 1954-5; Klepikov (1960) for 1957-8 and (1959) 1958-9; UNESCO World Survey of Education for 1958-9. They show some of the changes which took place towards the end of the fifties. The major changes were the introduction of socialist education, or politics, for one or two hours a week throughout the six years, and the introduction of productive work as part of the formal timetable. Politics replaced two one-year courses: politics in Junior 3, and Chinese constitution in Senior 3. Productive work only appears in Klepikov (1959). In Klepikov (1) there is a one-year course of basic agriculture in Junior 3 which he says is to 'give the young people sound knowledge and practical skills and prepare them for successful participation in productive activity after they finish the first stage of secondary school'. Another change was the separating of Chinese language from literature, the former stopping at the end of the junior stage. Subjects which have been dropped are hygiene, formerly 1 hour per week in Junior 1; basic Darwinism, formerly 2 hours per week in Senior 2; economic geography of foreign countries, formerly 2 hours per week in Senior 1; technical drawing, formerly 1 hour per week in Senior 1, 2 and 3; and astronomy, presumably part of the physics course.

The balance of the course proposed for 1957-8 was: humanities (Chinese language, literature, history, politics, economic geography of China and foreign language), 45.14 per cent of total school time; physics-mathematics, 27.44 per cent; natural science-geography (physical and regional geography, biology and chemistry), 16.22 per cent; basic agriculture, 1.12 per cent; physical education, 6.72 per cent; aesthetic education (music, drawing), 3.36 per cent; 20.16 per cent of the total time was devoted to Chinese language and literature. Estimates of the total weekly load, including extra-curricular work, varied from 29 hours to 32 hours, which compared with a 1946 estimate of 29.5 hours (Morrison). But this is probably a gross under-estimate when homework, meetings, and various other extra-class activities are included.

The new curriculum proposed for 1957–8

Subjects	Junior high school years			Senior high school years			Total number of hours in 6 year course
	hours per week						
	1	2	3	1	2	3	
1 Chinese language	2	2	2	0	0	0	204
2 Literature	5	5	5	5	5	5	1,010
3 Arithmetic	6/5*	0	0	0	0	0	187
4 Algebra	0	4	2	4/3	2	2	455
5 Geometry	0	2	3	2/3	2	2	389
6 Trigonometry	0	0	0	0	2	2	134
					Mathematics		1,165
7 History of China	3/2	3	0	0	3	3	385
8 World history	0	0	3	0	0	0	102
9 New and newest world history	0	0	0	3	0	0	102
					History		589
10 Politics	2	1	1	2	2	2	336
11 Physical geography	3/2	0	0	0	0	0	85
12 World geography	0	2/3	0	0	0	0	85
13 Chinese geography	0	0	3/2	0	0	0	85
14 Economic geography of China	0	0	0	0	2	0	68
					Geography		323

(*continued on following page*)

15 Botany	3	2	0	0	0	0	170
16 Zoology	0	2/4	2	0	0	0	170
17 Human anatomy and physiology	0	0	0	2	0	0	68
						Biology	408
18 Physics	0	3/2	2	3	3	4	485
19 Chemistry	0	0	2/3	2	2	3	317
20 Foreign language	3	0	0	4	4	4	510
21 Physical education	2	2	2	2	2	2	404
22 Music	1	1	1	0	0	0	102
23 Drawing	1	1	1	0	0	0	102
24 Basic agriculture	0	0	2	0	0	0	68
Weekly load	28/29	30	31	29	29	29	
						Grand total:	6,023

V. Klepikov, 1960, p. 73, ex *Renmin Jiaoyu*, undated.
* alternative figures refer to differences in the two terms.

As far as the spread of subjects and the allocation of time is concerned this curriculum would seem to suit the aims which various authorities have stated from time to time. For example, the *People's Daily* editorial of December 1959 (SCMP 2174, 1959) described secondary education as 'fundamental education' in which the emphasis should be on language, mathematics, physics and chemistry, and a foreign language, but without neglecting the moral and physical education of the students. The same theme was repeated in the *Hebei Ribao* in 1962, which gave secondary schools the aim of training a 'reserve labour force', and preparing students for higher education. The basic subjects, it said, were language, mathematics, and a foreign language (SCMP 2669, 1962). The arguments have been about the subject matter of the various courses, and the exact way in which moral-political education should be carried out.

Moral-political education

Moral-political education was, as has been stressed before, the central problem for Chinese education, whether the subject being studied was Chinese literature, world history, or that part of the curriculum which was specifically labelled Socialist Theory, or the

Chinese Constitution. Professor Fang Xiang-yi introduced what was surely a traditional attitude when he spoke to a conference on aesthetic education in Canton in 1962. He said that aesthetics included not only such subjects as literature, painting and music, but also the appreciation of good deeds and good people, tidiness and cleanliness, and courtesy and civilized behaviour (SCMP 2679, 1962).

Much of the organized activity whose purpose was moral-political education took place outside the formal curriculum. It took many forms, and may have involved only a limited number of students, or the whole school. Classes may have gone to a village to help with the harvest, or to build some irrigation works. Some students may have worked in a factory for a short period. Often the activity took place during the vacation. In 1962 the *Guangming Ribao* carried a eulogy for the activities of School 101 in the Yuanming Yuan, Peking, a special school for the children of higher cadres which was later to gain a different reputation. During the summer vacation of 1961 these students were reported to have set an example by their 'practice of thrift and hard work'. Some had worked on the 32 bus, helping old people on and off, and keeping order. One worked as a steward on a train. Others delivered newspapers or milk. The paper also mentioned that students had returned money and watches which they had found in the street.

From time to time all the students became involved in a particular campaign, or in an emulation movement like that to 'learn from Lei Feng' (February 1963). Another common theme was to learn from the past, either from old workers, or army heroes brought to the school to speak, or by going to the villages and taking down family histories. Xingmin Secondary School, in South China, regularly sent students to work in the nearby villages during the early sixties, and the *Nanfang Ribao* reported that in addition to working in the fields 'the school mobilized its students to write down data obtained as a result of their investigations' as family histories. The purpose of this exercise was rather unfortunately worded: 'with a view to making students learn their family histories by heart'! (SCMP 3049, 1963).

A personal account of these kinds of activities, described by one in whom they failed to inculcate the values intended, is given in *The Thought Revolution* (Tung and Evans, pp. 41–54). Assuming the account not to be greatly exaggerated, it shows the difficulties which such education faces in conditions of great poverty and hardship, and when high ideals of serving the people, and love of hard, socially valuable work have to be put over by individuals who are often weak and ignorant, and who are guided by quite different values.

The formal classes in political theory have varied in subject-matter and in quantity as was mentioned above. In 1957 the Ministry of Education set out new proposals with the aim of 'fostering an accurate world view and philosophy of life' (SCMP 1560, 1957). They proposed that two-thirds of the time should be devoted to lectures, and one-third of the time to current events and discussion of policies. The subjects proposed were 'youth training' for the first and second years of the junior high school; 'knowledge of the social sciences' for years 1 and 2 of the senior high school; and 'socialist construction' for the third year of the senior high school. No mention was made of particular books or writers.

Chinese language and literature

In July 1958 the *People's Daily* published two long articles which revealed some of the criticisms being made of the language and literature courses, and the ways in which they were being changed (SCMP 1825, 1958).

The first article, by Zhang Bi-lai, was entitled: 'Language teaching in secondary schools tends to give more weight to ancient than to modern things.' He began by analysing the content of the post-1956 textbooks. At the junior stage these devoted one-third of their lessons to classical material, i.e. material dating from before the May 4th Movement (1919). At the senior stage classical material occupied half the total material. All twelve books of the secondary course contained some classical material. As the material for the senior course was arranged chronologically, the greatest concentration was in the first three books. Zhang complained that this quantity of classical material was an increase on previous textbooks. Junior-stage books had previously had no classics, while senior-stage books had contained only 30 to 40 per cent of classical writings. Reference materials for the junior stage included *The Water Margin*, an abridged version of *The Three Kingdoms*, *The Legend of the Pilgrimage to the West* (*Monkey*), and *The Lives of the Scholars*.

Zhang then went on to state what he regarded as the aim of teaching literature. It should enlarge the student's knowledge of social life; and 'cultivate ethics and behaviour of a higher calibre through subtle and silent transformation'. Further on he adds that it should enhance the capacity for reading and writing.

Discussing the criteria for selecting extracts from literature, Zhang said:

> When *Roadside Mulberry Trees* is read, we come to know the life, thinking and feeling of an ancient woman by the name of Lo Fu, and cherish her chastity. When *Little Hero Yu Lai* is read, we come to know the life, thinking and feeling of a teenage youth who lived under the manifold oppression of the Japanese bandits and cherish the adamant revolutionary stand and unyielding fighting spirit which he was capable of displaying because of the education and cultivation of the Party. When the two are compared, the latter is no doubt more beneficial to the young people and teenage youth.

Zhang further argued that 'even under the most ideal conditions, in the circumstances under which the teachers are capable of teaching properly with the Marxist-Leninist stand, viewpoint and method, the teaching of classic literary works still takes double the time to achieve half the result . . .' And he added: 'As a matter of fact, many teachers are at present unable to teach with the Marxist-Leninist stand . . .'

The other article described how four CCP teachers and a group of third and fourth year students at the Peking Teachers' College revised their course in classical literature. The story is interesting for what it reveals of the basis of selection and interpretation, and because of the emphasis on speed, which would seem to be a general feature of such activities.

Thirty-five people participated in the work. They were divided into eight 'combat teams', each of which took a particular section of the syllabus. During the first 2 days they studied Mao Ze-dong's works in order to properly orientate themselves. Twenty-six of them read 291 books between them in between 4 and 5 days! They also collected folk songs such as the 'Chrysanthemum Poems' of Huang Chao, a Tang dynasty peasant leader whose poems were still circulating in Hubei, and the Taiping Tianguo poems in praise of Prince Zheng.

Examples of working at high speed included the re-writing of the Mongol period material by three men in a single night, and the reading and analysis of some 190 poems of Liu Yong by a group of students, again in one night.

Their approach to their work is shown by the following two quotations: The group studying the Lo Zhang Ji concluded that 'the poems of Liu Yong were decadent in theme and were devoted to the description of the decadent life in brothels. They pointed out that Liu Yong was an anti-realist poet'. A second-year student, participating in discussion, said: 'Du Fu [the Tang poet] owed his achievement to his contact with the people at his time and his reflection of the thinking and sentiment of the people. But the teachers said that he was influenced by the Confucian school of thought and humanitarianism. All my classmates disagree with the teachers in having history distorted in this way.'

Some language textbooks

The contents of those books which the author was able to examine suggest a process of patching and altering of the traditional scholastic contents, rather than a re-thinking of the course as a whole to meet the needs of contemporary society. This is more true of the literature books than those for language. The emphasis would appear to be preparation for higher studies rather than a general education for life.

We will examine first four out of the six language textbooks used in the junior high schools during 1960–4. In all they contain 118 texts. The inclusion of 28 (about 24 per cent) classical language texts shows the strong influence which traditional scholastic ideas still played. These texts include two pieces on studying, one from the Qing, and the other from the Confucian *Analects*; *Mencius* on learning chess; *Zhuangzi* on selling corn; some travel stories from the Song; and poems by Li Bo and Du Fu of the Tang.

There are 29 directly political texts, including seven pieces by Mao Ze-dong. Pavlov's letter to youth is also moral-political, and is presumably a relic of the Russian influence of the fifties, retained because of the author's scientific status.

Amongst the selections from literature there are excerpts from *The Water Margin* and *The Scholars*, and the writer Lu Xun is included four times. Only 9 texts deal with scientific and technical matters—about 7.5 per cent of the total. There is a description of squirrels; a text on fossils; a description of cotton; articles on meteors, and the universe; and the story of food.

Each text is followed by an exercise of three to six questions. Some are comprehension questions on the text. What is the meaning of a certain sentence? What is the importance of this or that event? Or even, 'after reading the story what do you feel?' Some attention is still paid to character recognition, especially in the early books, with instructions to note the pronunciation of a given list, and to copy each one into the student's notebook five times. But much more attention is paid to fine shades of meaning, and the use of idioms. There is also a great deal of formal grammar, noting word classes and dividing sentences into subject and predicate. Memorizing is still required for nearly all the classical texts, those by Mao, and a few others.

Fifteen short texts are practical instruction in various aspects of the writer's craft. In Book 1 students learn how to use various types of dictionary, and to write simple notes and receipts; how to note down observations and make descriptions; and how to plan an essay. Book 5 has another text on writing essays: 'Establish a standpoint'; and a piece on reporting.

The only language textbook for the senior school stage which the writer has seen is a copy of Book 2 published in Peking in 1960 and 1962. The exact place of this book in the curriculum is uncertain as according to the official timetables the language course is supposed to have ended in class 3 of the junior high school! The book follows the same pattern as the junior high school books. The only items perhaps worth mentioning are two of a series of short notes on logic: 'Reasoning: induction and deduction', and 'the basis of conclusions'. While the exercises continue to require certain items to be memorized, there seems to be no further study of characters, words, or grammar. Instead the questions are on content and style.

The first of the two literature textbooks which the writer has examined is volume 3 of the junior high school course. This is a much bigger book than the normal textbook, containing 336 pages of a larger size than usual. Lesson 1 is three poems from the *Shijing* (*Odes*) in the original. This is followed by a story from the *Shiji*, rewritten in modern Chinese, with the original classical passage as an appendix. Lesson 3 jumps to the Tang poet, Du Fu, and after a long biography in lesson 4 there are three poems from Bo Ju-yi in lesson 5. By lesson 9 *The Water Margin* is reached, and this is followed by an excerpt from *The Scholars* in lesson 10. By lesson 12 students are in the twentieth century, with Lu Xun, who has 5 chapters out of the total of 30. Each chapter ends with a number of comprehension questions, and most poems and certain other passages are to be memorized.

The second literature textbook is volume 2 of the senior high school course. Printed on the same large sheets, it is only 164 pages long. It was published in 1956 and 1957 in Shanghai. The whole book is devoted to Tang and Song poets, with the exception of a few essays, such as a political essay by Si Ma-guang.

History

The only material available to the writer has been three copies of textbooks used for the Chinese history course in the junior high school. Nothing is known about the course of Chinese history taken in the second and third years of the senior high school.

Two of the three textbooks were published in Shanghai, while the third, volume 3 of the course, was published in Peking. All were first published in 1955–6, but the Peking edition is a 1962 reprint. All three are illustrated by line drawings and maps, and there is a table of important dates at the end of each volume.

Volume 2 goes from the Sui dynasty to near the end of the Qing, at 'the beginning of European capitalist countries' aggression'. Chapters are devoted to Tang policy towards the peasants, artisans and merchants; to the various peasant wars in the Tang, Yuan, and Ming dynasties; to the culture and great inventions in the different dynasties; and to China's relations with the outside world. Zheng He's travels in the Ming (1405) get two pages, a map and a picture of artisans hammering out a huge anchor.

Volume 3 takes the story from the Opium War of 1840 to the May 4th Movement of 1919. Important topics dealt with are the Taiping Tianguo revolutionary movement; the birth of Chinese national capitalism; the reform of 1898; the Boxer Rising; and the 1911 Revolution. In this volume each chapter ends with three to six questions: what is the importance of this or that event? What was the cause of this, or the aim of that?

Volume 4 begins with the 'establishment of the CCP and the first revolutionary Civil war' and ends with 'the beginning of the construction of socialism', the first Five Year Plan and the new Constitution of the Chinese People's Republic. The twenty intervening chapters trace the struggle against the Japanese, and the struggle between the CCP and the Guomindang (Nationalists), culminating in the second revolutionary civil war, and the establishment of the People's Republic in 1949.

Other subjects

Almost no information seems to be available about the content of the remaining subjects of the curriculum. The only textbooks which the writer has encountered have been translations of Russian secondary school science books of the 1956–7 period, reprinted as late as 1963, or similar Chinese productions used to supplement the science courses. There would seem to be quite a wide variety of titles in these fields, and many of them are attractively illustrated and well laid out.

A number of secondary school wall-maps were on sale during 1965–6 which gave a glimpse of the geography course. Dealing with the climate and vegetation regions of China, they were clear and attractive, but being only printed on thin paper they would have a rather limited life. The only school atlas to be on sale during this period was a volume of 29 pages, each 5 inches by 7 inches (Dituce, 1965). Eighteen pages are devoted to China. There are two maps of the world, a map of Asia, and one page each to Africa, Europe, N. America, S. America, and Australia and Antartica. All but two maps are physical, with a selection of the railway systems and natural resources added. Because of the limited scale this produces unfortunate distortions, such as Britain having only one railway line, from Dover to Glasgow. It would be interesting to know to what extent these impressions are corrected in the classroom.

Third level schools

The institutions which will be discussed in this section were all described in Chinese sources as higher education institutions, and all had at least a majority of full-time students. Their students were normally expected to have completed a course of secondary education, or to be of equivalent standard.

The aim of all these institutions has been clearly and repeatedly stated. In the words of Peking University President, Ma Yin-chu, 'the task of higher educational institutions is to train advanced technical personnel and principal cadres for national construction' (Fraser, p. 119). Liu Shi said: '. . . higher education should be closely related to the construction needs of defence and production' (ibid, p. 129). Liu went on to emphasize the twin aspects of the training programme, later to be called 'red and expert'. 'They [the institutions] must train the personnel to carry out the tasks of national construction with a clear understanding of Marxism-Leninism and the teachings of Mao Ze-dong and of the various branches of knowledge' he said (Fraser, p. 129).

As in other levels of education, emphasis, at least in official speeches and writings, has more often been placed on 'red' than 'expert'. Looking back over the previous ten years at Xiamen (Amoy) University, Pan Mou-yuan wrote in 1959: 'We taught patriotism; love of the people, of science, of labour; care of public property; and inculcated a mind-set of serving the people' (JPRS 1165-D). These attitudes he contrasted with those which he said were typical before 1949: seeking personal enjoyment; using a diploma as a brick to knock on the door and become an official and make money. He went on: 'Bookworms who could not bind a chicken now can carry more than 100 jin (50 kg) in hill excavation.'

In 1949 the new government was faced with the need to expand third level education as quickly as possible, especially in the fields of engineering and science. Qian Jun-rui, Vice-Minister of Education, said in 1951, that 'the key to the reform of education lies in the ideological reform of the teachers' (Fraser, p. 123). After this it would be possible successfully to carry through the necessary curriculum reform, and re-structure the institutional pattern.

The institutional pattern

One of the first jobs which the new government undertook was the reorganization of the colleges and universities. Before 1949 there had been no attempt to plan higher education, and it had grown up, mainly in the big coastal centres, with limitations and duplications quite unsuited to the new needs. Probably influenced by Russian advice, the government decided to develop polytechnic institutions by regrouping the technical faculties of the old universities, and to set up a number of new specialized technical institutes. Universities were to teach the liberal arts and sciences, and there were to be various other special institutes, such as teacher-training institutes. These changes took place during the period 1949–52, and involved the taking over of some 250 privately or foreign owned institutions by the government (Fraser, p. 210).

Another aim of the reorganization was to establish a number of educational centres, each with one general university, one polytechnic, one teacher-training institute, one academy of medicine, and one or more specialized institutes adapted to the particular locality. Jiangsu is one such area, with a School of Silk at Suzhou, a Cement School at Nanjing, and a Mining School at Xuzhou (SCMP 2342, 1960). At first efforts were based on the large administrative areas, and 13 universities were designated. These were located in Peking and Tianjin in north China; Zhangqun in the north-east; Shanghai, Nanjing, Qingdao and Amoy in east China; Wuhan and Guangzhou (Canton) in central south China; Chengdu and Kunming in south-west China; and Xi'an (Sian) and Lanzhou (Lanchow) in the north-west (Fraser, p. 191). But later on some efforts were made to form smaller educational complexes in the administrative districts within the provinces. Jiangsu (Kiangsu) reported in 1960 having in each administrative district an industrial college, an agricultural college, a medical school, and a teacher-training college (SCMP 2342, 1960). The standard of most of these locally formed institutions is non-university, vocational training, and as many of them operate on a part-work basis they fall outside the scope of this chapter.

Special attention has been given to the national minorities. In Xinjiang (Sinkiang) eleven higher education institutions have been set up since 1949. At Urumchi there is Xinjiang University, and institutes for engineering, petroleum, railways, medicine, agriculture, and teacher-training. There are also agricultural and medical colleges in new towns in the Gobi desert. In other parts of China there are special institutes for national minorities, like those in Peking and Lanzhou (Lanchow). In the latter, the North-Western Institute for Nationalities, the Railway Department graduated its first group of Uighurs, Kazakhs and Uzbeks in 1962 (SCMP 2683, 1962).

In spite of all these efforts to re-locate third level institutions, a very high concentration remained in such places as Shanghai and Peking. In 1958 the latter had 50 institutions with a total of 121,000 students (UNESCO, 3), and since then new institutions have been set up there. It is therefore not surprising that pressure has continued to move some of these colleges to other areas.

Numbers

It is estimated that in 1940 there were some 143 third level institutions, of which 39 were universities, 50 were independent colleges, and 54 were technical institutions of various kinds. By 1949 there were 200 (UNESCO, 3) to 207 institutions (EPMC, p. 526). According to some figures given by the Minister of Education, Ma Xu-lun, in 1952, it would appear that there were 31 higher technical schools, 18 agricultural colleges, 30 teacher-training colleges, and 29 medical schools before the reorganization of higher education took place (Fraser, p. 134).

By 1953 the initial reorganization was complete and the total number of institutions had been reduced to 182. This included 13 universities, 26 specialized technical institutes, 20 polytechnical universities, 29 agricultural and forestry colleges, 34 teacher-training institutes, 32 medical colleges, 7 institutes of finance and economics, and 4 institutes for politics and law (Fraser, p. 191).

The number of institutions continued to grow. By 1957 there was a total of 227. Then during the Great Leap Forward in 1958–9 a large number of colleges were formed, bringing the total to 840. But by 1963 the situation was stabilized again and the total was then 400. This included 23 universities, 20 polytechnical universities, 100 engineering institutes, 90 agricultural colleges, 120 medical schools, and a number of colleges for teacher-training, economics, politics, physical education, fine arts and foreign languages (EPMC, p. 526). In 1965 a total of 664 third level institutions was given in a study by the Hong Kong *China Monthly*, which gave a detailed breakdown in terms of specialization (Tsang, 1968, p. 193).

Some of the newly-formed, specialized institutions quickly grew very big. The East China Chemical Engineering Institute in Shanghai, formed in 1952, had 5 departments with 19 specializations in 1962, with over 5,000 students (SCMP 2686, 1962). This institution was also significant because while in 1962 it was one of ten of its kind, before 1949 not a single chemical engineering institute existed in China. In its ten years of life it had already produced 3,000 graduates. Another institute to be set up in 1952 was the Peking Institute of Ferrous Metallurgy. Then it had 40 teachers and 400 students. By 1959 it had 600 teachers and 5,700 students, including evening and correspondence course students (G. N. Popov, JPRS 1176). It had 35 laboratories for mining, geology, iron and steel making, and electrical metallurgy, and a library of 450,000 volumes (SCMP 2727, 1962). The old institutions also expanded greatly in size. Peking University, housed in the campus originally built by the famous American Yanjing University (Yenching), reached a student total of 10,000 in 1958, some 5 to 6 times the 1952 figure (Goldman, 1961).

The total number of students enrolled in 191 higher education institutions in 1949 was 130,000. This figure rose to 660,000 in 1958, and then to 810,000 in 1959 (EPMC, p. 509). No enrolment totals have been given for later years, but Leo. A. Orleans estimates that a figure of 700,000 is probable for the middle sixties (EPMC, p. 509). This would mean about one in 1,000 of the total population.

The increase in the number of graduates is also impressive compared with pre-1949 figures. Between 1949 and 1963 nearly 1.2 million Chinese graduated from third level institutions, and the annual figure in recent years has been about 200,000. Thirty-three per cent graduated in engineering, 6 per cent in the natural sciences, 8 per cent in agriculture and forestry, and 10 per cent in medicine. Altogether there were a total of 671,000 science and technical graduates. This should be compared with a total of only 70,000 graduates in the same four fields during the longer period, 1928–48 (EPMC, p. 545). Zheng Ju-yuan (Chu-yuan Cheng) draws attention to the important increase in the number of women graduating in the sciences. During 1954–9 it rose from 19 per cent to 23 per cent (ibid, p. 545).

Administration

On 28 July 1950 the State Administrative Council passed an act placing all higher education establishments under the leadership of the central Ministry of Education. At the same time provisions were made for the participation of the various local Education Departments, or other ministries and government departments which might be concerned with particular institutions. Ordinary administration, teaching staff arrangements, equipment, and financial management were to be the direct concern of the local authority or government department (Fraser, p. 94). The function of the Ministry of Education was to be of general guidance and to control major policy decisions, together with directly controlling certain key institutions in the North China District (ibid, p. 93).

In 1952 a Ministry of Higher Education was set up which took over those functions of the Ministry of Education connected with higher education. Besides direct control over certain key institutions it acted as a supervisor on matters of educational policy. It approved unified regulations, and teaching materials, organized teacher training and transfer, and approved plans for the establishment of new courses and institutions.

The local education departments, or the branches of the central government directly responsible for particular institutions, while under the general supervision of the Ministry of Higher Education, were responsible for the day to day running of their institutions. They were responsible for the employment of teachers and other personnel, and for financing both capital construction, and general administration (Fraser, p. 248).

The Ministry of Higher Education was abolished in 1958 (UNESCO, 3) (1954 according to Tsang, p. 81), and its functions were transferred back to the Ministry of Education. The central Ministry retained direct control of People's University, Peking; Peking University; Qinghua University; Sichuan (Szechwan) University; Peking Teacher-training Institute; the Peking Russian-Mongolian Institute; and the Peking Foreign Language Institute (no. 1). In 1964 the Ministry of Higher Education was again set up (Tsang, p. 81).

This already complicated pattern of control was further complicated by the intervention of the Communist Party. In theory this organization was, at least until the period of the Great Leap Forward, only expected to play the role of a stimulant. But in practice it appears to have been much more. During the brief '100 Flowers' period in 1957 a number of complaints were made which suggested that decisions were largely made by the Party organizations, and the official administrative bodies were often by-passed, or used as rubber stamps. Lin Han-da, Vice-Chairman of the China Association for Promoting Democracy, said:

> . . . the entire Ministry of Education existed in name without any actual authority. The directives issued by the Ministry of Education did not mean anything to the lower-level organizations, while sometimes even a directive issued by the State Council encountered the same indifference among the lower-level organizations . . . the lower-level organizations only observed the directives jointly issued by the CP CC and the State Council . . . (MacFarquhar, p. 48).

Within the institutions there was apparently a similar state of affairs. Chen Ling, Principal of Nanjing School of Physical Training complained:

> The secretary of the Party faction is the head of the executive office of the school and can deal with many matters on his own . . . People are transferred in and out and I am kept in the dark; I did not even know of the arrival of a new secretary in the office. This man has all along mistaken me for the Deputy Principal and whenever he receives an official letter he hands it direct to the Party-member Deputy Principal. Only recently has he tumbled to the fact that I am the Principal (MacFarquhar, p. 67).

From 1958 onwards the role of the CCP has been strengthened. A. I. Belyayev, speaking of the N.E. Polytechnic Institute (JPRS 1176), said that academic, scientific and productive work was directed by the Party Committee through the Board of Directors and the Institute Council. Pan Mou-yuan, talking about Xiamen (Amoy) University (JPRS 1165), claimed that 'Party leadership and the mass line are the basis of success'. He went on to describe how the University Council and the Department Committees had 'responsibility under Party guidance'.

The internal administration of the various institutions followed a pattern first laid down in Ministry of Education regulations in June 1950 (Arens, pp. 94–101). The president (*xiaozhang* or *yuanzhang*) was appointed by the government and was responsible for representing the institution; directing all teaching, research and administration; guiding the political education of the staff and students;

appointment and dismissal of the teachers and workers of the institution; and approving the decisions of the institution council. In appointing teachers and workers the president was responsible to the government. In appointing the director of studies and the director of administrative affairs the president had to get the approval of the Ministry of (Higher) Education, but with minor appointments, like the librarian and heads of departments, it was only necessary for their names to be filed with the Ministry. One or more vice-presidents (*fu-xiaozhang* or *fu-yuanzhang*) were also appointed by the government. They took the place of the president when he was absent, or otherwise assisted him.

The director of studies (*jiaodao zhuren*) was appointed by the president with the approval of the Ministry of (Higher) Education, and could take over the full administration of the institution in the absence of both the president and vice-president(s). Otherwise his job was to plan, organize, direct and supervise all the work of both teaching and research departments.

The director of administrative affairs (*xingzheng ganbu*) was directly responsible to the president and was in charge of all administration.

The librarian was directly responsible to the director of studies.

The heads of department were also directly responsible to the director of studies. Their job was to plan and administer all departmental affairs. They supervised teaching and the examinations, and were responsible for the students' progress. They also made proposals to the president for the appointment and dismissal of department staff, both teaching and administrative.

Where the institution was divided into colleges (*xueyuan*) the president appointed a dean (*yuanzhang*) from among the teaching staff. The dean's job was to plan and administer the college, supervise the activities of its different departments, and propose the appointment and dismissal of staff.

These various officers worked within a framework of committees or councils, the most important of which was the school council (*xiaowu weiyuanhui*). Its chairman was the institution president, and the vice-presidents, director of studies, assistant director of studies, director of administrative affairs, the librarian and deans and department heads were all members. In addition there were a number of representatives of the teaching and working staff, and of the

students. According to A. I. Belyayev (JPRS 1176) the institute
council of the North-Eastern Polytechnical Institute consisted of
twenty-five to twenty-seven people and was elected by a 'general
meeting of representatives of the collective', but no doubt both its
composition and mode of formation varied widely.

The school council had wide powers of supervision and decision.
All plans relating to teaching, research, administration and finance
had to be approved by it. It also appointed various special committees to take charge of such matters as nominations or examinations.

In addition to the school council there were councils for each
department under the chairmanship of the Head of Department or
the Party Secretary of the Department.

Besides these formal councils there were numerous groups,
involving all the teachers, workers and students. All important plans
were discussed in these groups, and in big department, and even
institute meetings. In this way an attempt was made to involve
everyone in the carrying out of decisions, and even in some cases in
the process of minor decision-making (JPRS 1176).

Finance

The financing of higher education institutions was the direct
responsibility of the organizations responsible: the Ministry of
(Higher) Education in respect of a small number of universities;
local education departments; other central ministries; and various
enterprises. In addition to allocations from public funds, institutions have, since 1958, drawn upon funds accumulated as the
result of operating farms and factories. This was reflected in the
figures published for 1959, the last which were available (EPMC,
p. 527). It seems likely that productive activity for the market
declined during the middle sixties, but college labour was extensively
used for maintenance and equipping. According to Chinese sources,
state expenditure on higher education rose from 114 million yuan
in 1951 to 637 million yuan in 1957 (ibid, p. 528). No figures for
recent years, or for total expenditure are available.

The organizational pattern

Administratively the institutions were subdivided into departments,
and the departments contained one or more teaching-research

The full-time schools

groups (*jiaoyan-zu*). These, for which Zeng Zhao-lun uses the Russian term, *kafedra* (chair, or department) were concerned with carrying out the various study-plans, and with improving methods of teaching. They also directed research work in a particular field, and trained postgraduates and assistants.

Academically the institutions were divided along Russian lines into specialities (*zhuanye*) and specializations (*zhuanyehua*). 'The guiding principle of this system' wrote Zeng Zhao-lun, 'is that institutions of higher learning should aim at training cadres for specific jobs in the highly complex fabric of economic construction.' (Fraser, p. 192). Specialities were grouped together in departments of varying size. The Department of the Metallurgy of Nonferrous Metals at the North-eastern Polytechnical Institute provides an example of this system. In 1953 there were 61 members of staff. Eight held the rank of professor or assistant professor; 13 were lecturers and the remaining 40 were assistant lecturers (JPRS 1176). The department was divided as follows:

Specialities (*zhuanye*)	Number of students	Number of staff
Concentration of minerals	370	17
Metallurgy of light metals	136	12
Metallurgy of heavy metals	133	14
Metallurgy of rare metals	69	5
Dressing of non-ferrous metals and alloys by pressure	224	12
totals:	932	60

The English Language Department of the 2nd Foreign Language Institute, Peking, provides an example of a department with only one speciality, and one teaching-research group.

The length of the courses provided in the various specialities varied. The State Administrative Council Act of July 1950 laid down that courses were to range from 3 to 5 years, but both longer and shorter ones were developed in practice. According to the World Survey of Education (UNESCO, 3) technical courses lasted 5 years; medical courses, 5 years; finance and economics, 4 years, or sometimes 5; language institutes, 3 or 5 years; political science, 4 years; fine arts, 3 to 5 years; and courses in the special minority institutes, 2 to 5 years.

Each study year consisted of two terms (*xueqi*) lasting about 17 weeks. The first term began in October. Each week was to consist of between 44 and 50 hours of study, with no more than 6 hours of extra-curricular activities (Fraser, p. 96). In practice these hours were greatly exceeded and during the late fifties there were increasing complaints about pressure of work, and its effect on the health and academic standards of the students. Yang Xiu-feng, then Minister of Higher Education, drew the attention of the First National People's Congress to the problem in June 1956 (Fraser, pp. 248–9). But pressure continued, and in 1960 the *Guangming Ribao* published an editorial on the problem, stressing that even during political campaigns rest was essential (SCMP 2339, 1960). They referred to Mao Ze-dong's article: 'Take Care of the Living Conditions of the Masses and Attend to the Methods of Work' (Mao, 1965, vol. 1, p. 147), and published a separate account of how Qinghua University had tried to cope with the problem.

The impetus for 'labour with rest' came from the Qinghua CCP Committee which had 'led and pushed' (SCMP 2339, 1960). They proposed a schedule of 7 hours for social activities and physical training; 8 hours' sleep; and 9 hours for study. A daily routine was worked out, beginning at 6 a.m. when everyone got up. From 12.30 to 2.30 p.m. and from 4.30 to 7.30 p.m. was for meals and rest, and Saturday evening and all Sunday were also to be free. No meetings were to be allowed during this free time. Lights were to be out in the dormitories at 10 p.m.

Buildings and equipment

As at other stages of the educational process, the shortage of both buildings and equipment has been a very difficult problem. In the early fifties the government was able to take over the buildings and equipment of the foreign-owned colleges, but this was a transfer of ownership, rather than an addition to the total stock. The only gain was, perhaps, that more students obtained access to these facilities.

In the years 1950–8 the state built 11 million square metres of new buildings, including 1,000 new laboratories, and 10,000 workshops in the engineering colleges (CB 608, 1959). This was equal to three times the total of 3,400,000 square metres built in the previous fifty years. But it was still far from sufficient for the growing needs.

In the best colleges the laboratory equipment, engineering workshops, and other facilities compared well with those in the richer countries of the world. Libraries were extensive and contained many foreign books and periodicals (Wilson, 1959, pp. 169 and 189). But compared with national needs there were overall shortages, and even in such simple things as chairs and tables there was often a chronic shortage. In the foreign language institutes of Peking, students had to stand in the dining halls to eat their meals.

In order to deal with this problem the government has all along encouraged self-help and strict economy. Mass campaigns against waste, ironically all too wasteful in themselves, have involved students and teachers, as well as the general public. In 1960 a new method was advocated. The Minister of Education urged local education departments to produce their own building materials and to set up their own teams of designers and construction workers (Fraser, p. 373). He also urged local departments and higher education institutions to co-operate with each other in the production of all kinds of equipment on a mass scale, with the aim of producing 'self-sufficiency basically within three to five years'. How far this aim has been achieved it is impossible to tell. In the big polytechnics and engineering colleges, especially, much has been done. But in 1966, during the Cultural Revolution, there must have been a big setback. A great deal of furniture was destroyed, especially in Peking, where institutions were used as dormitories for the ten to twelve million youngsters who poured into the city. Paper was consumed in fantastic quantities for wall-posters (*dazibao*). And radio equipment of various kinds must have suffered heavy deterioration through inexpert use. It remains to be seen whether the future gains will outweigh these material losses.

The curriculum

The majority of the courses in Chinese third level institutions were at undergraduate level or below. Most of them led to the award of a college diploma (UNESCO, 3). Higher degrees were not awarded in Chinese universities before 1949. Instead, students were sent overseas, and this tradition was continued after 1949, with the majority of students going to the USSR. Only in 1955 were arrangements made with the Chinese Academy of Sciences to establish a higher degree, to be called associate doctor (*fu-boshi*). Candidates for this degree must be less than forty, must be graduates of a higher institution, and must have a minimum of two years' work experience, Much uncertainty appears to surround this degree and up to 1964 no degree appears to have been awarded (EPMC, pp. 510 and 526). In spite of this, however, large numbers of students have been retained in the universities and given post-graduate courses of one kind and another, for periods of from three to four years.

The need to reform the curriculum was already envisaged in the Common Programme of October 1949 (Fraser, p. 84). The act passed on 28 July 1950 criticized the majority of curricula for not being 'new democratic', which it defined as 'not national, scientific, and popular, and not in conformity with the needs of new China's reconstruction work'. In particular it stressed that 'politically reactionary curricula' should be abolished and replaced with ' "new democratic" revolutionary curricula' which would 'develop the ideal of serving the people' (Fraser, p. 95).

Some idea of the initial changes made in traditional fields can be obtained from a study of the curriculum laid down by the N. China Committee on Higher Education in September 1949 (Arens, p. 103). All colleges were expected to take an obligatory course in Marxism. This consisted of 3 hours per week in the first term devoted to dialectical and historical materialism, and the history of social development; 3 hours per week in the second term devoted to the theory of 'New Democracy', and the modern Chinese revolutionary movement; and 3 hours per week throughout the two terms of the second year devoted to political economy. With the exception of the literature departments, where courses were to follow a traditional pattern, all departments were to introduce courses aimed at inculcating an understanding of Marxism and the ideas of the Chinese Communist Party. Two examples will show the nature of the courses prescribed.

In the departments of philosophy the new objectives were to be the introduction of dialectical materialism and its use in solving real problems, and the training of secondary school teachers of logic. The basic course was to consist of (a) dialectical materialism, including its application in the natural sciences; (b) historical materialism; (c) the history of Chinese philosophy, with the emphasis placed on the period after the May 4th Movement of 1919, but with an outline of ancient thought; (d) a history of Western philosophy, concentrating on the differences between dialectical materialism and idealism; and (e) ethics. Included among a number of electives was a special research course on the ideas of Mao Ze-dong.

In the departments of economics the objective was again to be on the fostering of a Marxist viewpoint. 14 basic courses were to be offered, including economic reconstruction in the period of 'New Democracy'; research in Soviet economic reconstruction; and China's land problem and the land reform.

During the early and middle fifties change was slow. Traditional studies like the Chinese classics declined, and a number of subjects like law, which came under attack, also lost students (Arens, p. 109). At the same time a number of new fields were introduced, especially in engineering and the natural sciences. These included nuclear energy, electronics and electronic computers, automation, and semi-conductors (CB 608, 1959). In a majority of fields courses were taken directly from the Soviet Union, and even compressed into a shorter time. This naturally led to difficulties, which were forcibly expressed by the Director of Planning of the Ministry of Higher Education in 1955. Agreeing that it was 'no doubt a necessity' to copy the Soviet courses, he pleaded that consideration should be given to 'the existing cultural and scientific standard of the students and the quality of the teachers' (Fraser, p. 213).

The curriculum for all higher education students was divided into four parts. All were obligatory, except where chronic ill health prevented the student from doing physical exercise. The four parts were political-ideological training; academic-technical studies; productive work; and military-physical training. In 1952, in a technical institute, these courses were given the following time allocations.

1 Political studies: 400 hours, about 10 per cent of the total time.
2 Basic science: higher mathematics, physics and chemistry (no time given).
3 Basic technology: about 34 per cent of total time.
4 Specialized courses: 28 per cent of total time.
5 Russian: studied throughout 3 years.

6 Thesis planning: 10–12 weeks.
7 Experiment: 16–28 weeks.
8 Physical education: 2 hours per week for the first and second years of the course.
9 Vacations: 6 weeks in summer and 2 weeks in winter. (Hsu, p. 143).

A. I. Belyayev's description of the North Eastern Polytechnical Institute in 1959 only differs in detail from this picture. But it throws interesting light on the process of curriculum reform. During 1957–8 the curriculum had been revised twice, the first plan working for only six months. Changes included lengthening each term by a month at the expense of the vacations; intensifying political education; and rearranging the method of teaching basic science.

The political courses were increased from 370 hours to between 560 and 600 hours in all, together with 4 hours per week for 9 of the 10 terms for meetings on current affairs. The main politics course included a study of the policy of the CCP; the history of the Chinese revolution; the history of the international communist movement; political economy; and philosophy. It was carried out by the Party and YCL instructors attached to each group of students. These instructors also followed the scientific and technical training in order to understand the students and their work better.

The basic sciences, formerly taught separately, were now split up and combined with the applied science course. For example, electricity was studied with electrical engineering; heat with thermotechnics; and mechanics with mechanical engineering. Modern physics was an exception. There was a special course in year 3 on the structure of matter, the atom, the nucleus, and semi-conductors.

An attempt was also made to cut out repetition by not teaching in class what was already fully taught in the workshop. This was in line with a general movement throughout schools to apply a principle of 'less but essential' (*shao er jing*) (JPRS 1165—Amoy; Waiyu Jiaoxue yu yanjiu 4, p. 16). The failure of overcrowded courses had been realized and increasing efforts were being made to remedy the situation.

The treatment of the basic sciences in the North Eastern Polytechnical Institute cannot be taken as the rule, however. In other institutions exactly the opposite principle has been expressed.

Writing in January 1962, the Vice-President of the North Western Agricultural College (SCMP 2668, 1962), stressed the importance of the basic theoretical sciences, and of arranging studies according to a scientific system. He said: 'If we rigidly insist on going from practice first and theories later, and perceptual knowledge first and rational knowledge later, then by overemphasizing direct experience and perceptual knowledge, the result can only be the students will be restricted to a certain extent from acquiring complete knowledge.' The need to train 'all-round personnel' and the shortness of four- to five-year courses compared with what needed to be learnt were important factors to be considered.

Productive work

While practical work has been part of the process of education in engineering and the natural sciences, it was only after 1957 that serious attention was paid to making it an integral part of all Chinese higher education. The general espects of this policy were described in a *People's Daily* article in 1960 which claimed that 'as a result of implementing the correct policy of combining education with productive labour in the past two years, tremendously penetrating and pleasing changes have taken place in university education in China' (Fraser, p. 401). The writer was perhaps over-optimistic about the effects on the students when he wrote: 'They have become more and more enthusiastic in supporting the fatherland, the Party, labour, and the labouring people, and they have gained a deeper understanding of what they have learned from books.' But it was quite clear about the purpose of the work. On the one hand, productive work was to be directly related to studies, while on the other hand, a certain amount of unrelated work should be done in order to inculcate the right social attitudes (Fraser, p. 403).

During the Great Leap Forward a third element entered into the situation: productive work as economic activity, in the effort to reduce the cost of education by making it at least partly self-sufficient. This was not completely new, but the emphasis was so great as to bring about a qualitative difference. Articles of the period have numerous examples of schools and colleges setting up farms and factories to make all kinds of items. In many cases the work linked up with productive work as part of studies. This was clearest in the case of engineering schools, like that in the Peking Institute of Ferrous Metallurgy where the workshops turned out special steels, foundry iron and sheet strip (Popov, JPRS 1176), or the North-Eastern Polytechnical Institute, where they produced beryllium oxide and other materials (Belyayev, JPRS 1176).

The combination of economic and moral ends was recognized in an account of self-help methods at the Zhongzhan Industrial School (SCMP 2342, 1960). The students were ashamed to work in the buildings of the local secondary school, and so willingly set to and constructed their own. The *Guangming Ribao* commented that they 'built the school and the character of its students simultaneously'. Popov gives another example of students repairing and constructing academic buildings, and also equipping the laboratories (JPRS 1176).

Numbers of colleges reported making close links with the people's communes. In Jiangsu (SCMP 2336, 1960) 74 institutions had established links with 129 people's communes. Substantial aid was given in manpower: some 650,000 man-days in a year. This represented the moral education for the students. Other forms of aid, which included irrigation constructions, building a chemical fertilizer plant, curing animal diseases, establishing a spare-time school, and providing various equipment for culture and recreation, combined moral education with the students' special studies.

Shenyang Agricultural College (SCMP 2671, 1962) reported another aspect of work on the people's communes. It enabled the students to learn techniques from the peasants. The 26 people's communes on which the college students worked grew rice, fruit, silk, cotton and vegetables.

In some cases working on the farms could be combined with field work. Students of the Hydrology Department of Peking Geological Institute (SCMP 2664, 1962) worked in the Taihang Mountains during a drought. They studied local water resources during the morning, and helped the peasants on the land in the afternoons.

In other cases student diplomas were closely connected with economic activity. Qinghua Water Conservation Department reported in 1962 that 170 of its students' graduation diplomas were for actual construction projects, including some for the Bing-gu *xian*, Peking, irrigation project (SCMP 2677, 1962).

Teaching methods

Teaching methods in Chinese third level institutions were basically the same as those employed elsewhere in the world: the lecture; laboratory and field work in the practical subjects; discussions; and various forms of tests and examinations. The more formal American and Russian methods have been challenged by methods developed in the Communist university in Yan'an before 1949, particularly in relation to the role played by the students in the teaching process and teacher-student relations.

The Regulations of the Education Department of the North China Union University (Fraser, pp. 73-7) contain an interesting section on 'Methods of Teaching Leadership'. It is not that they say anything which would be considered startlingly new outside China. But they mark a complete break with traditional Chinese methods, and contain the seed of conflict with the more formal methods employed in other institutions in the years since 1949. It is therefore worth quoting this passage in full:

(1) Educational methods should be those which arouse interest and not those aimed at forcing knowledge. Every kind of course should make self-study, discussion, and research its main objectives. Such methods as asking for a summing-up report after a lecture should also be used. The democratic spirit of finding out and respecting the general feeling should be developed to make the content of study intimately connected with the students' thought and knowledge. Forcible methods of teaching should be opposed.

(2) This spirit of joining teaching and leadership should use the methods of teaching and leadership which join teaching and doing. Investigation, experiment, lecture, and discussion should be equally important . . . The doctrinaire spirit of dead book-learning should be thoroughly corrected.

The actual state of affairs in many institutions can be gauged by a few outspoken criticisms, most of which emerged during the brief '100 Flowers' period, and from the more numerous recommendations for reform since then. One example of the former spoke of a 'teacher reading his lecture notes and the students taking them down like recording machines' (Fraser, p. 256), and commented bitterly that, 'though incessantly talking about cultivating the students' independent work ability and co-ordinating theory with practice, the teachers, in practical teaching, only emphasize note-taking'. Foreign teachers, working in the various language schools, will recall the repetition of simple material and the stifling periods of 'revision'. D. Jenner describes a three-week intensive phonetics course to 'liquidate' faults. 'It is thought that by going at them very hard for a short period we achieve the best results', she writes. ' "Rectification" it is called. Never have I felt so much sympathy with third-degree interrogators. It hurts us as much as it hurts them.' (Jenner, 1967, p. 70).

A number of factors contributed to such dull, formal methods. Perhaps the biggest was the low standards of the majority of the teachers. Another was the enormous pressure to conform, especially in any subject with political implications. Fear of saying anything which might be politically wrong led to continual repetition of well-worn over-simplifications. If something had been published already, and not been criticized, then it was better to use that than something original which might lead to criticism, seems to have been the bureaucratic teacher's maxim. And the weaker and more lazy students preferred the traditional methods of learning by heart, for then they knew just what was expected of them, and did not have to think. Perhaps there was also a contradication at the very heart of the system, for the CCP appeared to genuinely desire people to think for themselves and take the initiative, while at the same time wanting them to do this only in such a manner as to develop socialism. The constant call is for 'positive criticism', or criticism within the field of socialism.

One way in which institutions have tried to improve teaching methods has involved cutting down the quantity of material, and giving students more free time. Qinghua reported doing this in 1962 (SCMP 2660, 1962), stressing that it would enable the students to read around their subjects after completing their homework assignments. In the Chemistry Department of Nankai University, Tianjin (Tientsin), teachers were asked to teach systematically according to the textbook 'so as to give a profound explanation of the main contents'. They were also asked to set out clearly the main points of each lesson, and to indicate the essential points made in various books which were used. Students were to be given a timetable of lessons, presumably setting out the content in outline. The Department of Political Economy at Nankai attacked pseudo-discussion, suggesting that students should not be coerced into taking part, and that discussions should not be prolonged at random (SCMP 2662, 1961). Perhaps less helpful was their suggestion that the reading lists given to students should only contain books considered absolutely necessary. Jiaotong University, Xi'an (Sian) at a meeting of chemistry teachers in 1961, called for shorter lectures outlining the main points of the subject and illustrating them with clear examples.

A second way advocated to improve teaching has been the development of practical, especially productive work. Replying to critics of this process in October 1959, Yang Xiu-feng said: 'There are facts to prove that the participation of the students in productive labour would not lower the quality of teaching but would raise it greatly, provided such labour were satisfactorily co-ordinated and arranged.' The proviso is the important point here, and available evidence suggests that much has still to be learnt before the arrangements can be regarded as 'satisfactory' (Fraser, p. 336).

Perhaps the most important development has been in student-teacher relations, and student participation in the teaching process. Traditionally the teacher has been respected by his students, and has been prone to keep aloof and carefully defend his dignity. But in recent years this relationship has been more and more replaced by that of a partnership in a common learning process. Long before the Cultural Revolution, with its 'three togethers' (live together, study together, and labour together), teachers in many institutions were taking part in productive labour with their students, and taking a serious interest in their out-of-class life. In 1961 the *Guangming Ribao* reported that the Peking People's University was making surveys of its students to discover their particular problems (SCMP 2658, 1961). In February 1962 the *People's Daily* wrote about the importance of 'grasping the actual conditions of the students' (SCMP 2695, 1962). In the Xi'an (Sian) Metallurgy College the teachers used special cards outlining the method and content of their lectures, on which the students then recorded their views (SCMP 2658, 1961).

Earlier the participation of student representatives on the various institution councils was noted. This, and their participation in the whole structure of discussion meetings, also helped to bring teachers and students together. Of course, especially where the teacher was weak and poorly qualified, the effect of being criticized by students could have a negative effect, and there is no doubt that some teachers were not helped by this system. But on the whole the system would seem to have been a useful development. Two foreigners who have seen it in action both praise it. A. I. Belyayev wrote (JPRS 1165) 'There is no doubt of the usefulness of the participation of students in the working out of training-methodological questions (curricula, schedules, programmes, training aids) and in the organization of the training process.' D. Jenner described a 'raise opinion meeting' at the Peking Radio Institute.

> Here the students told us what they thought of our teaching, what they liked, and what they thought should improve . . . I used to doubt the use of these meetings. I thought the students might be too shy to be frank, or that their ideas might be silly or just designed to get them out of some work. I see now that I was wrong. It gave everyone a chance to let off steam and some useful ideas were put forward, too. (Jenner, p. 77).

The teachers

One of the biggest problems which continues to trouble Chinese higher education is a shortage of teachers. In 1956 the then Minister of Higher Education put the problem very starkly to the third session of the First National People's Congress when he said:

> The demand for teachers has been particularly urgent in recent months, and comes into the greatest conflict with the demand of national construction departments and scientific research organs for cadres. In our opinion, it is particularly necessary . . . for all sides to assist the higher educational institutions to keep more graduates of good quality to be used as 'hens'. Otherwise, students enrolled will have no teachers to give them lessons, let alone to provide strenuous development of scientific research and improvement of teacher quality. (Fraser, p. 247).

By 1967 it was estimated there were about 1.7 million Chinese with a higher education (EPMC, p. 510). This is equivalent to 1/400 of the total population. Of these 1.7 million, about one-third were engineers, one-quarter were graduates in education, and about 6 per cent were graduates in one of the natural sciences. Orleans draws attention to the high number who have completed less than a four-year course. The number of persons with post-graduate training was estimated to be about 10,000 to 12,000, or about 1/70,000 of the population. Three-quarters of these were thought to be scientists and engineers. Another writer has estimated that some 4,500 of the scientists and engineers, including 900 to 1,000 with a Ph.D., were trained in Japan, Europe, or the U.S.A. (EPMC, p. 542). It is from this pool that national construction, research and teaching all have to draw, and its small size accounts for many of the difficulties which higher education institutions have to face.

One aspect of the shortage of trained people has been that the senior members of most institutions have been those trained, either at home or abroad, to fit into the Euro-American pattern of education. Mao Ze-dong recognized that this would make for difficulties and said that 'ideological reform—first of all the ideological reform of intellectuals—is one of the important conditions for our country's all-out complete democratic reform and gradual industrialization' (Fraser, p. 122). Qian Jun-rui, Vice-Minister of Education, quoting Mao, went on: 'It is thus obvious that the key to the reform of education lies in the ideological reform of the teachers.' (ibid, p. 123). From the early fifties the government gave considerable attention to this process, and a whole series of self-criticisms and denunciations were published (CB, nos. 169, 182 and 213). While there is no doubt that much misunderstanding was created, and much injustice done, it is necessary to see these events against the realities of the Chinese situation and the desperate need for change. In this connection it is interesting to read the comment of Dr. Y. C. Wang, author of the most detailed work on Chinese study abroad. He wrote:

Significantly, the intellectuals of Communist China are now confessing their sins of being detached from the masses and are atoning for them by living among the peasants. To be sure this action is politically induced, but it does not follow that the feelings are necessarily insincere. Virtually all the recantations are marked by cogent reasoning, internal consistency, and careful attention to details. Probably the most plausible explanation of this phenomenon is that because of their psychological vulnerability, these intellectuals were susceptible to coercive persuasion. Once the initial resistance was broken, they expressed their emotions readily. The self-condemnation may take an extreme form partly because the feelings are genuine. (Wang, p. xiii, footnote 4).

The aim of the criticism of the intelligentsia has been to win over as many as possible of them to support of the new government and its aims, and at the same time to destroy the influence of those who could not be won over. Ma Yin-chu, President of Peking University, put the first point in a speech delivered in October 1951. 'If the teachers' political consciousness is gradually raised to the same level as their professional training, greater accomplishments will be attained in various national construction work to be carried out henceforth. Only thus will "personal standpoint" be changed to "the people's standpoint" and the face of China be completely transformed' (Fraser, p. 118). Mao Ze-dong, speaking at the time of the '100 Flowers' movement, and just before the attack against the 'rightists' in which large numbers of the intelligentsia were condemned, put forward the milder view which has all along characterized top government pronouncements. He said:

> China needs as many intellectuals as she can get to carry through the colossal task of socialist construction. We should trust intellectuals who are really willing to serve the cause of socialism, radically improve our relations with them, and help them solve whatever problems have to be solved, so that they can give full play to their talents. Many of our comrades are not good at getting along with intellectuals. They are stiff with them, lack respect for their work, and interfere in scientific and cultural matters in a way that is uncalled for. We must do away with all such shortcomings. (Mao, 1966*b*, p. 108).

Nine years later, at the beginning of the Cultural Revolution, the CC CCP issued instructions for the guidance of the movement in which they laid down that:

> As regards scientists, technicians and ordinary members of working staffs, as long as they are patriotic, work energetically, are not against the Party and socialism, and maintain no illicit relations with any foreign country, we should in the present movement continue to apply the policy of 'unity, criticism, unity'.

163

Special care should be taken of those scientists and scientific and technical personnel who have made contributions. Efforts should be made to help them gradually transform their world outlook and their style of work. (CR docs 3, p. 11).

The results have no doubt been as much influenced by the rough ways of 'many of our comrades' as the good intentions of those higher up. A very high proportion of the intelligentsia have probably been moved by a genuine desire to help their country, but it is difficult to do so in an atmosphere of mistrust. Liu Xian, Professor of Biology at Fudan University, and author of *The History of the Development from Ape to Man* spoke of his own reactions to criticism of his book. 'In the first term of 1956 they [the department and the Marxist-Leninist study group of the university] devoted the whole term, holding a discussion meeting every two weeks, to criticizing my book, chapter by chapter and paragraph by paragraph . . . criticism has become a kind of spiritual pressure under which I was unable to express my own viewpoints fearlessly . . .' (MacFarquhar, p. 90-1). Such an atmosphere cannot assist the development of knowledge, yet it is hard to see how it could have been avoided in view of the wide divergences of attitudes and aims.

The second aspect of the shortage of trained people was the extreme youth of a high proportion of the teachers. Nanjing Mechanical Engineering College reported in 1960 that 9 of its 17 teachers were very young, and that 5 of them held positions of authority as department heads or heads of teaching and research teams (SCMP 2342, 1960). The Mathematical Mechanics Department of Anhui (Anhwei) University reported a majority of young teachers in 1962 (SCMP 2704, 1962). This state of affairs presented institutions with the problem of inservice training, as few teachers could be spared to go away on courses during term-time. As has been described elsewhere, elaborate methods were evolved, including, where possible, grouping the younger teachers around older, more experienced ones. Zhongshan University, Guangzhou (Canton), is one instance where this has been done. An article in 1961 (SCMP 2663, 1961) described how the History Department there used the older teachers as a 'hard core', while those of middle age were to 'learn from the old and enlighten the young'. It will be interesting to see how this rather traditional view survives the shock of the Cultural Revolution in which so much emphasis was placed on youth.

In the technical field the shortage of teachers could to some extent be overcome by the switching of skilled workers into teaching. The NCNA report of January 1962 that a former Shanghai steel welder had become a member of the Mechanical Engineering Department staff at Jiaotong University, Xi'an (Sian), is an example of this process. But the demands of production have been too great to make this common, and the alternative of developing part-work institutions at which workers could teach without moving from their production jobs was chosen as a major solution to the problem.

One of the first actions of the new government was to set up a salary scale for university teachers based on millet (Bodde, 1951, p. 116), which would eliminate the worst effects of inflation. In 1952 salaries were raised to a level 18.6 per cent better than 1951 (Fraser, p. 135). In 1959 Belyayev reported a scale with 12 categories ranging from 62 yuan per month to 345 yuan per month. Later these figures were adjusted, particularly to bring down the higher salaries, and the latest position is probably more in line with wages throughout industry. Here an eight-point scale operates, ranging from 35 yuan per month to 105 yuan per month (EPMC, p. 475).

In addition to a modest, but stable salary, higher education teachers enjoyed the benefits of social insurance.

Students : selection

Students of third level institutions have been selected from those who have completed the full secondary school course, or who could prove themselves to be of equivalent standard, and who were under thirty years of age. The age limit was waived in the case of certain workers, ex-soldiers and cadres.

In 1952 a central National Enrolment Committee was set up to run the entrance examinations for all but a handful of third level institutions. It produced annual plans, in accordance with the national economic plan, of the number and distribution of students, and it laid down detailed regulations for the examinations. Examinations were taken at special examination centres in the various provincial capitals and bigger towns. In 1954 there were 77 such centres, and in 1957 there were 91.

Beginning in 1958, a more decentralized system was set up. The central body continued to set targets for the numbers of students required in different parts of the economic and educational system, and their distribution between the various institutions, and the date of the examination. But the determination of where to hold the examinations, and the actual organization of them was delegated to the student-enrolment organizations to be set up by local education authorities and higher education establishments.

In order to register for the examination, candidates were expected to produce a registration form, and a medical certificate, and where possible, to show their secondary school graduation certificate. In addition, a letter of introduction was needed from the school or place of employment, or a letter of identification in the case of ex-soldiers, oversea Chinese, or 'other intellectual youth' (Fraser, p. 318). Except in the case of extreme hardship, where a subsidy could be applied for from the local education authorities, candidates were expected to bear their own expenses in connection with registration and sitting the examinations. In many cases this involved long journeys and maintenance during the two to three days of the examination itself.

The content of the examination was set out in a booklet published annually by the National Enrolment Committee. Outline syllabuses for the various subjects were given. These were wider in scope than the secondary school course, and some institutions organized voluntary preparatory classes to assist candidates. This problem was unavoidable because of the variation in standard and content of the school textbooks from place to place, and from one year to another, as attempts were made to improve the quality of secondary education.

Candidates had to take five or six subjects, depending on the field of study they wished to enter for. Fields of study were grouped as follows:

Fields of Study	Required Subjects
Group A 1 engineering	Chinese language
2 science	political knowledge
3 some branches of agriculture and forestry	mathematics
	physics
4 biochemistry and biophysics in medicine	chemistry
	(foreign language)

Group B 1 medicine   Chinese language
        2 agriculture and forestry   political knowledge
        3 biology   biology
        4 physical culture   chemistry
        5 psychology at comprehensive physics
          universities   (foreign language)

Group C 1 literature   Chinese language
        2 history   political knowledge
        3 political science and law   history
        4 finance and economics   geography
        5 philosophy and economic   (foreign language)
          geography at comprehensive
          universities

(Kunn, pp. 143–4 and Fraser, p. 319).

Central organization of enrolment work

Administrative Levels

National level	Ministry of Education
	(Ministry of Higher Education)
	National Enrolment Committee
	Question-setting Committee

— — — — — — — — — —

Regional level	Greater Administrative Area
	(after 1954: Regional Departments
	of Education and Higher Education)
	Greater Administrative (Regional)
	Enrolment Committees

— — — — — — — — — —

Provincial level	Provincial, municipal and
	autonomous region Departments
	of Education and Higher Education
	Provincial, municipal and
	autonomous region Enrolment
	Committee
	Examination Committees

— — — — — — — — — —

                Higher Educational Institutions

From: J. C. Kunn, 1961, p. 148.

A foreign language, either Russian or English, was not necessary for the years 1955 to 1958, but was required before and since. Exemption could be given for those candidates who did not study a foreign language at secondary school.

Kunn draws attention to the 1958 regulations section on 'political knowledge'. 'In political knowledge, the candidates will this year be examined from the important political events of domestic nature and other important events which took place during the year 1957–8. This is principally to test the awareness and attitude of the students concerning the rectification campaign and the anti-rightist struggle' (Kunn, p. 143).

In and after 1958 a special clause in the regulations allowed certion candidates to avoid the 'nationwide joint examination'. 'Workers, peasants, cadres of worker and peasant status and veteran cadres' could be recommended by the local education authorities for such exemption, but would then have to sit special examinations set by the institution to which they were sent.

In addition to the criterion of scholastic ability, health and 'political quality' have been major factors in selection. Section IX of the 1959 regulations instructed institutions to 'subject new students to another political and health check-up after their enrolment' and to disqualify those who failed it (Fraser, p. 321).

In some institutions, such as the big foreign language institutes, students were selected by cadres from the different departments, who travelled round the country interviewing candidates who had applied for entry (MacKerras & Hunter, 1968, p. 55).

Students: class composition

From the beginning, it was the intention of the Communist Party that higher education should be open equally to the children of workers and peasants. During the early fifties special schools were operated to prepare workers, peasants and their children, to overcome the handicap of insufficient preliminary education (Fraser, p. 194). As a result of this and other measures there was a steady rise in the percentage of these groups in the universities and other third level institutions. *Peking Review* for May 1958 published some figures:

Year	% of students of worker/peasant origin
1952–3	20.46
1955–6	29.20
1956–7	34.29
1957–8	36.42

Yang Xiu-feng (Fraser, p. 323) gave a figure of 48 per cent for 1958, and added that 62 per cent of new enrolments in that year came from worker-peasant families. S. Fraser, writing in 1965, referred to a figure of 'nearly half'. One way in which this substantial rise has taken place is the giving of priority to this formerly underprivileged group in cases where academic results in enrolment examinations are equal. All efforts have, however, failed to bring about a proportionate position equal to that of the group in the population, and the whole matter was raised very sharply during the Cultural Revolution.

Students: standards

From time to time grave anxiety has been expressed about the inadequate standards of the students, not only in academic matters, but also in health and 'political quality' (Fraser, p. 210). Health has been a particularly difficult problem, in spite of all the care taken to select healthy students. Zhu Wen-bin (Fraser, p. 253) refers to headaches, fatigue, insomnia and neurasthenia, and attributes them to worry caused by overwork and pressure of meetings. Another factor has also probably been an inadequate diet, especially during the hard years of 1960 and 1961. Defective eyesight was widespread, and there was a shortage of spectacles. Cases of tuberculosis have also been reported (MacKerras and Hunter, p. 61). Ill health was admitted to be the reason why many students had to give up their studies (Fraser, p. 211). In 1953, the only year for which a figure is available, this accounted for more than half of a figure of 3.5 per cent of the aggregate enrolment (Fraser, p. 217).

In 1955, at the first National People's Congress, Yang Xiu-feng made a strong attack on the moral-political quality of a number of the students. He accused them of being 'morally degenerate' and of leading a 'decadent life', and even of forming 'vagabond gangs to violate laws and discipline', (Fraser, p. 218). It is not clear just what these accusations referred to, but in many cases it was probably little more than an apathetic attitude to political education, then on the increase, and to formal studies. Since then there have been repeated references to the need to improve students' attitudes to study, to manual work, and to 'serving the people', but it is not clear what proportion of students err in this respect. Foreign observers all report a very high level of enthusiasm and devotion to study among students with whom they have been in contact.

One important question on which there has been a difference of opinion is the extent to which children of workers and peasants are able to benefit from higher education. Many of the older teachers have been hostile to, or at least fearful of, the introduction of such students. No one has denied that these students have special difficulties, and need more help than children from families in which education has been the rule. Many have praised them for their attitude to their studies, described as 'hard and dogged' in one example (SCMP 2664, 1962). Pan Mou-yuan, describing the situation at Xiamen (Amoy) University (JPRS 1165-D) comments that students of worker-peasant families are 'not naturally "dull" as many teachers assert'. In the first year they get easily tired, but with the right help they can keep up, and they have the right attitude to work. On the basis of working with students of English in Peking the present writer would agree.

Pan Mou-yuan goes on to give some comparative examination results to support his assertion. *See facing page.*

Students: conditions

The majority of Chinese students lived on the campus of their institutions. In many cases it was compulsory as it was thought to facilitate study (Popov JPRS 1176-D). From 1952 to 1955 tuition, board and lodging was free, but in 1955 this was replaced by a system of 'people's education subsidies'. Belyayev describes how these were allotted (JPRS 1176-D). They were independent of progress and depended on family income. The student's application was discussed by his student group, and then approved by the dean's office. In the N.E. Polytechnical Institute Department of Metallurgy of Nonferrous Metals, which Belyayev describes, 532 of the 935

Course	Grade	% among all students	% among worker-peasant students
1st Year Chinese language	Excellent	25.5	27.7
	Good	35.5	34.4
	Pass	33.3	28.8
	Fail	5.7	6.1
1st Year Economics	Excellent	29.8	28.7
	Good	39.8	40.4
	Pass	25.3	25.6
	Fail	5.4	5.9
1st year Electrical Machines	Excellent	13.5	13.2
	Good	47.0	44.0
	Pass	34.0	35.7
	Fail	5.5	6.9
1st year Mechanics	Excellent	16.1	16.1
	Good	43.3	42.8
	Pass	30.7	31.2
	Fail	9.9	9.8

students got subsidies, ranging from 14 yuan per month through 12, 9 and 6 to 3. Priority was given to children of workers and peasants, national minorities, and revolutionary orphans. According to the World Survey of Education (UNESCO, 3) most students received grants.

Institution fees went to pay for board and lodging. Tuition and medical treatment continued to be free, except in the case of special drugs, or prolonged or special treatment.

While student life was austere by European-American standards, there were sports clubs, music, drama and photography groups, and occasional outings to beauty spots and places of interest. Badminton, table-tennis and basket ball were played avidly, but travel, except during the early part of the Cultural Revolution, was rare. Colin MacKerras comments:

> The first thing Westerners notice about Chinese students is that, though roughly parallel in age with their Western counterparts, they behave and are treated in many ways like schoolchildren in the West. Yet Chinese students are not aware of this. I once

described to a group of them the kind of life a Western student
led. I gave them, I think, a fair picture. 'I'm glad I'm not a
Western student,' one of them said. 'I think we have a better life
here.' It was a sobering reply. (MacKerras and Hunter, p. 67).

Foreign language teaching—a case study

The various foreign language institutions have a special interest for
the student of Chinese education because they were the only places
where foreigners were able to teach alongside their Chinese colleagues and obtain first-hand experience. But care needs to be taken
in generalizing from these institutions to other areas of Chinese
education. Teaching languages is in some ways rather a special
problem. Compared with engineering and the natural sciences it is
more difficult to establish evaluating criteria, and there are more
direct political considerations. While the majority of graduates
probably became teachers, many went to work as interpreters at
home and abroad. Others translated foreign material for home
consumption, or Chinese material into foreign languages for
propagation overseas.

The number of students involved in the special foreign language
institutions was probably in the order of 12,000 plus or minus 3,000
in 1965–6. This would give a graduation figure in the order of under
2 per cent of total graduates from third level institutions. This does
not, of course, include all students of foreign languages, for there
were courses in the ordinary secondary schools and universities. It
should also be noted that there was a rapid increase in the number
of students in the special language institutions during the period
1964–6.

The majority of foreign language institutions were third level
institutions, taking their students from amongst the graduates of
the secondary schools. The two biggest and most important were the
1st Foreign Language Institute in Peking and the Foreign Language
Institute in Shanghai, each with some 2,000 students. Peking had a
number of small institutes, run by such Ministries as that for
Foreign Affairs, or Foreign Trade, or by the Radio. In 1964 a school
for training personnel for the Xinhua News Agency became the 2nd
Foreign Language Institute in Peking, and rapidly increased in size
and importance. In Xi'an (Sian) there was an institute which began

in 1952 as a Russian-language school, and by 1965 had about 1,000 students. Wuhan started a *zhuanke xuexiao*, or academy to teach English in 1964, but expanded this to include French in 1965, changing the title to *xueyuan*, or institute.

In addition to these third level institutions there were a number of schools at the second level, some like the Peking School of Foreign Languages, taking children as young as 8 years old. The Peking school was experimental and began in 1961. By 1966 it had 1,000 pupils from 8 to 18 years of age, 500 of whom were learning English, while others studied French, German, Spanish, Arabic or Japanese. There were other secondary schools in Guangzhou (Canton), Wuhan, Tianjin (Tientsin), Xi'an (Sian) and Chongqing (Chungking).

Administration and organization

The institutes were headed by a *yuanzhang*, or president, and a number of *fu-yuanzhang*, or vice-presidents. They were divided into departments on a language basis, each department headed by a *xi-zhuren*, variously called a dean, or head of department. While these were usually teachers with some knowledge of the language it was not unknown for an ex-soldier to be appointed, presumably for reasons of political reliability and organizational ability. In Xi'an (Sian) there was a *zhuren* with special responsibility for discipline throughout the institute. Within the departments there were various teaching groups (*jiaoyanzu*), each with its head and one or more deputy-heads.

Administration was by the usual institute and department committees, and Party organizations, only complicated where the number of foreign teachers was such that a special organization had to be devised to handle their affairs. In all cases a Chinese teacher was designated to act as guide, interpreter, and general helper to each foreign teacher.

The number of departments varied with the size of the institute. Where a large number of students learnt one language, as in the case of English, Russian, or Spanish, there might be one department for one language. In other cases languages were grouped, usually on an area basis. In the 2nd F.L.I., Peking, there was a Department of German and Japanese! The academic year was divided into the usual two terms, with a long break in the summer and a shorter one in January, where possible coinciding with the Chinese New Year. Other breaks were provided by the special holidays and by short periods of productive work, usually at harvest time, which the students all seemed to enjoy.

The day began early. Students got up at 5 o'clock in summer and 6 o'clock in winter. After a short period of physical exercises in the open air, and a cold wash, they had breakfast. Formal classes began at 8 o'clock and went on to 12 or 1 o'clock. Before morning classes students could be found all over the campus, reading their texts aloud. After the mid-day meal, and an hour in which students were supposed to rest, classes started again and went on for two to four hours. These were mainly non-vocational classes, history, and Chinese language. After supper at 6 o'clock there was private study and special coaching until half past nine. Most students went to bed about 10 o'clock.

Formal classes were divided by ten minute breaks, with a longer one at mid-morning. Accompanied by the din of music, and political or linguistic messages over the loud-speaker system, the students played table tennis, badminton, volley ball, or just roamed around chatting. Foreign teachers were waylaid by their own and other students, anxious to check up on what they had read or been told. Part of the long break was spent on further physical exercises. In some colleges there was a set time for a session of special massage to improve the circulation of fluids in the eyes, a cheap but doubtful substitute for the spectacles which so many students needed.

Political study occupied two afternoons a week in some institutes, and there was also a period of militia training. Saturday afternoons and Sundays were normally left free of organized activities, unless there was a special campaign on.

Courses ranged from 3 years to 5 years, except in those colleges with special short courses for older students, seconded from work. Such 'cadre classes' might be two-year courses. It appears to have been a policy to separate these cadre classes from the other classes in special Cadre Departments where numbers justified this. In the Peking Language Institute, where half the students were foreigners learning Chinese, there were special classes for army and air force students.

Classes ranged in size from 10 to 20 students. Little attempt was made to sort students according to their ability, though those with no previous study were usually separated from those who had done the language before. Where classes were noticeably backward, special efforts were made to raise their standard, and in all classes individual students were encouraged to help each other. Classes of the same year did not always use the same teaching materials. In 1965–6, in the 2nd F.L.I., Peking, year 1, class 8 who had never studied English before, were using the experimental material produced by the 1st F.L.I. Later in the same year a backward class in year 2 began to use some different experimental material based on work being done at the Foreign Trade Institute.

Buildings and equipment

As always, these were austere and functional. In Peking the concrete floors and central heating which was only switched on for two short periods in the morning and afternoon, made conditions very hard in winter, and students would huddle in their desks with overcoats, hats, gloves and even face-masks on very cold days. In the warm climate of the south such buildings would have been pleasantly light and airy.

A common building plan was the long, three-storey rectangle with rooms of varying size leading off central corridors. Some rooms were divided by temporary walls, allowing flexibility in use. The campus included teaching and administration blocks, a library, dormitory buildings, dining-halls and adjoining kitchens, bathhouse, printing works, clinic, and often blocks of flats for married staff. The grounds were usually planted with trees, under which there were scattered seats, and the open spaces were furnished with basket-ball posts. Some colleges had concrete table-tennis tables in the grounds, or there might be an open-air swimming pool, built by the students during their periods of productive work. In the winter in Peking a piece of open ground would be flooded and converted into an ice-rink for skating, which was a very popular sport in the north.

The institutions all had libraries of both Chinese and foreign-language books, and there were reading rooms where the various foreign language publications published in Peking were available. In the bigger colleges the libraries were quite extensive, but it is doubtful whether many of the foreign books were often read. In addition to the libraries available to students there were also in some colleges small collections for the staff. In the English Department of the 2nd F.L.I. in Peking there was an excellent collection of the latest British and American dictionaries, grammars, and of the latest books on methods of teaching English to foreigners. But during the writer's stay there, these were read by only a handful of the teachers.

Space was very limited, and students studied in the classroom, or when the weather allowed, in the open air. Classrooms were furnished with rather old-fashioned desks and separate chairs. Tiny, very low stools were popular for meetings and there were usually a number in each room. Teachers' desks were tall, square lectern-type objects on which notes could be rested during class, when the teacher was expected to stand. In the teachers' rooms, where they did their preparation, there were large table-desks with drawers.

As in all institutes, there was a well-equipped internal broadcasting system. Large quantities of foreign exchange had obviously been made available to buy Japanese, German and Dutch taperecorders, and German tape was common. The quality of Chinese tape-recorders and tape, though improving, was still well below that of foreign makes.

In addition to the loudspeakers in classrooms, corridors, and outside in the grounds, there were usually a number of taperecorders which could be used by groups of teachers or students. But as these were usually the older, poorer quality ones, their value was not as great as it might have been. Shortage of tape also often meant that results in the classroom were too poor to be of great use.

Both shortage of equipment and a lack of conviction about methods combined to produce language laboratories which were little more than libraries of tapes with facilities for group listening. There seemed to be very little recording of the student for purposes of self-correction and evaluation. In 1965-6 the writer was unable to find a single laboratory equipped in the manner now familiar in Europe, with two-way communication between teacher and the individual student.

The foreign teachers

In the early period after 1949 foreign teachers were drawn from those few foreigners who remained in China through sympathy with the new government, or because they were married to Chinese. It was only after the expansion of language work in the sixties that large numbers of foreigners were recruited. No attempt was made to recruit people qualified for the job. Some were recruited through friends already there. Others heard of the opportunity and went along to embassies and legations abroad and asked for work. A small handful could be classed as political refugees. The majority viewed the regime with varying degrees of sympathy. A very small number might be classed as hostile, there only for what they could get out of the experience.

All the foreign teachers lived at a higher standard of living than their Chinese colleagues, even where they shared similar accommodation. The majority lived in special hostels or hotels. Only a small minority were allowed to live on the institution campuses. Salaries ranged from six times to about twelve times that of a Chinese teacher. Hours of work were often much shorter. But probably the most important dividing factor was that the foreign teacher could never share the same responsibility. In the end he could always opt out and go home.

The kind of relationships which developed between foreign teachers and their Chinese colleagues and students seems to have been very much a personal question on both sides. During the period 1964–7 there were strong political pressures which tended to make contact official and superficial. The extreme care and courtesy with which the various authorities treated their guests, as they like to call them, often frustrated rather than helped. But here and there, in spite of custom and creed, real human contact was achieved and some mutual understanding was established.

Foreign teachers were employed in order to improve the standard of the spoken language. Almost all of them spent a lot of time recording material which was used not only in the institution to which they were attached, but also in other schools and colleges in China. This material might be phonetic exercises, or dialogues, texts or the works of Mao Ze-dong, but it almost all suffered from the general fault of being translated material rather than native. The greater part of a foreign teacher's time was probably spent in class teaching. In most cases one foreigner took two or three classes for the whole of their formal language work. His Chinese colleague, assigned to the same class, looked after the class organization, and did out-of-class coaching during the afternoons and evenings. The third job which most foreigners did was to assist in the in-service training of teachers. In its simplest form this involved giving demonstration lessons. In fact, every lesson was a demonstration lesson in many colleges, with one or more teachers from the same or another institution sitting at the back, busily taking notes. Some of the foreigners took the opportunity of visiting each other's classes, but usually not without warning, and the English-speaking teachers certainly did not encourage the practice, though it had obvious advantages where so few were trained teachers. The other form of teacher education was the formal class, usually on a once-a-week basis. In at least one case a foreigner was given a group of young teachers whose ability in English was for various reasons insufficient for them to teach it, and allowed to design and carry through a programme for 12 hours a week for nearly six months. Had the Cultural Revolution not intervened it would have continued for a whole year, when it was hoped that most of the class would be able to assume normal duties.

Finally, most teachers were involved in the preparation of teaching materials. In the majority of cases this involved correcting and commenting on material prepared by the Chinese teachers. While some textbooks existed and were used, in the majority of cases the material was prepared locally, all too often only a week or two ahead of its use. This work was probably the most difficult and frustrating which foreigners had to do, mainly because of political distrust. Delia Jenner gives a typical example and comments: 'Political texts are trying. If you try to dejargonize the texts they think you are twisting the meaning, but it's even more wicked to suggest we don't use political texts.' (Jenner, p. 87). Linguistic incompetence of the institution authorities was often a big factor. In English a minor nuisance was the confusion between dialects, particularly British and American, and the lack of any direction on how to handle this question. The same text would first be corrected by a British teacher, and then by an American. Then some Chinese would compile the final draft, without realizing the reason for the various corrections, and what was taught would be neither British, nor American, but a strange mixture of these and Chinese forms which the exasperated foreigner dubbed Chinglish (cf. the USSR where British and American English are taught separately).

In some cases foreigners actually wrote material themselves, usually based on everyday situations connected with student life, or with their future work as interpreters. Topics might be: going to see the doctor; or taking a foreign visitor to see the Ming Tombs. In the 2nd F.L.I., Peking, three British teachers spent the nine months before the Cultural Revolution writing a first-year textbook. In the Slavonic, and the African and Asian languages, foreign teachers seem to have had greater freedom in text-writing, though many of them expressed their frustration over similar difficulties.

In defence of the Chinese teachers it should be noted that many of the foreigners had only the qualification of being native speakers, and some displayed a remarkable ignorance of their own grammar. A number of foreign teachers felt that the Chinese would have got better value for their money if there had been more centralized control over them, and some attempt made to take advantage of what specialized talent there was. At least two teachers from Latin American countries had been trained at Ann Arbor, Michigan, under C. C. Fries, and one French teacher was trained in the methods of the Alliance Française. Much duplication of recording could have been avoided, and attention could have been given to the collection of materials in different dialects, e.g. standard British and standard American English. In fact, centralization and planning was the major element in the work which was missing, though it sometimes intruded into other aspects of the foreign teacher's life.

The Chinese teachers

The Chinese teachers were very mixed in age and qualifications. At one extreme there were the foreign-educated Chinese, with an excellent grasp of the spoken language, and also of the culture of the country concerned. Colin MacKerras recalled how the Dean of the English Department 'once asked me nostalgically whether the Backs at Cambridge were still as beautiful as ever' (MacKerras and Hunter, p. 56). At the other extreme there were the very young teachers who had struggled to grasp some language newly and badly taught, and who were without ability to read or speak it properly, or the aids which might have enabled them to do so. Between these two extremes the majority had a fair grasp of the language, with little idea of the life and literature of the country concerned.

The older, foreign-educated and university-trained teachers tended to favour courses using traditional literature. Dickens, Mark Twain and Bernard Shaw were used to convey what was thought to be a suitable message. Others preferred to analyse English grammar in their native Chinese. But by the sixties both of these were being gradually swept into the background by advocates of the oral approach, with the emphasis on Chinese political themes. The advocates of the pattern-drill approach embraced both foreign-educated and the products of the new institutes themselves.

The curriculum

The curriculum consisted of a single foreign language, which occupied the bulk of the students' time, together with Chinese, political studies, physical education, productive work and militia training. The last four were like courses in other third level establishments and will not be considered here. The Chinese language course lasted a few hours a week, and will also not be discussed.

The foreign language courses were aimed at enabling the students to acquire a working knowledge of the language without picking up any foreign ideas. Chen Yi, speaking to some foreign language students in 1962 on the need to master 'the foreign way of expression' and learn to think in the foreign language, stressed that this did not mean to learn the 'way of thinking of the foreigner' (SCMP 2713, 1962). Foreign languages were to be used 'in our own way'.

In practice, however, courses have included various selections from literature, and information of all kinds about life in the various countries. As in the use of foreign teachers, so here the basic characteristic was the absence of any overall planning, and a constant experimenting with new materials.

In the summer of 1965 some instructions relating to the curriculum were published, apparently on the direct orders of Mao Zedong. Worries about student health and standards of education dictated that time spent on meetings and compulsory extra-curricular work should be cut down. Students were to be given more time in which to relax, or to work on their particular interests. Such was the strange atmosphere in which some institutes worked that this matter was only disclosed to the foreign teachers in special meetings with a vice-principal some six months later, and requests for copies of the original instructions were refused.

Teaching methods

In this section the discussion will be limited to the teaching of English. From all accounts teaching methods in other languages were very similar.

The basis of the method used was a text which was memorized by the students, and in a high proportion of cases understood with the aid of translation. The older methods which employed Chinese to talk about English grammar seem to have gone out at least by the early sixties, though some teachers, unable to speak English fluently, still continued to speak more Chinese than English during lessons. In Xi'an (Sian) the third and fourth years still had one period a week of formal grammar in 1965-6.

Texts varied in origin, but were usually based on Chinese texts. The majority were chosen for their moral-political content, and little thought seems to have been given to their linguistic content. The Peking Institute under the Ministry of Foreign Affairs, and the Tianjin (Tientsin) Foreign Languages School both prepared first-year material based on simple sentence patterns, but in neither case was the order chosen successful. Only at the 1st F.L.I., Peking, was there a real understanding of modern methods, and for some reason other colleges seemed loath to learn from them.

Each text was taught for a week, or longer in the case of longer and more difficult texts in the more advanced classes. Teachers studied the texts beforehand and selected what they variously described as 'teaching points' or 'structures', depending on whether modern methods were being pushed in the department, and the jargon current. A varied collection of inflections, idioms and phrases was thus gathered and ways devised to drill them.

The texts were all recorded, where possible by a native speaker of English. In some cases the class teacher recorded material for his own class. But little if any attempt was made to ensure that beginners heard only one model until they had established their own pronunciation. Sometimes additional drills, phonetic and pattern, were recorded. This material was played to the students before and after formal classes, sometimes through a loudspeaker system of varying quality, and sometimes individual tape-recorders were available in the classrooms and students could listen as they pleased.

Apart from hearing the recorded text a number of times and repeating it in various ways in class, the students spent many hours reading it aloud. Describing how the Shanghai F.L.I. students were 'studying foreign languages with greater vigour than ever before' in 1962, the *Guangming Ribao* wrote: 'As they get up early in the morning, sounds of reading can be heard near the classrooms and in the sports ground' (SCMP 2724, 1962). Unfortunately such efforts were all too often an imprinting of error. When one of the foreign teachers took her English-speaking, foreign-educated Chinese principal into the school grounds to listen to one of these sessions the principal thought the students might be practising German. Another foreign teacher reported that one of his students had proudly announced that on the previous evening he had repeated the word 'bok', meaning 'book', a thousand times!

Foreigners had little access to their Chinese colleagues' discussions of teaching methods. On the whole they seem to have preferred this well-trod path to any new suggestions made. Memorizing came easily, and students knew what was expected of them. But a small number of the foreign teachers criticized the method, particularly in regard to the early period of study, on the following grounds. Successful language teaching depends on the careful selection and ordering of the structures of the particular language, and any texts used should illustrate these structures. It is also important to select and limit vocabulary, and to make sure that every word taught gets constantly revised in new sentence patterns.

Except in the 1st F.L.I., where the initiative seems to have come from the younger Chinese teachers, these ideas fell on stony ground. The change in emphasis from written to spoken English seemed to have taxed teachers to the limit for the time being. It should be emphasized that there was no shortage of material on the subject in most institutes. Books by H. L. Palmer, J. O. Gauntlett, A. S. Hornby, C. C. Fries, and the workbooks of Lado and Fries stood on the library shelves. Probably the opposition stemmed from a fear of the unknown on the one hand, and political considerations on the other. Simple sentence patterns do not lend themselves to the expression of abstract political concepts, dearly beloved of the text-writers. And the methods being advocated by teachers from 'imperialist' countries were of declared U.S. Origin. Finally, each institute seemed to regard it as a matter of pride to practise self-reliance, though considerable copying of material and use of published textbooks did go on.

While it was generally recognized that English should be the language of instruction as well as the subject taught, this was not always adhered to. Chinese teachers and students frequently lapsed into their mother tongue, and even one foreign teacher was known to use the opportunity to practise his Chinese. In the best cases, English was used outside the classroom, and in some institutes notices and posters used foreign languages, and loudspeakers purveyed further practice to accompany break-time activities.

In some institutions pictures were used to good effect in the early stages. Printed pictures seldom gave enough language practice, but often a student would make sketches on the blackboard in the interval between classes. In Xi'an (Sian) there was an artist engaged full-time on the production of visual aids. Teachers often seemed shy of exposing their weaknesses in this and in acting out a situation, preferring to stand stiffly in front of the class at the old-fashioned lectern.

A curious feature of most classes was their attitude to truth. On the one hand, it was assumed that the content of all sentences used in language practice must be correct, as well as their grammar. It would not occur to teacher or student to indulge in nonsense sentences or phantasy as a vehicle for grammatical exercise. But on the other hand, the text seems to have had a higher authority. If the students were asked what they found difficult about learning English they would all, with apparent sincerity, faithfully rehearse Comrade Wang's difficulties from the text on 'Studying English'. A colleague of the writer recalls a conversation which went: 'Good morning, teacher, how are you?' 'I'm tired out, comrade.' The student gaped in surprise, and said: 'But yesterday you taught us to say "Fine, thank you, how are you?" '

Method reforms

Compared with older methods which involved a high proportion of written translation and discussion in Chinese of foreign language grammar, the methods widely in use during the sixties have been a great advance. It remains only to comment on two experiments which received wide publicity in Peking, and perhaps farther afield, during 1965.

The first experiment took place in the 1st F.L.I., beginning in the autumn of 1964 with a number of first-year classes. The second took place in 1965-6 at the Foreign Trade Language Institute, and involved a special class in their second year. In some of the other institutes which discussed these two experiments there seemed to be some confusion, and the trade school method was treated as if it applied to first-year work. In the present discussion the experiments will be referred to as method 1 and method 2 respectively.

Method 1 (*Waiyu Jiaoxue Yu Yanjiu*, 4, 1965, pp. 13–20) was based on a careful study of teaching methods in China and abroad, and on a thorough analysis of the English language, to decide on a suitable teaching order for the various elements. The result was a carefully worked-out course of pattern drills and exercises with controlled vocabulary. In addition, students were expected to do a very much greater amount of reading than was usual in the other courses, and for this a number of books were rendered in versions using a controlled vocabulary. Much of this work was done by one of the British teachers. The whole course was to last three years, compared with the previous five. It was in its second year when the Cultural Revolution broke out.

Method 2 was the work, not of a team of teachers, but a single enthusiastic woman, who used group psychology to encourage enthusiasm and active participation. Many of the details of her work were not clear, even after prolonged discussion with her and observation of the class at work. It appeared that at least a majority of her students had learnt English at secondary school, before coming to the Foreign Trade Institute. The core of the work was a group of short texts, related in content, selected from the English translation of Mao Ze-dong's works, and speeches and editorials translated by the Xinhua News Agency, or the Foreign Language Press. From these the teacher selected various phrases for drilling. The more mundane English, needed to aid interpreters in handling foreign visitors' needs, was obtained from Eckersley, and by listening to old Linguaphone records. The concept of register was absent, and the students produced strange examples with machine-gun rapidity.

One of the more extreme, accepted in the presence of visitors, was:
'. . . plunging into the ocean of Chairman Mao's works . . .'

Method 1 was carefully tested by allowing students from the experimental and normal classes to sit the same examination, and ensuring that those marking the examination did not know from which group each candidate came. In the oral examination a microphone was hidden in a bowl of flowers so students would not be disturbed, and their performance could be more accurately compared afterwards. The results were in the main greatly in favour of the experimental classes.

Method 2 was not tested formally, perhaps because the Cultural Revolution broke out before the year ended, but there is little doubt that the class would have made a good showing if they had been. There was an impressive fluency among all its members.

The discussion of these two experiments at a third institute perhaps indicates some of the wider problems of education in present-day China. The majority of teachers, and especially those in leadership positions, seemed to favour method 2, without it appeared, grasping two important points. Firstly, the method relied mainly on the enthusiasm of teacher and class, and there was no evidence that this could be so easily generated under other conditions. Secondly, the real problem was in the first year, laying the basis for future work. Method 2 was used in the second year, when the basis was, however badly, already laid. But what made it so attractive, besides the obvious enthusiasm and success of the class, was the use of and constant reference to Mao Ze-dong's works. That in fact the two methods were not mutually exclusive, but could be combined, was pointed out by some of the foreign teachers, but the point was not taken.

Some examples of the content

In order to give an idea of the kind of material taught some extracts have been taken from English courses in three institutions. The first is a list of sentence patterns and other items taught during the first term of the first-year course at the Tianjin Foreign Language Secondary School in 1965. Each lesson was one week's work.

Lesson one :   I am a teacher.
You are a pupil.
Am I a teacher?
Yes, you are a teacher.

Then the words *boy, girl, cat* and *bag* were substituted. The expressions: *good morning; stand up; sit down;* and *good-bye* were also taught.

Lesson two :   New words: *worker ; peasant ; P.L.A. man ; cook and dog.*
New pattern: *No, I am not a worker.*

Lesson three :   I can see Li Ming.
Can I see Li Ming?

Other names were used, and the pronouns *you* and *me.*

Lesson four :   We are pupils.
They are boys.
No, they are not bags. They are bats.

Comment : Could this last be a phonetic exercise?

Lesson six :   This, that, these and those.
The definite article introduced with the nouns *sun, moon* and *sky.*

Lesson eight :   What is this? It is a flag.
Colours and uncountables were introduced: *what is this? It is chalk. What can you see? I can see ink.*

Comment : opportunity to consolidate the definite article was missed in the example: *I can see a blackboard.*

Lesson nine :   Today is National Day. The sky is blue. The sun is shining. We are happy.
This is a picture of Chairman Mao. Chairman Mao is our great leader. We love Chairman Mao. We are good pupils of Chairman Mao.
Special phrases at the bottom of the page were: *Do you love Chairman Mao? Yes, we love Chairman Mao. What does Chairman Mao say? Chairman Mao says, 'Study hard and make progress every day.'*

Comment : This kind of language can only be taught by translation.

Lesson ten: *What have you got?*
I have got two eyes. Further vocabulary: *my* and parts of the body. Then following: *She has got one nose. What can she do? She can smell.*
He has got two hands. What can he do? He can wash his scarf.

Lesson eleven: the cardinal numbers, one to twenty.
Can you count?
How many bowls have you got?

Lesson twelve: *Where are you? Where is the blackboard?* Replies drill: *in the dormitory; on the wall.*
The word *many* is used in one sentence: *I can see many desks in the classroom.*

Lesson thirteen: *Li Ming, go to the door.*
Where are you going?
I am going to the door.

Further drills with: *the window; to school; to the People's Park;* and other places. Special expressions: *Are you a red successor? Yes, I am a red successor. I love my red scarf. I love the three red flags.*

Lesson
  fourteen: *I can read.*
I am reading.
It can fly.

Comment: (1) Instead of verbs like *to fly* or *to shout*, it might, for instance, have been easier to use the verb *to lift* and heavy and light objects as an introduction. (2) Various meanings of *can* would probably be confused here, too.

Lesson fifteen: (the final and only continuous text). *At the zoo. Chen Fang and Chui Ling go to the zoo. They go by bus number three.*
In the zoo they can see many animals. In that cage there is a lion. It is big and strong. In that cage there are some monkeys. The monkeys jump and swing on the rope. The people laugh.
There is a tiger. The tiger is fierce. There is a peacock.

It is very beautiful.
The animals are interesting. Chen Fang and Chui Ling
have a good time at the zoo.

This kind of material is probably typical of what was taught in classes of this level, and it illustrates the transition which was taking place from old-fashioned translation methods to direct, oral methods. Much of the meaning could be put over by the use of drawings, but a great deal still depended on translation, especially the abstract words. The textbook is cyclostyled and locally produced, and compares unfavourably with the illustrated English textbook used in the ordinary full-time secondary schools.

The next example is taken from the second term of year 2 in an institute whose pupils were oversea Chinese. This was a third level institution, and the material was produced with the help of foreign teachers. The same text was used in the second year at the Xi'an (Sian) Institute.

The text was an 800-word long piece about 'Karl Marx—scientist and revolutionary' adapted from an article by Paul Lafargue. This was to be handled, according to the teaching plan, as follows:

		(45 minutes each)
1	Introduction of the text	3 periods
2	Reading the text	1 period
3	Language points	3 periods
4	Pattern drills	3 periods
5	Big question discussion	2 periods
6	Dictation	1 period
7	Aural comprehension	1 period
8	Quiz	1 period

Total: 15 periods

In addition to the text, students were provided with an English to English glossary, and some background notes about the origin of the text and the early life of Marx.

Teachers were provided with 63 questions, grouped by paragraph, with which to introduce the text. For example: paragraph 4 of the text read:

In early 1847, the two men [i.e. Marx and Engels] joined a secret propaganda society called the Communist League. This League was the first organization to emphasize the international class-character of the whole labour movement. Under Marx's guidance it began to organize international labour meetings and it was for this League that he and Engels wrote the Communist Manifesto in 1848 to explain the principles of scientific socialism.

The teachers' notes supplied the following comprehension questions:

1 What kind of organization did the two men join in 1847?
2 What was it called?
3 What was the new line that the League took?
4 Do you think it strengthened the labour movement to take an internationalist line for its struggles?
5 What did Marx begin to organize through the League?
6 What did he and Engels write for the League?
7 What did the Communist Manifesto explain to the workers?

Fifty-two language points were provided, listed under the paragraphs of the text in which they occurred. Some were explanations of words or phrases, like 'to spread', meaning to propagate; 'public life'; or 'to hold the view'. Others included the pattern 'to look at someone/something as something'; 'there' used emphatically; 'when' used with two meanings; and the pattern 'to use something to do something'.

Under the heading 'vocabulary and pattern drills' about ninety sentences were provided which had to be altered or completed to include a suggested phrase. A complete key was supplied. Some examples were:

Phrase: at the same time.
'Li Kung was not only a doctor but also a political worker.'
Key: 'Li Kung was a doctor and a political worker at the same time.'
Phrase: can only . . . if.
'We can only remould ourselves if . . .'
Key: 'We can only remould ourselves if we integrate with the workers and peasants.'
Phrase: It is not . . . It is . . .

o   189

'It isn't modern weapons that decide the outcome of war.'
Key: 'It isn't modern weapons that decide the outcome of war. It is the power of the people.'

Item 5, the big questions for discussion, were:

1 How do you interpret Marx's view about scientists and their relationship to society?
2 What have you learned from this lesson about some of Marx's contributions to the international working-class movement?

These were followed in the teaching plan by four pages of 'answer suggestions for teacher's reference'.

In the more advanced classes, especially in such institutes as that run by the Ministry of Foreign Affairs, a certain amount of native English material was used. Much of it was articles from various American and British left-wing magazines, but the London *Times* and the *New York Times* were also used.

Students and standards

The students varied considerably in background and aptitude. At one extreme there was the Shanghai middle class student whose parents spoke a foreign language, and may even have been abroad. At the other there was the peasant girl from a remote village who found Peking rather noisy and frightening, and who was the first person in her village to obtain a third level education. Some of them were excited by the opportunity to study a foreign language, while others obviously loathed it, and longed to be mathematicians or engineers. But all foreigners were struck by the general enthusiasm and capacity for persistent hard work. And the standard reached, bearing in mind all the difficulties, was remarkably good.

5

Part-time schools and classes

The schools and classes which will be described in this chapter cover the whole range of studies from basic literacy to university-level studies in engineering and science. A distinction will be made between spare-time and part-work education. The former essentially takes place in addition to a normal working day while the latter is an alternative to normal work, though in practice the distinction may become blurred. The term part-work is preferred to part-time because of the educative value which is ascribed to productive work, and the attempts which have been made to relate work and study in these schools.

Spare-time education

Spare-time education did not begin with the new government in 1949. Literacy classes were organized for the Chinese workers in France during the First World War. James Y. C. Yen of the Y.M.C.A. worked in France, and then in China. In 1923 a National Association of Mass Education was set up. In 1922 Mao Ze-dong himself set up a similar movement in Hunan, based on the Y.M.C.A. work, but using different textbooks (Schram, 1966, p. 68). The method of using 'husband teach wife, son teach father, those-knowing-more-characters teach those-knowing-fewer' was instituted by Xu Te-li, the well-known communist teacher of Mao Ze-dong, and Commissioner of Education at Yan'an (Yenan) (Schram, 1966, p. 207; *Hanyu Keben*, 1, p. 225). The same method was used by Tao Zhi-xing (Tao, 1938). But only the government support and stable conditions of the past eighteen years have enabled a comprehensive spare-time education system to be developed.

The aims of the new system were first set out in June 1950, in the directive on spare-time education issued by the Government Administration Council of the Central People's Government

Part-time schools and classes

(NPC docs, 2, pp. 81–8). Spare-time education was seen as 'the most important means of raising the political, educational and technical levels of the masses of workers and staff members'. While suggestions were made for more advanced courses, the emphasis was on political education and literacy classes. In 1960, after several years of renewed attention, the same aims were repeated. 'Several hundred million young and grown-up labouring people will, through spare-time education, gradually raise their political, technological, and cultural standards' wrote the CC CCP and the State Council (Fraser, p. 349). The role of these schools in popularizing education also began to be emphasized, a role which the state-operated full-time schools were said to be incapable of (Fraser, p. 363). Speakers like Tao Lu-jia, first secretary of the CCP Shanxi Provincial Committee, waxed eloquent on 'turning the workers and peasants into intellectuals' and 'eliminating the difference between manual labour and mental labour', themes which were to be heard again with increased intensity during the Cultural Revolution.

Development and organization

The 1950 directive laid down that spare-time education should be organized by the government education departments, and by the trade unions. At the central level it envisaged a national Committee on Spare-time Education for Workers and Staff Members, set up by the Ministry of Education, the All-China Federation of Trade Unions (ACFTU), the Ministry of Labour and other bodies. At the local level similar committees were set up with an education department representative as chairman and a trade unionist as vice-chairman. The central body was to be concerned with 'policy, planning curricula, expenditure and rules', while the local committees concerned themselves with local problems. Within the factories, mines and offices the detailed organizational work was carried out by the trade union organization. For a time the management, whose job was initially only to supply facilities for classes, took over the running of cultural and technical studies, while the unions continued to run political education.

In 1958 a directive of the CC CCP and State Council handed over control of workers' education to the Party committee of each enterprise. The control of cultural and technical studies reverted from the management to the trade unions. P. Harper points out that a Party committee, with 'a much wider spectrum of interests' has a 'greater ultimate stake in education for the working class', and that this move was probably therefore in the right direction for the development of education. He also draws attention to the overlapping of Party and trade union responsibility and membership, and concludes that 'most of the work done in the plants' educational programmes, other than actual teaching of cultural or technical classes, is performed by trade union cadres' (Harper, 1964, pp. 20–1).

While at the local level organization of spare-time education was being decentralized, in Peking the CC CCP and State Council were again turning their attention to the question of a spare-time education committee. They issued a notification setting out its powers and composition. Besides officials concerned with education, culture, science, economics and military affairs, it was to include representatives of the trade unions, the Young Communist League, the women's organizations and other similar bodies.

According to the June 1950 directive, spare-time education was to be financed from the cultural and educational fund which the factory or enterprise contributed to the trade union organization. Any deficit was to be made up by a subsidy from the local government educational fund. It initially suggested a figure of 60 per cent of the fund. In 1956 the two Education Ministries and the trade unions altered the figure to 75 per cent, equivalent to 2 per cent of wages. But in 1957 it was reduced to 50 per cent. The 1950 directive clearly stated that such money should only be used for 'the payment of teachers' wages, allowances, prizes, subsidies for the purchase of books and small sundry purchases, *and any waste must be avoided*' (NPC docs, 2, p. 87, emphasis added).

One of the biggest problems in developing spare-time education has been the provision of teachers in sufficient numbers and of the right quality. The 1950 directive clearly foresaw the difficulties and attempted to meet them. To teach the literacy classes it called on organizers to 'mobilize all literate staff members, workers and members of their families . . . to teach in primary classes and make them understand that teaching illiterates is a glorious task and duty'. It went on: 'In principle, teaching primary classes shall be a non-remunerative or quasi-remunerative work, while honourable mentions and material awards shall be given to teachers who have done outstanding work.' Political education was to be given by 'leading comrades in the factories', or teachers of political courses in the local secondary and higher schools. Finally it urged that 'all technical personnel in the factories and enterprises shall be mobilized to take up the glorious task of training technical workers for the country and to volunteer to be the teachers' (ibid, pp. 82, 84 and 85). By the beginning of 1960 such measures had led to the establishment of a teaching force of about 430,000 people, 60,000 of whom were professional teachers transferred from the full-time schools to work wholly in the spare-time system (Harper, p. 18). The 1950 directive envisaged, besides literacy classes and political education, a system of both general and technical education. General education classes were to be organized at 'intermediate' and 'advanced' levels, the former to correspond to classes 5 and 6 of the primary school, and the latter to the secondary school. The time to be taken was to be flexible, but two years was suggested for the intermediate class and five years for the advanced. Government education classes were to issue certificates at the end of the courses which would be equivalent to those of the regular schools.

The directive's suggestions for technical education were training classes, research classes and master-apprentice contracts, depending on local conditions. But it stressed the need for regular examinations, and the desirability of rewarding good students with promotion, and teachers with a prize or award.

Time allocations were also made in the directive. Primary and technical classes were to meet 'at least twice a week', while the intermediate, higher and political classes were to meet 'at least three times a week', each time for 'at least 90 minutes'. An important provision which was probably often ignored was that 'on study days the students may be free from overtime work or from taking part in meetings'.

Teaching materials for the intermediate and higher general education classes were to be similar to those used in the regular schools, or the short-term secondary schools for workers and peasants, but were to be condensed. A special editing committee was to be set up jointly by the Ministry of Education, the ACFTU, the Ministry of Labour and the Publications Administration. Local teachers were given the responsibility for drafting technical and supplementary materials, which then had to receive the approval of the local spare-time education committee.

In 1955 the Ministry of Machine Industry published directives on the establishment and running of technical education at the secondary and higher education level. Specialist courses for training technicians were to be either a five-year course of 12 hours per week, or a six-year course of 9 hours per week. Throughout the following year the ACFTU was busy drawing up a twelve-year plan for spare-time education.

In 1957 the Ministry of Higher Education issued a directive on the revision of the curriculum in spare-time higher educational institutions. It differed from that in the full-time institutions in its emphasis on basic general and technical subjects, and the reduction in the number of special subjects. Special subjects were only to be studied during the two final years of the course. Technology students were not expected to study a foreign language or take part in physical or military training. Political education, however, was compulsory. Standards were expected to be equivalent to those of the full-time four-year course. The six-year course consisted of 38 to 40 weeks of 9 hours per week, with 4 weeks of examinations. The total number of hours for the course was to be about 2,160. Classes were normally to be held for 3 hours on 3 evenings a week, but might be extended to occupy 12 hours per week, where work allowed. Regulations prevented the total time being shortened in an attempt to prevent the students being overburdened. Vacations were from 8 to 11 weeks per year. Workers were guaranteed 4 hours per week for homework and 2 weeks a term for examinations. No uniform conditions were laid down for admission to these courses. Workers could apply for entry to any term of the academic year. Examinations and certification for each separate part of the course benefited students who for some reason wished only to study a more limited field.

The record

Between 1949 and 1955 most of the effort went into political education and the eradication of illiteracy. What technical education there was took the form of master-apprentice contracts, mutual study with a master, and special lectures by engineers and specialists. More serious training took place in full-time institutions to which workers were sent for varying periods.

At a National Work Conference on Spare-time Education for Industrial Workers held by the Ministries of Education and Higher Education and the ACFTU in December 1955, Yang Xiu-feng, then Minister of Higher Education, made the following criticisms: the establishment of a complete scheme of spare-time education from primary school through to university level education was too slow; workers were not guaranteed time for study; there were inadequate numbers of qualified teachers; the students' qualifications were low; and there was a lack of funds. The conference criticized the 'rightist conservative thought' of many of the cadres concerned. Local government officials tended to concern themselves only with the regular full-time system, while cadres in industry, including trade union and youth league leaders, concentrated on immediate production tasks (Harper, p. 10).

During the Great Leap Forward of 1958–9 the numbers of students in spare-time education greatly increased. Later, more realistic targets for enrolment and graduation emerged. In February 1963, the Municipal TUC and Education Bureau of Xi'an (Sian) set a target figure of 30 per cent of young workers to be enrolled in local factory classes. In Jinan (Tsinan) enrollees went from over 200,000 in 1958, through 800,000 in mid-1960, 70,000 in 1962, to 130,000 in 1963 (Harper, pp. 14–15).

A number of figures issued during 1959 give some measure of the then state of education of the workers in industry. According to Lu Ding-yi, 20 to 30 per cent were still illiterate, while 50 per cent had reached primary school level, 20 to 30 per cent had reached secondary school level, and 1 to 2 per cent had college or specialized technical education. An NCNA report for the same year gave the figure of illiterates at just over 20 per cent of the total, many of them having reverted to illiteracy through the absence of a literacy course follow-up programme (Harper, p. 22). By November 1959 some 9 million workers had reached secondary school standard and over 400,000 were at college level. P. Harper points out that while this is only a quarter of the total number of workers it represents a significant advance compared with pre-1949 conditions. How much of the credit for this should go to the industrial schools is uncertain. There is some evidence that the better-educated peasants formed a big part of those migrating to the cities, and the pressure of applicants for work in industry enabled the selection of the better educated.

Another measure of the success of the system is the way in which individual enterprises have been able to train their own leading personnel. Peking's No. 1 Lathe and Machinery Plant trained the deputy secretary and the propaganda director of the CCP committee, the chairman of the trade union, a Youth League secretary, 61 per cent of cadres at the section level, and the directors of all five research divisions, all of whom were formerly ordinary workers. The Chang-chun Municipal Gas Company trained half of its engineers and workshop directors. The Xin-xiang Electric Power Plant in Henan trained 18 out of its 26 engineers and technicians, 7 of whom had been illiterates when the programme began in 1951 (Harper, p. 25).

Figures for the number of students taking part in spare-time education are both hard to obtain and to evaluate. What figures do exist suffer from changes in the definition of such key categories as 'workers' or 'workers and employees'. P. Harper gives the following global figures, compiled from a number of Chinese sources.

Number of workers attending spare-time education classes

1949	..	..	..	..	276,432
1950	..	..	..	..	764,199
1951	..	..	..	..	2,026,381
1952	..	..	..	..	2,344,272
1953	..	..	..	..	2,587,967
1954	..	..	..	..	3,050,000
1957	..	..	..	..	10,000,000
1959	..	..	..	..	13,000,000
1960 (February)	..	..	..	19,000,000
1960 (August)	..	..	..	25,000,000

Abe (1961) quotes more detailed figures which show the breakdown between the different types of spare-time education. His totals do not correspond with those given by P. Harper (*see p.* 198).

Some examples of spare-time education

(1) *Factory-organized*

P. Harper describes the education which took place in a widely publicised factory, the Wusan industrial works of north-east China,

Part-time schools and classes

Number of spare-time school students (in thousands)

Year	Higher	Semi-professional	Secondary	Primary	Graduates from literacy classes
1949	0.1	0.1	—	—	657
1950	0.4	0.1	—	—	1,372
1951	1.6	0.3	—	—	1,375
1952	4.1	0.7	249	1,375	656
1953	9.7	1.1	404	1,523	2,954
1954	13.2	186.0	760	2,088	2,637
1955	15.9	185.0	1,167	4,538	3,678
1956	63.8	563.0	2,236	5,195	7,434
1957	75.9	588.0	2,714	6,267	7,208
1958	150.0	—	5,000	26,000	40,000
1960	160.0	—	5,000	8,800	4,600*

* number of students, not graduates.

Figures from 1949 to 1958 from *Great Progress in 10 Years—Statistics Concerning Economic and Cultural Construction in the People's Republic of China*, Peking: State Statistical Bureau, 1959, p. 176, *quoted* M. Abe, 1961. Figures for 1960 from the report of the Minister of Education to the National People's Congress in April 1960, quoted ibid, p. 157.

during the early fifties. The trade union organized a weekly programme consisting of one hour of inspection and discussion of the work of the trade union production teams, three hours of political education (current affairs), two hours of political theory, and one and a half hours on each of four nights devoted to cultural education. The party, trade union and administrative cadres had a separate programme of study each evening after the workers had finished. Technical education was limited to master-apprentice contracts and occasional lectures and campaigns to promote advanced techniques (Harper, p. 4).

The mining industry was one of the earliest to organize a comprehensive system of education. The NCNA reported that by November 1955 every mining centre had at least one spare-time school. In all the industry operated a total of 349 schools, with an attendance of 140,000 miners and other workers. The majority of classes were still literacy classes at that time, but numerous short technical courses, especially to introduce modern Soviet techniques, were also held (Harper, p. 10).

Some idea of the difficulties of organizing spare-time education can be seen from the experience of the Harbin United Meat Processing Plant. This plant began spare-time education in 1948, and by 1959 had a complete range of courses from literacy classes to university level. In 1958 the management and workers took part in a lengthy discussion of aims and ways to achieve them, and a ten-year plan for education was adopted. An immediate target of training 45 veterinary surgeons, 110 refrigeration and processing technicians and 28 administrative cadres was set. There was also talk of all workers being 'trained to be university graduates' (Harper, p. 13). A more realistic aim of a minimum educational level of junior high school standard was put forward in 1961.

The plant had a total of 5 full-time and 127 part-time teachers, but of these only 9 were qualified to teach to university standard, and only another 16 could teach senior high school or technical course materials.

In October 1959 98 per cent of the young workers were enrolled in classes, and during the year 1958-9 they maintained a 95 per cent attendance record. The target set for graduation from classes in 1960 was 90 per cent, but only 80 per cent actually did. Following discussion of the reasons for this the classes were reorganized into three grades, each moving at a different speed. Workers were able to choose which to attend on the basis of their aptitude and the amount of spare time which they had.

In 1961 the plant began to have difficulties owing to the irregular supply of carcases following the bad harvest. This led to transfer of workers from shop to shop and shift work was introduced. Many workers were sent to work in the rural areas. Education was completely disrupted, largely because it was organized on the basis of the workshop and production team. After discussion classes were reorganized so that teaching shifts corresponded to production shifts, so that workers who changed their jobs also changed their teacher and study course, and during the summer months teachers were sent to the rural areas. In this way it was possible to provide 5 hours of education per week for 40 weeks during 1961. Seventy per cent of young workers enrolled and they maintained a 68 per cent attendance record. While this was a big drop compared with 1959 it was, in the circumstances, a solid achievement.

An example of joint enterprise was the technical college set up by the Peking Electric Tube Factory, the North China Radio Factory and the Peking Telephone Factory in 1960. Seven hundred students were enrolled, more than half of whom were reported to be workers or peasants. The remainder were technicians who had graduated from secondary technical schools, or other cadres. Classes were to be held for 4 hours per day on 3 days a week for 5 years. Specialized courses were provided in telegraphy, manufacturing of radios and their parts, manufacturing of electrical apparatus, machine production, and semi-conductor production. The 40 teachers were drawn from different factories and given special training at Qinghua University, Peking University and the Peking Technical College. Lecturers from Qinghua University also gave refresher courses from time to time in the technical college (Abe, p. 159).

Qinghua was also involved in the establishment of an Evening University in 1957. It provided five-year courses in six different specialities. In 1960 it had 700 students, 16 per cent of whom were reported to be Peking workers, while the rest were government technicians and cadres.

China Reconstructs for July 1962 reported on the spare-time college set up by the Wuhan Heavy Machinery Plant. Students attended for 9 to 14 hours a week on Monday, Wednesday and Friday evenings and Sunday mornings. Workers got half a day off a week with pay to study, and one to two days to revise before examinations. Tuition was free, but workers had to pay for books and mimeographed texts.

The first spare-time sports school started in Shanghai in 1956, and by 1962 a total of 200 had been established in different parts of the country (*China Reconstructs*, April, 1962).

(2) Correspondence Courses

Education by correspondence was not unknown in pre-1949 China. The Commercial Press in Shanghai had run the first courses in 1914, in Chinese language, English, mathematics and various commercial subjects. Later other courses were started, nearly all in the coastal cities. But it was only after 1949 that the necessary official support was forthcoming, and correspondence courses developed into a serious alternative way of getting qualified.

Late in 1952 the first signs of the new growth emerged, at the People's University in Peking, and at the Jilin (Kirin) Teachers' Training Institute. By 1956 it was a regular part of many colleges' work, and there were independent correspondence colleges in Peking, Changchun, Shenyang, Wuhan and several other cities.

Many full-time third level institutions set up special departments to run correspondence courses. These departments had a full-time staff whose job it was to enrol students, prepare curricula and teaching materials, and to run an advisory service for students. The last was often provided in special branch offices. The Peking Mining Institute had such offices in every major mining centre in north and north-west China. The Postal and Telecommunications Institute ran 222 local branch offices. Tongji University, Shanghai, together with local government Public Works Departments, had offices in Hangzhou, Jinan (Tsinan), Hefei, Foozhou, Chengdu, Huhehot and other cities.

Until 1963 courses were financed by the sponsoring institution, but then the Ministry of Education began giving special grants for correspondence course work. Students were charged very low fees to offset costs of tuition and books. In many cases courses were provided free, or were paid for by the management of the student's workplace. Fares to and from the local centre might also be paid for by the management or trade union concerned.

Correspondence courses were provided at three levels. The highest level were four- to six-year courses in such subjects as mining, engineering, Chinese literature, or history. The second level were two- to three-year courses in such subjects as mathematics or meteorology. Below this there were a number of limited courses in accounting, the cultivation of special crops, or the study of a particular period of history, which ranged from a few months to a year in length. The courses were graded so that it was possible for a student to graduate from one to another, ending up with one at the highest level.

Some institutions ran a wide spectrum of courses. People's University, Peking, ran courses ranging from a six-month course in logic to a five-year course in factory management. Xiamen (Amoy)

University ran a course for oversea Chinese. Nanchang University, Jiangxi (Kiangsi), ran one in traditional medicine.

Students taking courses were supplied with textbooks, notes and study guides. Where possible lectures and laboratory work was also provided. Lectures were sometimes given over the radio, or on tapes which were lent to the students. One of the more spectacular examples of such additional aid was that provided by the Peking Television College, set up in March 1960 under the city education department, the Peking broadcasting authority, and three local universities. Courses in mathematics, physics and chemistry were supported by T.V. instruction for four hours a week. Teaching staff were drawn from Peking University, the Peking Teachers' Training Institute and the Peking Teachers' Training College. In 1960 there were 6,000 students in over 800 factories, mines, research institutions and schools (Abe, p. 159).

Various tests are given during the courses. There is an entrance examination; terminal tests; and at the highest level students write a thesis or submit design projects which are defended orally. Those failing at any stage must repeat that stage.

In 1963 *Peking Review* (17 May) reported that People's University and Jilin (Kirin) Teachers' Training Institute alone had graduated 10,000 students in economics, finance, political science and factory management, and more than 3,000 secondary school teachers since their courses began.

Literacy campaigns

Mass illiteracy was one of the main problems facing the new government in 1949. It was the main obstacle to technical progress, both in industry and in the village. The exact extent of the problem is uncertain. In commerce, especially in the cities, literacy of a level sufficient to do business was common. But the efforts of the National Association of Mass Education, and of the Communists in the liberated areas, had hardly begun to affect the position. Lu Ding-yi, in October 1950, remarked that 'the overwhelming majority of the people today are illiterate', Liu Shi, in the same month, referred to a figure of 85 per cent (Fraser, p. 112), while Ma Xu-lun, in 1952, used a figure of 90 per cent (Fraser, p. 131). Whatever the real figure may have been, there is no doubt of the gravity of the problem.

Tackling the problem

The first directive of the new government to deal with the problem was that of June 1950 on spare-time education for workers. A literacy campaign was to be begun immediately after 'elementary political education has been carried out among the workers and staff members for a certain period'. Political education was thought necessary in order to explain why literacy was so important, and to thus arouse the necessary enthusiasm for the task of learning. Classes were to be voluntary and the aim was to teach all illiterate workers about 1,000 characters within three to five years, to enable them 'to read simple publications', (NPC docs. 2, p. 82).

While some literacy classes were held in the villages during the early years, it was not until 1956 that government attention was seriously turned towards the peasants. In March of that year the CCP and State Council issued a directive setting out the aim of wiping out 'word-blindness' in five to seven years. Within two to three years it was aimed to make all officials and cadres literate, while 95 per cent of the illiterates among the workers were to be made literate within three to five years (*Notes et Etudes Documentaires*, n. 3197, p. 23).

Aims and standards

In the pre-1949 literacy movement, organized by the Chinese National Y.M.C.A., the aim was to teach a basic vocabulary of 1,200 characters. These were supposed to be equally useful to Shanxi peasants or Shanghai textile workers. The aim set by the more recent movement has been about 1,500 characters for peasants, and 2,000 for workers, and in each case these have been chosen according to the requirements of the particular group being taught. Mao Ze-dong, commenting on an article describing the experience of literacy classes in a Shandong village (*Socialist Upsurge*, pp. 425-6), stressed the economic necessity of literacy when peasants begin to form co-operatives, and recommended that local people should compile a basic textbook for use in recording work points and the like. He added: 'Each place should compile its own text; there cannot be one unified text for all.' This is because names of people and places will form a high proportion of the characters. Mao proposed a second textbook, also compiled by local people, but to be approved by the local education authorities, containing a few hundred characters devoted to the activities of the region, with a few devoted to provincial and national matters. Above this standard the provincial or city education authorities should prepare suitable textbooks.

Teaching methods

One *xiang* for which detailed information is available is Yinda in Gansu (Kansu) Province. Mutual-aid and co-operatives were already developing there in 1950, and produced a demand for winter schools. In 1952 these were changed to 'quick-method literacy classes', details of which are not given. In 1954 the May 4th Yongfeng Agricultural Producers' Co-operative was formed with 5 branches and 25 production brigades, involving 242 households out of a total of 318. Estimates were then made of the need for literate workers. A total of 46 were required, including 8 book-keepers, 33 tallymen, 1 radio monitor, and 4 literacy-school teachers. But the whole *xiang* could only find 32 people with four to six years of schooling, and only 21 of these were poor or middle peasants, that is, those organized in mutual-aid and co-operatives requiring education for their work.

In order to meet the need the four winter schools were converted to a single literacy class of 173 students. This met in three groups, located near to members' homes. There were four teachers, one of them the town clerk. The teachers received help once a week from one of the teachers in the *xiang* primary school.

The *xiang* Party branch arranged the study programme. Monday, Tuesday, Thursday and Friday evenings were allocated for language and arithmetic classes. Wednesday was set aside for meetings. Saturday was for political study, and Sunday was for Party and Youth League lectures and meetings.

The literacy classes used the *Peasants' Vocabulary Textbook*. Ninety-two people used Book 1. Thirty-five of them learnt to read 500 characters, while the remaining fifty-seven managed only 300 characters. Forty-three people studied Book 3, and by the winter of 1955 aimed to learn 800 characters. A senior class of seventeen students used *Chinese Reader for Peasants, Book 1*. A three-volume textbook, *General Arithmetic for Workers and Peasants* was used by all classes.

In 1955 some reorganization took place. The secretary of the Y.C.L. branch, the head of the Women's Federation, the chairmen of the various branches of the co-operative and the principal of the primary school were made responsible for planning the studies and for encouraging students to attend regularly. In spite of their heavy work-load, 52 of the 89 cadres took part in studies. A method of learning two characters a day, with a test every three days was tried, and proved very successful (Mao, 1956, pp. 433–8).

Another interesting example is the Red Banner Agricultural Producers' Co-operative in Gaojialiukou Village, Shandong (Shantung). In 1955 this found itself with trouble over book-keeping and turned to the Y.C.L. for help. They tested their members and found seven who could read over 100 characters. But on attempting to record work-points they produced only chaos, as they could neither record names, nor the various agricultural operations clearly. So the Y.C.L. turned to and organized a literacy class. At first doubts were expressed. 'I've been attending literacy classes for I don't know how many years,' complained a committee-member. 'Now I'm a father of three children and I still can't read more than a dozen characters. Just imagine how long it would take to train a book-keeper.'

However, in spite of doubts, 26 members were assembled, and 4 teachers were found who had graduated from primary school. They began by preparing a vocabulary. In order to write down the 59 names of the co-operative members 68 characters were needed. To locate the 39 fields in which they worked a further 52 characters were added. The various farming operations required 54 more. The names of various tools, animals, and the numerals brought the total up to 243 characters. After two and a half months' study the class memorized all these and left the class to become book-keepers.

The initial success of this class inspired others in the co-operative. A number of people began to 'learn-from-work', memorizing the characters for the different operations as they performed them in the fields: *gengdi* when they ploughed; *song fen* when they carted manure; or *hong zhi zhu* (red spiders) when they were catching these pests. Each production brigade appointed an assistant to help members revise during rest periods in the fields. In the evenings members went to classes to consolidate. Of the 115 members who attended classes for two and a half months, 19 qualified as book-keepers and 92 were able to record work points.

By the end of 1955 the chaos in recording work-points had been straightened out and the peasants began to see the value of learning to read and write. Parents encouraged their children to join classes, and the co-operative management allowed its office to be used as a classroom, even providing the paraffin required for the lamps (Mao, 1956, pp. 427–32).

The textbook which the Gaojialiukou Y.C.L. teachers produced was so successful that it was adopted by the local Bureau of Culture and Education, who had it printed. After 1956 a group of local teachers produced another textbook, using 1,300 characters. Lessons were in the form of folk and work songs. Lessons using the textbooks were reinforced by creating a 'literacy environment'. The method of 'learn-from-work' was extended and objects all over the villages were carefully labelled: 'table'; 'chair'; 'tree'. Boards were placed in the fields with the place and type of work written on them, for use during breaks. It was claimed that in one year these methods enabled 240 people to 'doff their illiteracy caps'. In 1958 the village, now a production brigade of the Wentuan People's Commune, set up a primary school, and four spare-time education classes, three of primary grade, and one junior high school standard. An improved textbook was produced with 1,500 characters. 'Literacy checkpoints' were set up in the market and village streets, where passers-by were stopped and given a reading test. By 1960 it was estimated that two-thirds of the young and middle-aged villagers were literate (*China Reconstructs*, March 1964).

In other parts of the country similar methods were being used. Photographs in Chinese magazines show peasants with placards on their backs with characters and the new *hanyu pinyin* transcription, introduced into the literacy campaign in 1958. In Shanxi and Jilin Wayfarers' Schools were organized to help carters study during their work. Inn-keepers turned teacher. They tested the carters during their evening stop, taught them a few more characters and set them a dozen or so to memorize as they plodded on over the hills to the next stop the following day. During the building of the Miyun Reservoir, north of Peking, one to two hours a day were used during the nearly two years of construction to bring all 3,500 former peasants up to literacy standards. Previously some 80 per cent of them had been illiterate.

The radio, lantern-lectures, exhibitions, films and plays were all used to encourage people to study. In the Cultural Revolution of 1966 the 'literacy environment' was almost overwhelming, with every available space plastered with wall-posters (*dazibao*). The streets of towns, and even country roads were lined with boards carrying quotations from the works of Mao Ze-dong. Mass distribution of the *Quotations* and their regular recitation must have rubbed home previously unfamiliar characters, especially amongst the younger members of the community, thus assisting them to understand the newspapers, which were writing about similar subjects.

The use of *hanyu pinyin*, it is claimed, greatly increased the rate of learning. Using the old look-and-say methods, self-study was almost impossible. But after some 20 hours' coaching a peasant could learn *pinyin*, and then continue studying in his free time, using books in which the pronunciation of the characters was given underneath in *pinyin*. Hu Yu-zhi estimates that using old methods it took between 40 and 90 hours to learn the 1,500 to 2,000 characters required for literacy, but that using *pinyin* the time could be cut down to some 12 to 20 hours.

Books for peasants

Unfortunately none of the basic literacy campaign materials have been available to the writer, but some idea of the aids available to literacy class teachers and students who have already made some progress towards literacy can be gained from other more advanced material which was on sale in bookshops in China during 1965–7.

Nongcun Shiyong Shouce: (*Village Practical Handbook*), published by the Shanghai Cultural Publishing House, in 1964 and twice in 1966, in a total edition of 660,000 copies. This devotes 84 of its 504 pages to 'cultural knowledge'. The section begins with 4 pages on the art of writing: how to sit, place the paper, hold the pen, and detailed hints on how to write the characters correctly. Then follow 36 pages of 'practical writing': detailed instructions on writing letters, making out receipts, writing notices and circulars, recommendations and certificates, agreements and contracts, and other documents connected with village life. Specimens are included, neatly laid out, and there are tables to show how to begin and end letters according to the relative position of writer and recipient. Two pages are devoted to diary-writing, with an extract from Lei Feng's famous diary as an example. Three pages explain how to take notes from books, and four pages are devoted to setting down plans. Ten pages are devoted to *chunlian*, the red strips of paper with wise sayings which from ancient times have been used for decorations at Chinese New Year. Now, of course, the sayings are political, classified here according to the number of characters used. A page on punctuation and other marks is followed by the *pinyin* alphabet with the sounds shown by a common character.

After that comes an 18-page illustrated dictionary of common objects and actions: plants and insects; baskets and hoes; ploughing and cooking. Each character is followed by a better-known character of the same sound, together with the *pinyin* transcription. They are classified by subject and radical.

After the dictionary comes a list of the simplified characters, arranged according to the number of strokes in the old forms, ranging from 7 to 32. The section ends with 30 pages on calculations: use of the abacus, including multiplication and division; and mensuration.

Zenyang Xie Xin? (*How to Write Letters?*). This is one of the Worker and Peasant Popular Library, published by the Shanghai Education Press. Published in 1964, it only numbered 25,000 copies. Its 33 small pages are devoted to proving that letter-writing is as easy as talking. A specimen layout shows the five essential parts of any letter, which are then described in detail with tables showing the forms of address and ways to begin and end letters, depending on relationships between writer and recipient. Seventeen specimen letters are included.

Gongnong Shuxin Bidu: (*Worker and Peasant Correspondence Manual*). This is a larger variant of the last booklet, published by the Hunan People's Press. The two editions of 1965 and 1966 total 40,000 copies. It begins by explaining that writing letters is not difficult, and has the usual specimen layout with its five divisions which it goes on to explain in detail. It includes examples of 'ordinary letters' and 'special documents', devoting 20 and 14 pages of its total of 49 pages respectively to each.

Part-time schools and classes

Rongyi Yong Cuode Ci: (Words Easily Used Wrongly) is another of the Shanghai Education Press's 'Worker and Peasant Popular Library'. Two editions, in 1963 and 1964, totalled 395,000 copies. The dictionary uses *hanyu pinyin*, and arranges the words in alphabetical order. There are 99 pairs, or trios, of homophones or near homophones, usually differing in one of the tones, e.g. *jingzhi*, two identical sounds; *jùjī* versus *jùjí*; or *kaizhan* versus *zhankai*.

Rongyi Ren-cuo Xie-cuo De Zi: (Characters Which are Easy to Misread and Miswrite). Another of the 'Worker and Peasant Popular Library', published in 1962 and 1964 in a total edition of 494,000 copies. Again, *hanyu pinyin* is used, but this time the 365-odd characters are grouped into five classes: those with identical sounds and similar forms; those with different sounds and similar forms; those with the same sound and different form; those with almost the same sound and similar form; and those with almost the same sound and different form. Various words using each character are shown, but no explanation of the word is given.

Nongcun Yingyong Wen: (Village Practical Culture). This 96-page booklet was published by the Peking Publishing House in 1963 and 1965 in a total edition of 791,000 copies. In addition to the usual information on writing letters and special documents, it has a long section on note-making, including making notes for speeches, with an example using Mao Ze-dong's article on *Norman Bethune.* Another section deals with taking notes at meetings, with a list of special points to be noted, such as when and where the meeting was held, who took the chair, who spoke for and against the different motions, and who recorded the minutes. Another section deals with field experiment plans and reports. The book ends with 15 examples of decorative couplets.

Nongcun Wenhua: (Village Culture), no. 5 for 1966. This is a monthly, published by the Peking Publishing House in an unspecified edition. It contains 64 pages measuring 7 inches by 5 inches. The gay cover is decorated with photographs on the inside, while the texts are enlivened by line drawings. There are two 'comic-strip'-type features: the first on a model peasant, a story in 19 pictures and texts taken from the *Hebei Pictorial*; and the second, 10 pictures and texts telling how Vietnamese sailors captured some American airmen who had been shot down in the sea. Many of the articles deal with 'applying Mao Ze-dong's ideas in a living way', and there are short quotations scattered through the book. Several pages are devoted to 'U.S. Imperialism's days are truly numbered', and the Vietnam war. The People's Militia has its section, with a diagram of a hand-grenade. Three pages are devoted to agricultural techniques. There is a 7-page extract from the novel, *The Song of Ouyang Hai*. In lighter vein, though still, of course, political, there are 2 pages on 'quick talk', a popular form of recitation to the accompaniment of bamboo clappers, and some songs with tonic-solfa rendering.

Evaluation

The exact success of all these efforts to eradicate illiteracy and raise the cultural standards of the people is very difficult to estimate. It was recognized from the beginning that old people would be unlikely to succeed in becoming literate and efforts have been concentrated on the young and middle-aged. Reports from time to time have revealed what one would suspect: that after each campaign was over a number of people who made no use of their literacy skills in their work soon began to relapse into illiteracy. One of the biggest problems must be the shortage of suitable material to read, and the lack of the physical conditions which make reading a habit. In the villages almost all the daylight is used for work. Too few homes can provide sufficient light to read. Visitors to the outskirts of Peking will recall the families sitting out under the street lamps during the summer months, the studious taking advantage of the higher illumination provided.

No official figures have been given in the past few years. In the years 1959 and 1960 a number of speakers recorded figures of 60 or 100 million who had taken part in literacy classes (Fraser, p. 323—Yang Xiu-feng; p. 377—Lin Feng). But all of them echoed the words of Zhou En-lai when he said: 'much has been done' to abolish illiteracy, but 'the work of wiping out illiteracy must be energetically carried out with the participation of the masses' (Fraser, pp. 309 and 311). The problem today (1968) is probably not so much illiteracy, as an inadequate standard of literacy and general education for the needs of the country.

Part-work schools

The various types of school which will be described in this section have been developed to meet different needs, and cannot be sharply distinguished from spare-time education on the one side, and those full-time institutions where productive labour plays a big part on the other. But typically the characteristic feature of part-work schools is that the pupils can be regarded as primarily workers of some kind, whose working time is shortened to allow them to study. For this reason they are often referred to in Chinese sources as part-work, part-study schools (*ban-gong ban-du xuexiao*), or in rural areas, cultivate-study primary schools (*geng-du xiaoxue*).

Definitions and aims

The relationship between studies and work depends on the level of the school. The first part-work schools to be set up were agricultural high schools (*nongye zhongxue*), intended to provide peasant children with a form of secondary education which would be economically viable and directly related to the needs of the local community (Barendsen, 1964). These began in 1958, at the time of the Great Leap Forward. More recently, in 1963–4, the emphasis has turned to the problem of making primary education universal, and many schools and classes have been started where there is little or no relation between what the child does at work and what he studies during school hours. In the third level, non-university institutions which have been set up there is a direct relationship between the productive work done, and the schooling provided. These colleges are intended to provide technical-vocational training.

Writing in 1958, Lu Ding-yi pointed out that part-work schools were one facet of the CCP policy of combining education with productive work with the aim of ultimately eliminating class differences. Workers and peasants were to acquire culture, and the intellectuals to 'eliminate [their] bourgeois thinking' (Lu, p. 21). Already at that time it was foreseen that as society got richer the distinctions between different forms of schooling would break down. 'As production grows further and working hours can be shortened, the present spare-time schools will be similar to part-work part-study schools' wrote Lu (ibid, p. 25).

The 1958 education conference, on the basis of which Lu Ding-yi wrote his pamphlet, advocated the setting up of schools by all kinds of local bodies. Lu criticized the 'bourgeois pedagogues' for maintaining that running schools is the job of experts (ibid, pp. 17–18). But he admitted that traditional ideas about the superiority of mental work were strongly held and could only be broken down by a 'protracted' struggle (ibid, pp. 26–7).

The aim of reducing the gulf between worker and peasant, and between mental and manual work was emphasized again and again during the following years. Another aspect of this was expressed in a headline which appeared in the *People's Daily* on 24 August 1965. It read: 'Try to conduct "from the commune and back to the commune" agricultural education properly' (SCMP 3538, 1965). Part-work schools were seen as the best way of encouraging young people to see work in the rural areas as a worthwhile career. The same point was brought out in a forum on education organized in Guangdong in February, 1965. Graduates from part-work secondary schools were praised for their industry, practice of economy, for obeying the Party's orders, for being able both to write and to labour, and for 'working in the countryside with a composed mind' (SCMP 3419, 1965).

The Guangdong (Kwangtung) Provincial Party Secretary, Ou Meng-jue, made an important point when he spoke about the experience gained in his province in the running of part-work schools. He pointed to the danger that if the poor and lower middle peasants remained without education they would also have no political power. Part-work schools were the only way to remedy this situation (SCMP 3333, 1964).

Many of the articles on part-work schools emphasize that they are cheap to run, and therefore often the only way in which the children of poor and lower middle peasant families can obtain an education. Ou Meng-jue gave some comparative figures to support this argument. Xinhui *xian*: cost of keeping one student at

a full-time junior high school	76 yuan/year
a state-subsidized agricultural high school	6 yuan/year
a full-time agricultural technical high school	350 yuan/year
a part-time agricultural technical high school	140 yuan/year

Gujing Commune: cost of keeping one student at:

a full-time junior high school	130 yuan/year
a part-time junior high school	14 yuan/year

(SCMP 3333, 1964).

First-level schools

Details of the development of part-work primary schools began to appear after the National Conference on Rural Part-work Schools, held in March–April 1965 (SCMP 3481, 1965). The conference decided that the part-work principle was to be 'the future mainstay of the educational system for secondary and higher education', and should also be extended in the primary field. The conference, whose delegates were received by Liu Shao-qi and addressed by Lu Ding-yi, talked a lot about popularizing primary education. On 18 May the *People's Daily* carried an article entitled 'Universalize education with greater, faster, better and more economical results', which stated that there were some 30 million children of school-age 'who have yet to enter school', (SCMP 3475, 1965). That works out at an overall figure of about one in every six children. But of course the distribution was very uneven. In the cities attendance was probably in the order of 98 per cent, but in many rural areas it was probably below 70 per cent (cf. *Geng-du Xiaoxue* . . . p. 64). Many villages were reported to be without schools (ibid, pp. 19 and 64). In isolated villages with only a few children, or among such groups as the boat people attendance might have been almost zero. Poor families rely on their children's help in such work as gathering fuel or fodder, and watching grazing animals (buffaloes). Full-time primary schools were often located too far for the children to walk. And many parents remained unconvinced that the schooling provided would be of value to children whose future was to be in the village.

In 1965 the *People's Daily* published some figures for Yangxin *xian* in Hubei Province which showed how important the part-work schools were in raising school attendance figures (SCMP 3475, 1965).

Percentage of children in school

	1956	1958	1963	1964
Publicly run full-time schools	34.3	43.2	31.3	41.6
Privately run full-time schools	3.1	10.7	11.4	17.2
Farm-study schools	—	—	—	20.8
Totals:	37.4	53.9	42.7	79.6

Here 'privately-run' refers to schools run by factories, co-operatives and communes with little if any state aid. The fall in the number of schoolchildren between 1958 and 1963 is probably accounted for by the economic effect of the bad years 1959–61, combined with the continued population increase.

Part-work primary schools are of different kinds, depending on the local need. Sometimes the school runs full-time during the slack season and then on a part-time basis, or closes altogether during the busy season. Part-time classes may be held in the building of the full-time school, or they may operate in offices or even the children's homes. The last may be the case in small villages with few children, where the teacher travels round from village to village, teaching a day here and a day there. In the smaller Mongol nomadic villages some of the children learn from an elder brother or sister who attends school, or from a local cadre or head of the family, and instruction can be little more than simple literacy (*Geng-du Xiaoxue* ... p. 148).

In one example of a part-work primary school the emphasis was placed on language work and arithmetic, but 'simplified and essential' courses were given in history, geography, nature study, physical education and map/plan drawing. It was specifically noted that the third year evening class studied only the use of the abacus, and not arithmetic in general (ibid, p. 133).

Part-work primary schools have been cited in some areas for their use in raising the attendance figures for girls. In Maji Commune, Yizheng *xian*, where the girls had previously been unable to attend school because they were needed at home to make pig food and look after the younger children, the organization of half-day schools brought the proportion of girls up to 100 out of 150 pupils in nine schools. Others who still could not get to school were visited by the teacher and taught in their homes (SCMP 3463, 1965). During 1964 and 1965 figures for a few areas were published. In Guangdong (Kwangtung) 36,000 part-work primary schools were reported to have raised school attendance in the province from 69 per cent in 1964 to over 80 per cent in 1965 (SCMP 3572, 1965). In Qinghai (Chinghai) Province, 300 schools in six *xian* surrounding the provincial capital, Xi'ning (Sining), had 10,000 students in 1964. Part-work schools in the province enabled 8 per cent of the age-group to attend school, including some 90 per cent of those children from poor and lower middle peasant families (SCMP 3350, 1964). Qinghai (Chinghai) also reported 100 'tent-schools', moving with the herdsmen over the grazing grounds. Children attended school in the early morning and in the evenings, and worked with the herds in the afternoons. In the Ningxia Hui Autonomous Region 1,500 out of 3,800 primary schools worked a part-work system in 1965, and enrolled 66,000 out of a total of 270,000 pupils (SCMP 3385, 1965). The NCNA also reported that there were 1,000 part-work primary schools in the villages surrounding Peking (ibid).

Second-level schools

The pioneers of the part-work principle were the agricultural high schools set up in Jiangsu (Kiangsu) and other areas during 1958, 1959 and 1960. In those years large numbers of schools were started with enthusiasm but inadequate preparation, and many of them were closed down again in the early sixties. But by 1964–5 reports from different parts of China showed that a steady expansion had been going on, not only in the rural areas, but also in the cities.

The schools have largely been set up and maintained by the local communities. In Liaoning and some other areas it was reported that special offices had been set up by the CCP and local government to supervise them (SCMP 3345, 1964). In the cities schools are mostly run by factories and mines (SCMP 3549, 1965). In some cases the schools are financed by the local communities, while in other cases there is a big state subsidy. Teachers may be paid by the state, as in the forestry school on the Khorcin grasslands in Inner Mongolia (SCMP 3360, 1964).

Part-time schools and classes

At the second level productive labour really fulfils an educational role in a high proportion of schools. How much it also contributes to paying the expenses of running the schools is uncertain, though this was certainly one of the aims of the system. In 1960 the Jiangsu delegate to the National People's Congress claimed that 19 per cent of the agricultural high schools in his province were 'wholly self-supporting', 18.6 per cent were 'to a large extent self-supporting', and 31.8 per cent were 'partly-self-supporting' (Barendsen, pp. 16–17). In some cases the money is earned from the product of land or workshops worked by the schools, but in other cases it would appear that students work as part of the normal commune teams and contribute money in fees.

The type of work performed and the time allocation depend on the type of school. At first most of the rural schools were half-day, but this was later changed to full-day school during the slack season, and full-day work in the fields at busy times. This change must have weakened the link between theory and practice, though this may have been balanced by an increase in concentration. No discussion of this important question has so far become available. At the 1965 National Conference on Part-Work Schools in Cities it was stressed that labour should be directly related to specialization where possible, but that in other cases labour should be performed in order to temper the students' labour viewpoint. A four-hour work, four-hour study day was recommended on the grounds that it was best suited to the 'physical conditions of man' (SCMP 3598, 1965).

By the early sixties a number of different kinds of second level part-work schools existed. Reporting on 'current problems of the character of the agricultural high schools' in 1965 the *People's Daily* described three different types of school. The first was a technical school, specializing in training people for agriculture and technical jobs. The second was a general agricultural school, equivalent in standard to, and often taking pupils from the full-time high schools. The third, and most numerous type, was a school teaching elementary courses in only four subjects: politics, language, arithmetic and principles of agriculture. According to the same article, in schools in Jiangsu (Kiangsu) and Shandong (Shantung) 10 per cent of time was spent on politics, 30 per cent on 'production knowledge', and 60 per cent on 'cultural subjects' (SCMP 3585, 1965).

Part-time schools and classes

An NCNA report from Xi'an, describing the Hongzi Agricultural High School which began part-work in 1960, described how at first the curriculum followed that used in the full-time high schools. Lack of success was followed by discussions between parents, teachers and former students, and as a result the course was pruned to politics, language, arithmetic, agriculture and some physics and chemistry in the second and third year. The article also described what it called the 'four-combination teaching method'. This was a combination of book knowledge with production practice; general teaching with specific points; classroom teaching with on-the-spot teaching; and productive labour with scientific experiment (SCMP 3341, 1964). Students at Hongqi worked an average of 50 man days a year on the land, and up to 100 man days a year in the case of the older age-groups.

All reports on the graduates from the part-work high schools stress that the majority remain at work on the farms. Many take over key jobs as accountants, cashiers, sideline managers, or other administrative posts (SCMP 3538, 1965). Others take on more technical work, becoming tractor drivers, electrical engineers, horticulture and forestry experts, veterinary surgeons or even medical workers.

A small number of second level schools are highly specialized. In 1965 the *Guangming Ribao* reported the setting up of a medical class in Xiangyin *xian*. In the area concerned there was only a clinic for Chinese medicine and many of the local peasants could not afford to go to town to see a Western-style doctor. Therefore, under the leadership of a medical team from the Chinese Academy of Medicine, a farming-study medical class was set up in April 1965. The course was to last for two years, six months in each year being devoted to study and six months to work in the fields. During the first two months a crash course, concentrating on common summer diseases, was given so that students could begin to put their knowledge into practice as quickly as possible. Thirty students, mostly graduates from junior high school, were enrolled (SCMP 3471, 1965).

Third-level institutions

A number of institutions have been set up at the third level standard of education. In Chinese the majority of them are either called *daxue*

217

or *xueyuan*, misleadingly translated as university and academy respectively. It would probably be better to refer to all these institutions as colleges, as will be done here. Their standards vary widely from second level, second cycle, to third level non-university vocational training (UNESCO, 4).

The first such institution to be described was the Communist Labour College (*Gongchanzhuyi Laodong Daxue*) set up at Nanchang, Jiangxi (Kiangsi) Province, in mid-1958. It was intended to take in students with little previous formal education from worker and peasant families, and to train them for two to four years, either in a central college, or at one of a number of branch colleges scattered around the province. Total enrolment for 1959 was about 55,000 (Barendsen). In February 1960, a second such institution was set up, the Industrial Labour College (*Gongye Laodong Daxue*), also in Jiangxi (Kiangsi). While the former college specialised in agriculture and forestry, the new college was to train specialists for industry and communications. By April 1960 it was already in operation with some 30,000 students spread among 35 branches throughout the province.

A number of part-work teacher training colleges have been reported, using the part-work principle to train teachers for part-work schools. In 1965 Shanghai reported a school with 139 students taking a five-year course in mathematics, physics, and radio and mechanical engineering. The course included some 131 weeks of study, including examinations, and 104 weeks of productive labour. Twenty-five weeks were to be vacations. The students began by helping to build their own workshops (SCMP 3332, 1964). Also in 1965, the Zhejiang (Chekiang) Teachers' Training College announced that it was moving to Jinhua *xian*, in the country, and changing over to a part-work system. Plans for the change-over were still being worked out, but the intention was to become more flexible, and to learn to teach less, but essential material (SCMP 3560, 1965).

In 1965 the NCNA reported the setting up of three 'institutions of higher learning' in Guiyang, Guizhou (Kweichow) Province. The first, the part-work Industrial Teachers' Training College, offered specialist courses in mathematics and physics; mechanics; and chemical engineering. The Farming Teachers' Training College offered courses in politics and language; agronomy; and mathematics and physics. The Guiyang College of Chinese Traditional Medicine offered a four-year or a two-year course, and had a 160-bed hospital attached to the college. It also ran an intermediate technical school class which trained students in the planting and gathering of medicinal herbs (SCMP 3560, 1965).

The Agricultural Labour College set up in Xuntian *xian*, Yun'nan Province in 1965 had courses in agronomy, animal husbandry, veterinary science and forestry. Special courses included teacher training, an intermediate technical course, and a junior high school course. One thousand, four hundred students were enrolled, a majority from local minority peoples: Hui, Pai, Tai, Yi, Naxi, Hanyi, Miao, Zhuang and Wa. Some were graduates of senior high schools; others came from agricultural high schools. Some students came from the urban areas, while a few came from overseas. They began work by constructing the campus and 3,500 sq.m. of buildings (SCMP 3560, 1965).

A similar college was established in Yongning *xian*, Guangxi (Kwangsi) Province in 1965. It had a staff of 60, and 500 students, many drawn from the minority peoples, the Zhuang, Miao, Yao and Tong. There were departments of agriculture and horticulture; animal husbandry; and veterinary science. These ran four-year courses. There was also a one-and-a-half-year course in political science (ibid).

The Labour College, set up in Jiangsu (Kiangsu) Province in May 1965 on the site of a tea farm, drew its teachers from various full-time colleges in Nanjing (Nanking). Its 150 students, 'taking their copies of Chairman Mao's works and their labouring tools with them', were all ex-senior high school. Specialist courses were to be given in agriculture and forestry, teacher training, and rural medicine and public health.

An example of an urban college is that set up in Wuhan. Called the Communist Labour College, it had four departments: agriculture and forestry; agricultural machinery; agronomy; and agricultural economics. Students were enrolled after graduation from either senior or junior high schools, for courses to last four or five years. Those from junior high schools were first to do a two-year preparation course. The 370 students and 20 members of staff began work by building the college (SCMP 3471, 1965).

The future of part-work schools

Dr Tsang C.S., concluding his description of part-work schools, says: 'In spite of the publicity and propaganda surrounding the rise of these schools, it seems that they are only a transient phase of education in China and doomed to failure.' (Tsang, p. 187). To the present writer it would seem that, taking into account the present situation, and the need which these schools have been established to meet, the majority of them can only be regarded as a success. Without them there would have been no education for the students concerned. It is obvious, of course, that with the passing of time and the growth in wealth of China, many of the present forms of part-work school will disappear. But within the foreseeable future it would seem that the part-work principle is going to be strengthened, and there will be a growing together of the different forms of school, full-time, spare-time and part-work.

6

The teachers

Quantity and quality

Traditionally China has honoured and respected the teacher. The value of learning and the qualities of the ideal teacher have been extolled in the ancient books, and have been chanted (albeit often without understanding) by schoolchildren for more than a thousand years. The classical primer, the *San Zi Jing* (*Three Character Classic*), composed in A.D. 960 and still taught to their sons by a few peasant fathers in the 1950s, though long laid aside as a school textbook, contains the lines: 'The most important thing in education is close co-operation between teacher and pupil . . . If teachers are not strict in their duty, they are idle teachers.'

Those who went on to study the classics proper learnt the following lines of Mencius:

> There are three things in which the Superior Man delights, and to be a sovereign of the empire is not one of them. That his parents are both living and that his brothers are upright, is one delight. That he can look up to heaven with a clear conscience, and look out upon men without shame, is his second delight. That he can obtain the young men of finest talent in the empire and educate them, is his third delight. (*Mencius*, 7.1.20, quoted Galt, p. 98).

Understanding between teacher and pupil is again stressed in the *Xue Ji* of the Li Ji. 'When the Superior Man knows how to approach students who find learning difficult and those who find it easy, and knows those who are going right and those who are going wrong, then he can give comprehensive instruction and is qualified to be a teacher.' The same theme is returned to by Xun Zi: 'In learning there is nothing better than establishing rapport with the teacher . . . Therefore it is said in learning nothing helps progress better than intimacy with one's teacher, and nothing quickens progress more than affection for one's teacher.' (Galt, p. 138).

Galt, commenting on the passage from Mencius above, remarks: 'It would be difficult to find the expression of a higher ideal in all the literature of education . . . such high ideals of life and of education for upward of two thousand years kept before the minds of Chinese students, account in a measure for the stability of Chinese society and for the high standard of Chinese culture and scholarship.' (Galt, p. 98)

Another foreign teacher, long in China, testified for the 1930s. 'China has always reverenced teachers', he wrote. 'They were never insulted by having their learning bought by "wage" or "salary". Instead they received as honorarium "wood and water", or the monetary equivalents of these necessities of life.' And he went on to describe how 'in the midst of chaos there has been steady growth' in education; '. . . devoted teachers have kept to their work, often without salaries for many months together.' (Sewell, 1933, p. 108).

Chinese, writing about teachers during this century have expressed more qualified opinions. Not uncommon in the old classical schools was this experience, described by Wu Yun-duo. 'I soon found it very dull and boring at Master Hu's. I recited the Chinese classics, but didn't understand a word of it. The master never explained anything, and when I asked a question, he simply stared me into silence.' (Wu, 1956, p. 8). Ye Sheng-tao, in the novel *The Schoolmaster, Ni Huan-zhi*, written in 1929, describes teachers good and bad. When the hero is first asked to become a teacher his mother worries 'when she remembered what she had seen of primary schools, with the teacher run off his feet and shouting himself hoarse from morning till night trying to keep the boys in order'. And the first headmaster Mr. Ni works under 'had held the post of headmaster at the Sixth Primary four or five years now—that is to say, for the last four or five years he had been feathering his nest in that capacity.' Finally one should remember that teaching was traditionally done, except in the highest institutions, by those who had failed to pass examinations and gain office, or by office holders who had, perhaps for political reasons, been forced to retire. The old sneer about 'those who can do, and those who can't teach' certainly applied to China of the classical examination period, and this tradition may also have persisted to some extent into more recent periods.

Since 1949 there have been great efforts to raise the status of teachers and make the profession more attractive. Nevertheless old problems remain, and perhaps a new factor has appeared. Fear of being considered politically weak or unreliable adds to the teacher's difficulties and may even be taken advantage of. In *The Thought Revolution* Dong Ji Bing (Tung Chi-Ping) describes such a situation in 1953, when his teacher was scolded and wept over his group's poor examination marks. 'What I learned from this test', he says, 'was that my position as a student was stronger than the girl's position as the teacher.' During the Cultural Revolution some teachers were beaten by their pupils, and all of them indulged in self-criticism to an extent that must have greatly weakened their authority. Against this it would probably be claimed that group self-discipline is the aim, and that the teacher is only the leading member of the group. But the doubt remains, for outside China the power of the pupil, bent on disruption, to influence his fellows is well known. Pupil-teacher relations will certainly be an important question to study in the coming years, as the post-Cultural Revolution pattern takes shape.

Some of the reasons why teaching does not attract more people have been expressed in the press. In 1956 a delegate to the National Conference of the Union of Educational Workers listed three grievances: the political status of teachers was low; their salaries and living conditions were inadequate; and they worked so hard that many of them developed nervous illnesses (Chen, 1960, p. 32). The shortage and inadequacy of teachers' housing was dealt with in an editorial of the *Teachers' Daily* on 20 July 1956, while numerous complaints were published during the '100 Flowers' period.

In 1956 the Ministry of Education announced a 32.8 per cent increase in the salaries of primary school teachers, providing a minimum salary of about 20 yuan per month. But many teachers have continued to receive less. Ten yuan per month has not been unusual, and some have received as little as four yuan, according to Chen. Salaries are dependent on qualifications, as shown in the following table.

Qualification	Minimum	Maximum
	yuan/month	
3 years' junior teachers' training school or equivalent	20	26
2 years' senior teachers' training school, or senior high school	24	31
Graduate of 2-year college course	34	44
Graduate of 4-year college or institute course ..	40	52

Deductions from salaries are made to build up welfare funds. But the extent to which these are adequate is uncertain. Chen T.H. quotes a number of complaints about misuse of funds, or discrimination against teachers on personal or political grounds (Chen, p. 34). Medical attention, at least in the cities, is free, though dependents may have to pay.

In 1951 estimates of needs during the coming five years were given at the first National Conference on Primary and Teacher Education (Chen, p. 26).

Type of school	Need over 5 years
Kindergarten	Tens of thousands
Primary	1,000,000
Spare-time	200,000
Secondary	130,000
Higher education	10,000

Total: over 1,340,000

In 1956 the Ministry of Education estimated a need of over a million new teachers during the coming seven years. Against these figures the total of graduates from the teacher training establishments was pitifully inadequate. An article in *China Reconstructs* for September 1956 noted that in 1955 12,000 new teachers had graduated, but the deficit in the schools was 'at least 5,000'. (*China in Transition*, p. 328). The same journal in 1959 claimed a 300 per cent increase in the number of teachers trained between 1949 and 1959, but at the same time noted that pupil enrolment had increased during the same time by 363 per cent in primary schools, by 570 per cent in secondary schools, and by 440 per cent in higher education establishments. Thus the position would seem to be worse than before. (Chen, p. 27).

Estimates for shortages of teachers in secondary schools have been made on the basis of one teacher for every 28 pupils in the junior grades (13 to 16 years), and one for every 25 in the senior grades (16 to 19 years). (*China in Transition*, p. 328). The basis for the primary school estimates is uncertain.

The difficulty of persuading junior high school graduates to train as teachers was noted by the *Teachers' Daily* (15 June 1956). It pointed out that only 5 per cent of graduates opted for teacher-training, against the 15 per cent planned for by the government. In one *xian* in Hebei (Hopei) only 2 students out of 500 put down teaching as their first choice. Sometimes as many as 90 per cent of teachers' training school students do not want to teach. Also in 1954 the *Xinjiang Ribao* reported that 45 students out of 110 in one teachers' training school announced that they had no intention of becoming teachers. (Chen, p. 43).

The absence of any data for the sixties makes it very difficult to estimate the effect of the considerable efforts which have been made in teacher education, both full- and part-time, during this time.

In addition to the shortage of teachers, their qualifications also lag far behind requirements. In 1955 the Ministry of Education noted that 43 per cent of primary school teachers were below the standard of the junior teachers' training school graduate, and that 80 per cent were below that of a senior teachers' training school graduate (Chen, p. 29). In a December 1955 edition of the *People's Education*, an editorial noted that more than half the secondary school teachers were below the level of the teachers' training college graduate (Chen, p. 30).

Amongst those teachers, often teaching only part-time, in the spare-time and part-work schools, the situation is also far from satisfactory. In the early period one *xian* reported that out of 428 teachers given short-term training, 15 were found to be illiterate, and 239 semi-illiterate, while out of a total of 4,000 teachers given short-term training, only 170 could be considered qualified to teach (Chen, p. 48). While it is probable that these are extreme examples there can be no doubt about the seriousness of the problem. The hope for a solution would seem to be the development of a close relation between schooling and production and the use of skilled, and enthusiastic (?), workers as a source of teachers (see ch. 20). The resulting practical success would then, perhaps, encourage a respect for schooling which poor quality academic teaching so often destroys, and pave the way for a more general and genuine raising of standards.

The Teachers' Union

In 1950, following a conference of education workers from different parts of the country, the All-China Union of Educational Workers was set up. Like other trade unions, this was attached to the All-China Federation of Trade Unions, and following communist principles it has an industrial rather than craft basis. This meant that its members consisted not only of teachers, but also of office workers, caretakers, labourers, school police, and all other people employed by the various educational establishments of the country. By the second National Congress of the Union, in August 1956, the membership was reported to be 1,351,134, which was about 60 per cent of the total number of potential members. Wu Yu-zhang, then Chairman of the Union National Committee, set out its aims at the inauguration conference in 1950. 'The aim of the Union of Educational Workers', he said, 'like other trade unions, is to protect the interests of the working class and to guarantee the fulfilment of the production plans of the state' (Chen, p. 39). Chen notes that:

> 'the constitution provides that the Union must be under the direct supervision of the All-China Federation of Trade Unions and that the organization must follow the principle of democratic centralism, with lower levels subordinate to the higher (provincial and national) levels and the minority pledged to obey the majority. The duties of members are listed as follows: (1) to observe labour discipline; (2) to engage in political, cultural, and professional study in order to raise the level of political consciousness and professional work; (3) to carry out the resolutions of the Union and take an active part in its work and social activities; (4) to unite with and educate non-members, and (5) to pay monthly dues.' (Chen, p. 40).

The union is affiliated to the World Federation of Teachers' Unions and observes 20 November as the 'International Day of the

Teachers' Charter'. The Union has played an active part in the various campaigns of the World Peace Movement and the internal campaigns, such as the Aid-Korea, Resist America campaign. It was resolved at the second Union Congress that one of its most important functions was to be a 'school for Communism' to 'produce loyal and faithful workers to carry out the educational programme of the Party and state' (ibid, p. 41).

Its function may become clearer if the following quotation from the preamble to the Constitution of the All-China Federation of Trade Unions is considered: 'The trade unions should educate the workers and recognize the unity of interests between the state and the individual and, when these two conflict, realize that individual interests should be subordinated to state interests.' (ibid, p. 40).

In 1958 the National Committee of the Union called for a campaign of ideological self-education and in various parts of the country 'thought reform emulation campaigns' were started, to raise the 'level of socialist consciousness'. (ibid, p. 42).

Teacher education

The aims

The aims of teacher education are basically the same as those of all other parts of the educational system: the education of people who are at the same time 'red and expert'. At different times during the past eighteen years the stress has been put on one or other of these concepts. In 1952 the president of the newly-established Tianjin (Tientsin) Teachers' Training College said with reference to his college: 'learning from the advanced experience of the Soviet Union and employing the revolutionary methods of uniting theory with practice, we aim to produce people's teachers for the secondary schools who are armed with Marxism-Leninism, the thought of Mao Ze-dong, advanced scientific knowledge, and familiarity with the techniques of teaching.' (ibid, p. 14). In the following year Premier Zhou En-lai directed higher teachers' colleges to pay special attention to political study amongst teachers, and reforming the intellectuals; to reorganize the teaching materials to bring them into line with 'the standpoint, the viewpoint, and the method of Marxism';

227

and to integrate what they were learning from the Soviet Union with the actual conditions in China. (ibid, p. 15).

The institutions

Linked with the system of full-time schools, there is a system of full-time teacher-training schools and colleges, and parallel with them a system of spare-time institutions. In the following account the American terminology for these institutions is given in parenthesis.

The junior teachers' training school (junior normal school) is the lowest grade, taking graduates from the upper primary schools and training them for 3 to 4 years, before returning them as teachers to the lower primary schools. It also takes some graduates from the junior high schools and trains them for periods ranging from 6 months to 2 years in preparation for work in the lower primary schools. These short courses may also be run in the junior high school itself. Kindergarten teachers are trained in a separate section which may be attached to the training school, or be a separate institution.

The senior teachers' training school (normal school) takes in graduates from the junior high schools and trains them for 3 years. They are then able to teach in all six grades of the primary school. Some senior teachers' training schools also have a kindergarten section. At the third level of education there are three types of institution: the teachers' training institute (higher normal university), the teachers' training college (higher normal colleges), and the teachers' training (junior) college (higher professional normal school). The first two offer four-year courses to graduates of the senior high schools and prepare them for teaching in all six grades of secondary school. The two institutions differ in the number of departments and type of organization, the Institutes being rather broader and more elaborate. The teachers' training (junior) colleges also take graduates from the senior high schools, but only train them for two years before returning them as teachers to the junior high schools.

The curriculum

The curriculum can be divided into academic subjects, moral-political training, productive work, education, and practice teaching.

The academic subjects studied at teachers' training schools are: Chinese language and literature; mathematics; physics; chemistry; biology; a biology course which is mainly human anatomy and physiology in some schools; history; geography; music; and drawing. Students at the college level specialize in a smaller number of related subjects. Colleges are divided into departments. Peking Teachers' Training Institute has 12. The South China Teachers' Training College has 10 in its four-year course, 8 in the two-year course, and 6 in the one-year course (Chen, p. 17). Most colleges provide courses in Chinese, foreign languages, history, geography, mathematics, physics, chemistry and biology.

The education course provided in the teachers' training schools includes special lectures in education, psychology, and subject method lectures in language and literature, arithmetic, and sometimes in other subjects.

Teaching practice in the teachers' training schools is provided for in a special primary school attached for this purpose. According to T. H. Chen (p. 16) after 1958 students helped to establish schools (presumably part-work schools) in communes and factories, thus gaining experience which made 'the "practice teaching" part of the teacher training curriculum . . . unnecessary'. But accounts of such schools reported in the press after 1960 do not bear this out.

The extent to which teachers' training schools and colleges make the recommended contact with the ordinary schools is uncertain. The *Guangming Ribao* reported in 1958 (18 April) that Zhejiang (Chekiang) Teachers' Training College teachers must spend at least a sixth of their time teaching in secondary schools, while the young inexperienced teachers must spend one or two years out of every five teaching in secondary schools. (Chen, p. 16). College students are expected to observe and practise teaching in secondary schools. But the tone of a report in the *People's Daily* of 21 March 1962 about the Huazhong Teachers' Training College making contact with ten local secondary schools suggest that for them at least this was a new venture.

The importance attached to moral-political training will be clear from the discussion of aims above. In the teachers' training schools courses may include such subjects as 'Character Formation for Youth', or 'Common Knowledge of Politics'. In the colleges the courses are more theoretical.

Training outside the training school system

Short courses

A large number of short courses are run by different institutions to raise the academic level of the teachers. Some are run by the teachers' training schools and colleges; others by the secondary schools and higher institutions. The duration of the courses varies from a few weeks to one or two years. At the lowest level one finds the young part-work school teacher visiting the local junior high

Timetable for senior teachers' training schools, 1957–8

Subjects	Weekly hours by year and term					
	1		2		3	
	1	2	1	2	1	2
Language and literature						
Chinese language	2	2	2	2	2	2
Literature	4	4	4	4	5	5
Teaching methods	—	—	—	—	2	2
Mathematics						
Arithmetic	—	—	2	2	—	—
Algebra	3	3	—	—	—	—
Geometry	2	2	2	2	2	—
Teaching methods—arithmetic	—	—	—	—	2	3
Physics	2	2	3	3	2	—
Chemistry	3	3	—	—	—	—
Human anatomy and physiology	2	2	—	—	—	—
Geography						
Physical geography	2	—	—	—	—	—
Chinese geography..	—	2	2	—	—	—
Foreign geography..	—	—	—	2	—	—
History						
Modern world history	2	2	—	—	—	—
Chinese history	—	—	3	3	3	3
Politics..	2	2	—	—	—	—
Psychology	—	—	2	1	—	—
Education	—	—	2	2	3	3
Physical activities	2	2	2	2	2	2
Music	2	2	1	2	1	2

Drawing	..	..	..	..	2	2	2	1	1	2
Practice teaching	..	..	..	..	—	—	1	1	3	4
TOTAL ..	..	..	..	..	30	30	28	27	28	28
Weeks per term	..	..	..	..	18	17	18	17	18	13

From: Chen T.H. p. 18, based on timetables published in the *Jiaoshi Bao* (*Teacher's Newspaper*) 23 and 26 July 1957

Timetable for kindergarten teachers' training school, 1957–8

Subjects	Weekly hours by year and term					
	1		2		3	
	1	2	1	2	1	2
Language and literature						
Chinese language	2	2	2	2	2	2
Literature	4	4	4	4	5	5
Mathematics						
Algebra	3	2	—	—	—	—
Plane geometry	2	2	—	—	—	—
Physics	—	—	2	—	2	—
Chemistry	2	2	—	—	—	—
Human anatomy and physiology ..	2	2	—	—	—	—
Chinese geography	2	2	2	—	—	—
Chinese history	3	3	3	3	3	3
Politics..	2	2	2	2	2	2
Psychology of small children ..	—	—	2	2	—	—
Education of small children	—	2	2	2	2	3
Hygiene for small children	—	—	—	—	1	1
Methods of teaching						
Language	—	—	—	2	2	—
Nature study	—	—	—	2	1	2
Games and physical activities ..	2	2	2	2	2	3
Music	3	2	2	2	2	3
Drawing and handiwork	2	2	2	2	2	2
Practice teaching	—	—	2	2	4	4
TOTAL	29	29	27	27	30	30
Weeks per term	18	17	18	17	18	13

From Chen, T.H. p. 19, (ibid).

school to learn what is little more than the rudiments of reading, simple arithmetic, and perhaps some science to pass on to his village pupils. At the other extreme, the North-Western University, Xi'an, trained teachers from fraternal colleges. Between 1959 and 1962 it trained 300 teachers from colleges in Xinjiang (Sinkiang), Inner Mongolia, Heilungjiang (Heilungkiang), Guangxi (Kwangsi), Hebei (Hopei) and other provinces (SCMP 2696, 1962). In 1960 the Ministry of Education ordered a number of universities to provide short-courses to training teachers (*People's Daily*, 5 February 1960).

Spare-time courses

In 1952 the Ministry of Education called for a 'regular and orderly system of spare-time study to raise the quality of teachers' (Chen, p. 28). A *People's Education* editorial commented that spare-time study must be considered a 'fundamental method of raising the quality of teachers'. In 1955 further instructions were issued by the Ministry of Education, urging the development of spare-time teacher education along three lines: schools; correspondence courses; and study groups.

Schools

These are really only feasible in the towns and cities. Courses provided at the junior level require the teachers to attend for 6 hours per week, and a continuous period of 10 to 20 days during the winter and summer vacations, when in addition to intensive study, examinations are held. Ministry regulations, issued in 1957, require a course of 3 to 4 years. At the senior level attendance requirements are the same, but the course lasts 4 to 5 years. The content is similar to that in the full-time teacher training schools, but more attention is paid to language and mathematics.

Spare-time higher education is to raise the academic standard of secondary school teachers to that of a teachers' training school graduate, according to a Ministry of Education directive in 1955 (Chen, p. 30). A three-year course of 10 to 12 hours per week was recommended, consisting of political studies, academic studies and education courses. Earlier, more specialized courses had been run. Wuhan Spare-time Senior Teachers' Training School had held a two-year course, 4 hours per week, enabling secondary teachers to study two subjects at a time. Tianjin Senior Teachers' Training School had run a special spare-time department to train selected primary school teachers for work in junior high schools, and junior high school teachers to work in senior high schools. Teachers had attended for 6 hours per week for a period of 5 years. (Chen, p. 29).

With the formation of the communes and the Great Leap Forward an attempt was made to rapidly increase the number of teachers. A number of provinces reported the setting up of spare-time training schools by communes, but standards were probably very limited and many of them were probably of short duration. Jiangsu reported that 21 communes had set up 25 higher schools, 132 schools and 21 kindergarten teachers' training schools. Some were on a part-work basis. Henan reported setting up more than 10 teachers' training colleges to train secondary teachers. (Chen, p. 30).

In the middle sixties the increasing emphasis on the part-work principle had its effect on teacher training. A number of new, part-work training establishments were set up, some of which were described in the previous chapter (ch. 5 p. 218).

Correspondence courses

Special correspondence courses to train teachers have been set up at approximately junior teachers' training school and senior teachers' training school standard. They are run by both the senior teachers' training schools, and by separate institutions. Regulations were published in 1957. Students are expected to study for 6 to 8 hours a week for 4 to 5 years (i.e. 1 to 2 years longer than the full-time course), and to attend an all-day session at a 'guidance station' once or twice a month. A large number of these stations was reported for Henan in 1959 (Chen, p. 31) and in Sichuan in 1962 (SCMP 2694, 1962). Sichuan (Szechwan) reported a growth in the number of students from 1,000 high school teachers in 1960 to 4,800 in 1961. They were providing four-year courses in mathematics, physics, chemistry, biology and history. In a number of Sichuan schools teachers taking correspondence courses had organized themselves into study groups.

In-service training

There are a number of ways in which inexperienced teachers are given guidance during their early years as teachers. In many cases the new teacher is assigned to work with a more experienced teacher. He may only observe classes for a time, perhaps taking occasional classes, or giving help during the private study periods (it should be remembered that most secondary schools and colleges are boarding schools).

Zhejiang University Mathematics Department required its young teachers to rehearse their lectures in front of older teachers (SCMP 2710, 1962). Zhongshan University in Guangzhou (Canton) reported its apprenticeship methods at length (SCMP 2724, 1962). The same university reported that difficult and specially important parts of the syllabus were assigned to older teachers (SCMP 2663, 1961).

It is often difficult in practice to distinguish between training of the inexperienced, and the increasing emphasis on collective ways of working. In the larger schools and colleges where more than one teacher teaches the same subject, meetings are held to discuss teaching plans. These plans are drawn up very formally and in great detail. The writer has himself participated in such meetings which ranged from perfunctory to very useful. A hint of the traditional ways they are trying to escape from was given in the *People's Daily* account of the work of young physics teachers at Peking University (SCMP 2667, 1962). It spoke of long hours of preparation; preparing as many as seven or eight different versions of the same lecture over a few years; of using familiar situations to illustrate physical principles; and, almost as an aside it added that they did not just read the textbook!

In all this work guidance comes from above, but the detailed working out is left to the institution concerned. The writer taught a group of nine young teachers at one of the big Foreign Language Institutes in Peking for the first six months of 1966. Because of illness or other special circumstances their level of English was too low for them to teach and it was decided to set up a special class to remedy this. It met for 12 hours per week, and the content of the course was left in the hands of the writer, including the choice of books. A number of standard British and American language works were used, and the students became enthusiastic supporters of pattern drills and the oral approach.

Another institute to take training seriously was the Peking Aeronautical Institute. In 1952 they had 8 teachers, only one of whom had been formally trained in theoretical mechanics. By 1963 they had 17 teachers (2 assistant professors, 10 lecturers, and 5 teaching assistants) and they had trained and sent elsewhere a further 22. In this period they had worked out a training course with set books and a graded practice. During the first term the teacher was on probation and studied and observed. After that he took classes in the review of exercises for two years—repeating the material a second time. In the third year he prepared and gave trial lectures, while continuing to supervise the revision of exercises classes. Only after that was he allowed to lecture.

At least in the early years after 1949, teachers for the higher levels were found from amongst the better teachers of lower levels. Shanghai, in 1954, transferred hundreds of primary teachers to junior high schools. In the central-south region, in the same year, junior high school teachers with two years' experience were given a five months training course and transferred to senior high schools. Xiamen (Amoy) University ran a six months course in physics and mathematics for teachers from junior high school who would then go and teach these subjects in senior high schools. At the same time there were reports of high school teachers being transferred to higher institutions to train teachers. (Chen, pp. 27–8).

7

The moral-political educators

No study of Chinese communist education would be complete without some consideration of those organizations which, acting both within and outside the school system, play a dominant role in shaping education. Because of their special emphasis they can conveniently be grouped together as the moral-political educators, though some of them are also concerned with purely organizational or technical matters. In addition to the political and youth organizations, publishing and the radio will be described. Here, too, the emphasis is on moral-political education.

The Communist Party

The aims and organization of the Communist Party during the period covered by the present book are set out in the Constitutions of 1945 and 1956. During the 9th Party Congress in the spring of 1969 a new and much shorter Constitution was adopted, laying great emphasis on Mao Ze-dong's thought, and sanctioning a number of the principles established during the Cultural Revolution. But while emphases have been changed, the fundamental role of the Party remains the same.

Aims

The Chinese Communist Party sees itself both as an organizer and as an educator. Under the heading 'General Programme' it states the 'aim of the Party' as 'the achievement of socialism and communism in China' (1945), and goes on to describe how it takes Marxism-Leninism as 'its guide to action'. On page 3 it states 'the Party must do everything possible to stimulate progress in China's science, culture and technology so as to catch up with the world's advanced levels in these fields'. Referring to the need to help the various national minorities to develop, the Constitution advocates the training of leadership cadres from amongst them, while at the same time preventing and correcting great-nation chauvinist tendencies amongst Han Party and government workers. Finally, referring to the Party's 'mass line' policy, the Constitution states: 'as a result of its propaganda and organizational work among the masses' it 'transforms Party policy into the views and actions of the masses themselves'.

Organization

The Communist Party has a network of branches all over the country, and within all the institutions and enterprises. These are grouped in a hierarchy, through municipalities, counties and provinces, to the Central Committee in Peking. According to the Constitution the supreme body is the National Party Congress, but this meets infrequently and its place is normally taken by the CC which it elects. The organizational principle of the Party is democratic centralism, some of whose features are described in the Constitution. All leading bodies are to be elected, and all leading bodies 'must pay constant heed to the views of their lower organizations and the rank-and-file Party members, study their experience and promptly help to solve their problems' (article 19, (3)). Lower organizations must report regularly and 'in good time for instructions on questions which need a decision by higher Party organizations'. 'All Party organizations operate on the principle of collective leadership combined with individual responsibility'. Article 25 tries to delimit national and local problems and divide responsibility for each between the central and local Party organizations. Article 26 is concerned with 'free and practical discussions' by lower Party organizations before decisions are taken by central bodies.

Membership of the Party is open to persons over eighteen years of age who have been recommended by two full members. They have to serve a probationary period of one year. Resignation is allowed for in article 11, and measures are outlined for disciplining, and finally expelling members who do not fulfil required standards.

The first duty of a Party member (article 2, (1)) is 'to study Marxism-Leninism diligently and strive unceasingly to raise the level of his understanding'. Paragraph (4) refers to behaving in 'accordance with communist ethics', and paragraph (6) states their duty to 'serve the masses of the people heart and soul, strengthen their ties with them, learn from them, listen with an open mind to their wishes and opinions and report these without delay to the Party, and explain Party policy and decisions to the people'. Party members failing in their duties are to be 'criticized and educated'.

Article 50 deals with the work of the primary Party organizations, the branches at grass-roots level. Again the first duty is 'to carry out propaganda and organizational work among the masses'. Then they should 'pay constant attention to the material and cultural life of the masses and strive to improve it'. They must 'organize Party members to study Marxism-Leninism and the Party's policy and experience and raise the levels of their ideology and political understanding'.

Propaganda is considered so important that there is a special Propaganda Department (*Xuanchuan Bu*), set up by the CC and working under the direct supervision of the Political Bureau and the Chairman of the CC. No doubt this committee is concerned with the contents of the two important central organs of the Party, the *People's Daily* and *Red Flag*. At the various levels down the hierarchy there are similar propaganda departments.

Comment

This conception of an elite whose function it is to govern the people, and at the same time educate them, has both striking similarities with and interesting differences from the Confucian scholar-bureaucrats of the past. J. Needham remarks: 'Surely the basic conception of a non-hereditary elite in a non-competitive society has much in common with the conception of membership of an organization like the Communist Party' (Needham, *The Past in China's Present*, pp. 2–3). In the past it was the scholar-bureaucrat who was to instruct the people. The *Zhou Li* has a number of passages describing how the minister of education should instruct the people in the 'six virtues', 'six actions', and 'six arts' (Galt, pp. 126–7). But always the distinction of ruler and ruled, of the Superior Man and the Small Man, was kept in mind. As Confucius said: 'Require the people to follow, but do not try to make them understand' (*Analects*, 8.9). The Communist Party denies these distinctions and is greatly concerned with making the ordinary people understand.

The Party puts over its message by endless meetings, by slogans, wall-newspapers, by special campaigns, or simply in conversation between Party and non-party persons (Yu, 1964, p. 81). How well these methods work is hard to judge at this stage. We hear mainly from critics of the system who point to bureaucratic privilege, and the pressure of the security system (Lin Xi-ling in Doolin, 1964). But whether the system works well or ill, the virtues of 'serving the people', putting the collective good before the private good, unselfishness and thought for others, are constantly placed before the people. Whatever the pressure practised, the ideal held out is that of self-help and a critical attitude. And all this is done on a vast scale, similar perhaps, but much greater than that of the medieval Christian Church.

The People's Liberation Army (the PLA)

It may seem strange to include the army in a book on education, but there is both a general and a particular reason why it should be considered as an educational force. As in many other basically peasant countries, the recruit is taken away from his native village and introduced to many modern things which he might otherwise not encounter. He may learn to handle engines, or radio, or he may simply visit a big city, or learn to read. In China the army has been particularly important as a source of manpower for the bureaucracy, and as a model for the masses, and it has a highly developed system of moral-political education which has served as the model for similar education in other spheres of Chinese society, including the formal educational system.

While the system has been developed and extended, it is not a new one. It goes back to the Eighth Route and New Fourth Armies of the 1938–45 period. Gittings estimates that some one and a quarter million soldiers were recruited to these two armies, and that by the end of the civil war in 1949 as many as four and a quarter million were involved, plus a further million taken over from the Guomindang armies. With a further one and a half millions to replace demobilized soldiers, and losses through the Korean War, this gives a total of some eight million for the period 1938–53 (Gittings, 1967, p. 48). While the quality and quantity of education must have varied in time and place, the very length of time which a

239

high proportion of these soldiers served in the army must have had a profound effect, not to mention the nature of the struggles in which they had been involved.

Compulsory conscription was begun in 1955 (ibid, p. 148) and as far as is known approximately half a million young people have been enlisted annually since that time. Very roughly, this is about 1 in 20 of the affected age group, but decreases as a proportion as the population increases. Length of service was increased in 1965. It has varied with both arm, and rank within the forces, from 3 years for an infantryman in 1955 to 6 years for a sailor in the fleet in 1965. On demobilization reservists continue to receive regular training until the age of forty (ibid, p. 105).

Until compulsory conscription was introduced the Communist army had always relied on volunteers. Because of the traditional low regard in which army service was held, elaborate measures were taken to encourage young people to volunteer. Gittings describes some of these, and quotes from a NCNA report of a meeting of a Peking trade union branch, called to get recruits for the Korean war:

'Suddenly someone shouted that he wanted to go to Korea . . . thereupon many other people rose to their feet . . . After two hours had passed the trade union secretary said that it appeared to him that everybody wished to volunteer. This was "magnificent but not practical". He suggested that the branch should consider these applications and recommend who should be allowed to step forward . . . Everybody would "have a chance" '. (Gittings, p. 85).

The result of such a system on the composition of recruits is uncertain, but the majority must have been peasants. During 1950 and 1951 a total of 520,000 high school students and graduates between the ages of 16 and 25 appear to have been recruited, a figure equal to some 40 per cent of the total second and third level school enrolment for 1950–1 (Gittings, pp. 81–2). The enrolment of students seems to have been dictated by the need for more educated cadres in the armed services, and perhaps by the surplus of junior high school graduates (Gittings, p. 81). During the years of conscription the number of students recruited must have been low, as senior high school and higher education students were allowed to apply for exemption.

Attitudes and skills taught

The PLA has, except for a short period of Soviet influence, concentrated on highly mobile warfare, and the military skills taught have been largely those of small-group tactics, hand-to-hand fighting, and guerilla tactics. Great attention has been paid to sport and physical fitness, subjects very much neglected in pre-1949 China.

The numerical extent of technical training in the armed forces is impossible to estimate as none of the necessary figures are published. Some recruits have already been students at technical colleges and schools. But substantial numbers of young people will have passed through the supply, medical, signal and other specialized corps, or through the Aviation, Artillery or Naval Schools. Here they will have acquired many skills which can be applied in civilian life: driving; storage and maintenance of various supplies; cooking and preparing food on a large scale; and various repair and construction jobs. Some of these activities are described in the fictionalized account of the life of a recent army hero, Ou-yang Hai (Chin, 1966).

Of decreasing importance as the years have gone by has been the acquisition of the ability to read. In 1952 illiteracy was widespread, and its elimination was one of the aims mentioned in the Army Day speech of that year by General Xiao Hua (Gittings, p. 132). Already by that date campaigns to teach up to some 2,000 Chinese characters had been launched. According to a method evolved by a PLA teacher, Ji Jian-hua, it was claimed that 1,500 to 2,000 characters could be learnt within fifteen days. Elementary mathematics and calligraphy were taught at the same time. By the middle of 1953 it was claimed that the great majority of the ordinary soldiers were able to read military textbooks and take notes at lectures (Gittings, p. 145).

That a great deal of time was devoted to such education and training was testified to by the then Chief of Staff, Lo Rui-ching in 1961. He said after an inspection of army units that 'the term of service for soldiers with technical skill is too short. An automobile driver who has just learned to drive is soon entitled to be discharged from the service. That is why many automobiles cannot move.' (Gittings, p. 149).

More important from the point of view of the philosophy of

education held by Mao Ze-dong are the values and habits acquired during the long hours of moral-political training. In fact, to suggest that certain 'hours' are devoted to it is probably wrong. The whole structure and functioning of the PLA ensures that every waking moment is concerned with this matter.

The basis of moral-political training is the groups of three mentioned earlier, into which the PLA squads are divided. Each member of the group is expected to criticize the behaviour of the other two, for whom he has a special responsibility, as well as to indulge in self-criticism. Frequent meetings are held for this purpose at squad, platoon and company level. At such meetings the behaviour of both commissioned and non-commissioned officers can be criticized. Available evidence suggests that the soldiers dislike public criticism very strongly and modify their behaviour accordingly to prevent it (George, pp. 77–81). But more than modified behaviour is required. The system is really intended to alter the soldier's way of thinking. The analogy is used of beetroots and radishes, the former being 'red all through' while the latter are only red on the surface (George, p. 89). Evidence of the success in changing soldiers' attitudes is almost impossible to obtain. The study of prisoners taken in Korea suggests that in this limited group there were a number of 'radishes' (George, p. 80), but more rigorous selection in recent years has probably reduced their number.

The attitudes which the system attempts to instil were described by George as: 'anti-individualism, dedication of self to the interests of the "people", acceptance of leadership of the Party. This was part of the effort to create a new communist "conscience" in the individual, which would make him deeply dissatisfied with things as they are, cause him to maintain a constant alertness and watchfulness against the appearance of "evil" in himself or in others around him, and impel him to be an "activist" on behalf of political and social reform and in the performance of his military duties.' (George, p. 32).

In the propaganda and campaigns used to develop them, the desired qualities are grouped under numerical phrases, from ancient times so typical of Chinese thought. A 'four good' company is one which is good in: (1) political and ideological work; (2) the three-eight working style; (3) military training; and (4) arrangements for the well-being of the fighters. The 'three-eight working style' refers to three slogans: (1) keep firmly to the correct political orientation; (2) maintain an industrious and simple style of work, and (3) be flexible in strategy and tactics; and to eight characters which mean: unity, alertness, earnestness and liveliness. The 'four firsts' refers to the correct handling of the following relationships: (1) between man and weapons, giving first place to man; (2) between political and other work, giving first place to political work; (3) between ideological and routine tasks in political work, giving first place to ideological work; and (4) between ideas in books and living ideas currently in people's minds in ideological work, giving first place to living ideas. These slogans, first developed in the army before 1949, continue to be used and have been taken out into civilian life.

An important aspect of political education is what is described as the 'recollection of past bitterness and appreciation of present sweetness'. Lin Biao has commented that 'one who knows nothing about exploitation knows nothing about revolution' (Gittings, p. 249). During the pre-1949 days regular 'speak bitterness' meetings were held, when soldiers poured out their grievances and found unity in common misery. In more recent times young soldiers have listened to veterans telling tales of the past, seen exhibitions of photographs and relics, and read stories of the lives of heroes of the anti-Japanese and Civil Wars.

In the special political study classes lectures are given on current topics. Articles and editorials from the army papers and *People's Daily* are read. And increasingly the writings of Mao Ze-dong are studied, especially the book of quotations, and the 'three good old articles'. Officers are expected to make a more theoretical study of such subjects as the history of the Chinese Communist Party, political economy, dialectical materialism and the party constitution (Gittings, p. 168).

The PLA contributions to civilian life

1 To the bureaucracy

Military officers had long experience of civil administration in the 'liberated areas' under communist control before 1949. This was extended, and in December 1949 China was divided into six major administrative regions (North-West, South-West, Central-South, East, North, North-East) each with a Military Control Committee.

Direct military control was rapidly replaced by civil control, but large numbers of key personnel were former PLA officers. The need for trained personnel, sympathetic to the new government, was enormous. The role of the army envisaged by Mao Ze-dong is shown in this quotation from his report to the CC in March 1949: 'We must prepare to turn all the field armies, 2,100,000 strong, into a working force. In that event, there will be enough cadres and the work can develop over large areas. We must look upon the field armies with their 2,100,000 men as a gigantic school for cadres' (Mao, 1965, vol. 4, p. 363).

In the succeeding years large numbers of cadres have been trained through other channels, but the PLA continues to make an important contribution. Work teams which include army officers have been set up from time to time to handle particular jobs. In 1956 the 'Programme for Participation and Support by Army Units in the Agricultural Co-operative Movement and Agricultural Production' states:

> In areas where army cadres are required to take part in construction and reorganization of co-operatives (particularly in late liberated areas, border regions, islands along the coast and minority nationality areas), work teams of officers and men should be placed under the leadership of the local party committee to help in agricultural work. Officers should be specifically assigned to these areas to support socialist construction. (Gittings, p. 179).

In the Foreign-language Institute where the writer worked, both the Dean of English and his deputy were ex-PLA officers who knew no English, and whose qualifications were administrative rather than academic. During the 'learn from the PLA' campaign in 1964, and also in 1963, large numbers of officers were transferred to business and financial enterprises, principally to prevent curruption and waste. At the same time many civilian cadres went into the PLA for short political courses. (Gittings, p. 257). It is obviously felt that the political contribution which ex-PLA-men can make outweighs any lack of technical knowledge.

2 'Learn from the PLA'

Individual army heroes, and the Eight Route Army have always been held up as models of virtue for people to emulate. The exact combination of virtues has varied from hero to hero, but in recent years the stress has been on studying Mao's works, and through their inspiration serving the people to the point of risking and usually sacrificing one's life (Sheridan, 1968). After an extensive political education campaign in the PLA in the early sixties a mass 'learn from the PLA' campaign was launched. It began with an editorial in the *People's Daily* on 1 February 1964. Gittings draws attention to a special feature of the campaign: the reorganizing of party branches and the setting up of new ones to conform with the pattern within the PLA. ' "In the PLA" it was explained, "the basic-level combat unit is the company. In the industrial enterprise, the basic-level production unit is the workshop" ' (Gittings, p. 256). Institutions began to set up political departments modelled on that of the PLA. It will be interesting to see whether this trend is intensified or reversed when the new administrative structures emerge from the Cultural Revolution. Plans for reorganizing Tongji University in Shanghai suggest the trend will be towards closer identification with the 'PLA spirit'.

The Youth League

Organization

In the 1965 *People's Handbook* the Chinese Communist Youth League (*Zhongguo Gongchanzhuyi Qingnian Tuan*) was the second organization to be listed, coming immediately after the Communist Party itself, and before all other political parties and political and cultural organizations (*People's Handbook*, p. 132). Headed by a First Secretary, it had a Secretariat of 8 members, and a Standing Committee of 29 members. In addition it had a Central Committee of 178 full members and 74 alternate members elected at the periodical Congresses. Provincial, municipal and district committees, and a network of branches within the nation's industries, rural communes, and armed forces completed its structure.

The basic units of the League are branches and general branches. A branch could be set up where there were more than 3 members and less than 100. A general branch required between 10 and 300 members. The setting-up of a branch or general branch required the approval of a League committee of municipal or *xian* rank.

245

Branches with fewer than 7 members functioned with the aid of an elected secretary, and sometimes a deputy secretary. Bigger branches might have a branch committee. General branches had a general branch committee, and in enterprises and organizations having more than 300 members, or where the work demanded it and the membership was over 100, a League Committee was formed. The setting up of such a League Committee had to be approved by the provincial League Committee or its equivalent. According to the 1953 Constitution all such committees normally held office for six months to one year.

Membership of the League was open to girls and boys between the ages of 15 and 25. Before 1957 youth of 14 were admitted. Throughout its history a large number of older people retained their membership, often occupying the leading positions. They retained full rights, 'to speak and to be elected' (Fraser, p. 201).

Published membership figures showed a rise through 5,180,000 in September 1951 (*Guide to New China*, p. 57), to 9.9 million in 180,000 units at the time of the 2nd Congress in July 1953, and to some 25 million in 1959 and 1962 (CNA, no. 633, p. 3). Since then no national figures have been given, but dissatisfaction has been expressed editorially in the League's *Youth Daily* editorials. Breakdown figures for membership at the time of the 3rd Congress in 1957 show that of the total of 23 million, 16.4 million were in the villages, 3.6 million were in schools, 2.28 million were in industry, 1.8 million were in the army, 970,000 were in government offices, and 680,000 were in commerce. 600,000 were from the national minorities. (CNA, no. 633, p. 2). In April 1964 a *Youth Daily* editorial complained that only 13 per cent of youth in the villages were members of the League, and that 10 per cent of the production brigades did not have a single member (i.e. about half of the villages). It also warned of the effect of failing to recruit new members, when over-age members might form a majority and the organization lose its character as representing the youth.

The conditions for membership laid down in the constitution of the League are recognition of the League constitution, participation in the work of one of its organizations, implementation of its decisions, and payment of membership dues. Apart from the lower age limit, membership is in theory open to all youth, 'irrespective of sex'. But in practice there appears to have been considerable discrimination on class and other grounds. During 1965, after the CC 2nd Plenum of March-April, a number of articles appeared in the *Youth Daily* and the Magazine, *Chinese Youth*, stressing the importance of recruiting the sons and daughters of former landlords and rich peasants, and of judging young people on their merits, rather than on those of their family. The point was also made that youth should be judged on their main characteristics, rather than on minor matters. Political attitude and attitude to work were the most important things. Articles like that from the Miaodi Production Brigade (ECMM 483) echoed the CC editorials in reporting fears of being regarded as reactionary if they associated with 'backward elements' and the children of former landlords and rich peasants. The Miaodi YCL described how they corrected their attitude, encouraging 'backward' youth by praising their good points, getting them to work with the YCL teams in the field, and assisting them over such difficulties as a broken tool. In this way they claimed to have won over a number of youngsters to the point where they wanted to join the YCL.

The 1953 Constitution stated that the League was 'led by the Communist Party of China and [was] also the lieutenant and reserve force of the Party'. In the revised Constitution of 1956 the relationship was spelled out in greater detail. 'The CC of the YCL accepts the leadership of the Party's CC. The YCL local organizations are simultaneously under the leadership of the Party organizations at the corresponding levels and of higher League organizations'. (Fraser, p. 266). Party organizations 'at all levels (had to) take a deep interest' in the work of the YCL and guide it.

The special nature of work in the PLA was already recognized in the 1953 constitution. Article 34 laid down that YCL work must be done under the direct leadership of the basic-level Party organ, in accordance with the instructions of both the Party committee and the military leaders. Overall policy was to be the joint responsibility of the CC of the League and the general political department of the People's Revolutionary Military Council of the Central People's Government. At the same time YCL branches in the PLA were expected to take part in the activities of the local, civilian YCL branches.

The constitution is laconic on the question of finance. Article 37 states: 'The funds of the League shall come from the membership dues and other incomes of the League'.

The decision to set up what was then called the China New Democratic Youth League (*Zhongguo Xin Minzhuzhuyi Qingnian Tuan*) was taken by the CC CCP in January 1949, and the new organization held its first congress in Peking from 11 to 18 April of that year. (*Guide to New China*, p. 57). 323 delegates attended, representing 190,000 members. A constitution and programme of work was adopted.

At the second congress, in June–July 1953, an amended constitution was adopted. At the third congress, in May 1957, the name of the organization was changed to the Chinese Communist Youth League. What was really the fourth congress, held in June 1964, was called the ninth because of a desire to link the post-1949 organization with Marxist youth organizations which had existed during the pre-1949 period. An attempt to describe the history of these earlier organizations was made by *Chinese Youth* in 1957 (nos. 4, 5 and 6), Research Material for the History of the Youth League.

Aims

The aims of the League were set out in the preamble to the constitution (Fraser, p. 198). The League's job was to assist the Party in moral-political education among the youth and its members were expected to be models for the youth to follow. The constitution listed the following desirable qualities: 'a deep love for the motherland, being loyal to the people, educated, disciplined, brave, industrious, lively, and ready to face any hardship'. Members were expected to set an example in observing the state law, and to foster good relations between the various nationalities in the country. Education was to include advanced production techniques. National construction and national defence were both included.

Activities

The main activities of local YCL branches were study meetings and propaganda, particularly in the field of production. In the village described by Myrdal there were one or two branch meetings a month to plan the work. The smaller groups met once a week to discuss agricultural production, for the success of which they took some responsibility. In addition, a study circle met once a week to study the League programme, day-to-day politics, and Mao's works (Myrdal, p. 250). Branches also organized visits to places of interest, entertainments, and sports events such as swimming, which was regarded as important in developing the people's health.

The Young Pioneers

Origins and aims

The Young Pioneers were closely linked organizationally with the YCL. In October 1949 the CC YCL set up a Children's Corps of China. In June 1953 this became the Young Pioneers of China (*Zhongguo Xiaonian Xianfengdui*). The YPC was based on the tradition established in the Red Army base areas before 1949, where the CCP established various children's organizations. At that time their aims were cultural and military. Children learnt to read, and then passed their knowledge on to their parents and other relatives. They also delivered messages, served as guides to the Red Army, helped to look after servicemen's dependents, and worked in many other ways. No film about this period is complete without the village children's guard, armed with red-tasselled spears. They formed the eyes and ears of the communist army and militia.

While conditions have changed, the aims of the YPC have remained in many ways the same. One of the lectures on the YCL Constitution in the *Youth Daily* (CB 680) says: 'The Young Pioneers enlightens children on communism and trains them to be a new generation that loves the fatherland, the people, labour and science, that takes good care of public property, is healthy, active, courageous, honest, and creative in spirit.' It differed from the YCL in being a mass organization whose members were not expected to be perfect models for the rest of the children. The same lecture tried to distinguish it from the school, with which it shared the same aims, and firmly stated that it was not to be regarded as an accessory organ of the school. It was especially to be concerned with developing initiative, creativeness and independence.

In June 1953 the then leader of the YCL, Hu Yao-bang, gave a membership figure for the YPC of 7 million members (Fraser, p. 188). By 1962 the figure had risen to 50 million (CB 680).

Organization

All children between the ages of 9 and 15 were eligible to apply to join the YPC. They had to submit an application to the Brigade Committee, which discussed the matter and then decided. The YPC had a three-tier hierarchy. Seven to thirteen members formed a group, two to five groups formed a team and two or more teams formed a brigade. Brigades or teams were based in primary and secondary schools or in a street or production brigade of a commune.

One of the functions of the YPC was to train children in leadership, and aiding in this was an elaborate leadership structure. Each group elected a head and two deputy heads. The teams and brigades elected a small committee each. Leadership was strengthened by tutors who were provided by the YCL. In many cases these were primary and secondary school teachers, but they may also have included secondary school students and workers. They were chosen, says the *Youth Daily*, because they were progressive, upright and loved children.

The YPC had the usual ritual which children everywhere enjoy. New members were admitted at an impressive ceremony at which they took an oath of allegiance. At the same time they had to plant a tree, or do some other socially useful task.

The YPC had its own flag, and the red scarf which every member wore represented a corner of this flag. It symbolized a banner of revolutionary victory. There was also a special salute, and a call which was shouted out at the end of every meeting. The leader cried: 'Be ready to struggle for the Communist cause!' and the members replied. 'Ever ready!'

Activities

The importance of relating the activities of the YPC to the needs and abilities of children was pointed out on a number of occasions. Hu Yao-bang, at the 2nd National Congress of the New Democratic Youth League in 1953 (Fraser, p. 188) said: 'We should show concern for the children like our own brothers and sisters. At present, some activities of the Young Pioneers are still not suitable to the children, as they impose upon them too much social work.

This should be corrected.' Speaking of the responsibilities of teachers and youth leaders he said: 'They should ceaselessly improve their work, patiently enrich the knowledge of children according to their physical and mental conditions as well as use their exemplary acts for setting a good example to the children and train the children to be a new generation of high moral quality.' The 1962 lecture (CB 680) pointed out that the YPC was not just for play, but 'it is not right either to think that, inasmuch as the YPC is an organization of communist education for children, abstract political theories are to be infused into the minds of children regardless of the degree of their ability of acceptance.' The lecture went on to describe the various activities of the YPC, grouping them according to the various aims which they were intended to fulfil.

A primary aim of the YPC was to help the children to learn to read and to study well. It tried to make children see the object of studying hard, and to value their time. It also tried to instil disciplined habits and serious study methods. To this end it organized visits to factories and construction works, meetings with model workers, and discussions on such topics as 'we are heirs to communism', 'the tasks of the reserve force', 'how important arithmetic is', or 'the value of one minute'. Patriotism was encouraged by meetings with combat heroes and visits to units of the PLA. Groups were also organized to study methods of plant cultivation, and to look after animals. In the towns groups made model aeroplanes and ships, studied radio, meteorology, or read science fiction.

In order to foster revolutionary traditions the YPC officially participated in the celebration of national days, such as 1 May, 1 October, 1 July and 1 August. This, the lecture on the YCL constitution pointed out, was to help the children understand exploitation and oppression, and who should be hated and who should be supported.

Similarly a great emphasis was placed on social activities. These ranged from participating in the various political campaigns to collecting manure, cutting grass, or helping to exterminate pests. Guo Lin (JPRS 1165-D) described how Young Pioneers in Hebei (Hopei) and Zhongjing collected scrap metal, and in the latter place started a movement to make straw shoes for local workmen which finally achieved 30,000 pairs.

A great deal of emphasis was placed on work. 'Interesting and light labour' was expected both to cultivate a love of work, and to help the children's physical and mental development. YPC units were expected to teach their members to help in the home, to look after themselves, and to practise 'industrious living and frugal habits' (CB 680).

Finally, the YPC encouraged cultural activities and physical exercise. Singing groups, dance groups, recitation and drama each found participants. There were evening parties and camp fires at which these groups performed. Then there were ball games, swimming, skating, and in some places, rowing and skiing. These physical activities merged into the national call for preparations to defend the country, and for the older children there were military drills and marches.

The Red Guards

The Red Guards were formed during the Cultural Revolution of 1966 and the YCL and YPC appeared to fade out of existence. Some confusion has been caused by speaking about *the* Red Guards, as if they were a single organization. Certainly there is reason to believe that at the beginning their formation was encouraged from above. But to see them as puppets, manipulated by the firm hand of Mao Ze-dong, is quite wrong. Their authority was paragraph 9 of the CC CCP decision on the Cultural Revolution of 8 August 1966, which welcomed as 'something new and of great historic importance' the emergence of 'cultural revolutionary groups, committees and other organizational forms created by the masses in many schools and units'. (CR docs. 3). Outwardly the appearance of all Red Guards was the same: PLA-type uniforms with a red arm-band, and a firmly grasped copy of Mao's *Quotations;* marching columns; sacred portraits; and the sound of gongs and drums between the chanting of slogans. But underneath all this there were significant differences, both in numbers and methods. Determined critics of the Party officials in some cases emerged from imprisonment and severe ill-treatment to become leaders of Red Guard organizations of several thousand students and teachers, and to wield considerable power for several months. When the movement spread to the factories, young workers found themselves in managerial positions through their leadership of Red Guard organizations. The writer found some of them a refreshing change from the former party-bureaucrat type during his tour of Shanghai factories in March 1967. At the opposite end of the Red Guard scale could be found groups of a few friends, teachers or students, who for some reason or other could not agree to join one of the bigger groups. In the writer's Institute in Peking there were 8 different groups at one time. In Peking University, centre of student activities, there were at times over 20 organizations. Conflicts between such big groups as the Shanghai Revolutionary Rebels (*Zaofan Dui*) and the Scarlet Guards (*Chi-wei Dui*) were sometimes violent.

As the Cultural Revolution developed more and more attempts were made to bring the different Red Guard organizations together. Congresses of Red Guard organizations were held, like that in Peking in February 1967. At the time of writing both the organization and the possible future of such organizations is unclear. All that can be said is that probably for the first time in history the youth of China has been free to organize itself, and that some sections of it have shown their ability to exercise considerable power in a responsible manner. But wider sections of the student body have proved incapable of responsibility, and workers have had to be brought in to restore order.

Activities

The Red Guards burst upon an incredulous world during the last week of August 1966. First in Peking, and later in Shanghai and other major cities, they swept through the streets, tearing down shop signs, changing the names of streets, cutting off girls' braids, and attacking all kinds of things which they regarded as representing the 'four olds' (old ideas, old culture, old customs, old habits—*Peking Review*, 36, 2 September 1966, p. 17).

During this period of violence the homes of many people were invaded and offending books, gramophone records, and other items were removed and often destroyed. Red guards invaded the churches and temples and removed the idols, tore up the hymn books, and set up portraits of, and quotations from the works of Chairman Mao.

But the main activity of the Red Guards lay elsewhere, in almost endless discussion, reading and writing of wall posters (*dazibao*, or big character papers). The wall poster might be a factual description of some incident (often highly exaggerated), a criticism of someone in authority, a self-criticism, or a suggestion for action. It might be written by one person, or by some organization. It was usually written by hand on large sheets of paper which were then fastened with home-made paste to the nearest suitable surface.

Red Guard reading consisted of newspaper articles, especially the editorials of the *People's Daily;* the works of Mao, especially the book of *Quotations;* and various wall posters and Red Guard papers and leaflets. Discussion, it seemed from the outside, tended to centre on the attitudes taken by different people and organizations to the conduct of the Cultural Revolution itself. But it would also seem that considerable attention was given to questions of a moral-political character. How should a revolutionary journalist behave when sent to write about peasant life in a commune? What does 'serving the people' mean when applied to a student or a worker in a shop? Other students discussed such questions as what constitutes linking theory and practice in the teaching of a foreign language.

There can be no doubt that large numbers of young people learnt a lot about organizing during this period. Each group had its committee, and many ran news-sheets, and broadcast over loudspeaker networks which they set up themselves with equipment 'borrowed' from the institution in which they lived. In Peking the various institutes and colleges played host to literally millions of youngsters from all over China. This meant housing them, feeding them, guiding them about the city, and organizing activities for them, a task which must have taught many a useful lesson.

During November and December 1966 large numbers of Red Guards went off in small groups on what they called for historic reasons, 'long marches'. Usually these were aimed at such places as Yan'an, cradle of the revolution, or Mao's birthplace in the south. On the way the marchers were expected to carry the message of the Cultural Revolution to the villages through which they passed. In this way large numbers of youth were able to visit many parts of China which they would probably otherwise never have seen, and to realise at first hand the wide differences which exist, and the problems which their country faces. Some teachers and students from the north went as far as the minority areas bordering Burma, while a few even penetrated forbidden Tibet. A number of such groups stopped on their journey and worked, sometimes for several months, at some factory or enterprise where they had been made welcome. The unlucky or less well-behaved groups learnt what it means to be unwelcome!

Finally, all the Red Guard groups were involved in the detailed examination of the activities of their particular institution, whether it was a school, an office or a factory. Meetings resembling a court of law interrogated officials about their past activities. Red Guards went off to other parts of China to investigate accusations made at meetings. For the majority it probably meant little more than slogan shouting, but for a few in each institution this was a valuable opportunity to acquire experience and knowledge about the running of the enterprise.

The written and the spoken word

The written word

While the exact effect of the written word on public opinion probably lies outside the realm of strict proof, few modern societies doubt its importance, and all take varying steps to regulate and control it. Communists have always taken this medium very seriously. Lenin, in *What is to be done?* in 1902, argued at length on the importance of a party newspaper as a 'collective propandist and collective agitator' and 'also a collective organizer' (Lenin, 1947, pp. 256–71). In an article written in 1918, Lenin urged Russian newspapers to 'get closer to life', to pay more attention to 'training the masses' by paying 'more attention to the way the masses of workers and peasants are *actually* building something *new* in their everyday work. More *testing* to ascertain to what extent this something new is *communistic*'. (Lenin, 1937, p. 505). Mao Ze-dong has written similarly on numerous occasions (cf. *Yenan Forum on Literature and Art; On New Democracy; Intervention at the CCP National Conference on Propaganda*). He sees culture as a weapon in the revolutionary struggle, and the writers as educators, but only truly 'serving the people' to the extent that they immerse themselves in ordinary life. Writing specifically on the role of provincial newspapers in 1958, he said it was 'to organize, to stimulate, to agitate, to criticize, and to propel' (Yu, p. 103).

Production and control

Holding such views on the importance of the printed word, it is not surprising that the new Chinese government introduced legislation to control book and periodical publication during its second year of office. All publishing enterprises, or responsible persons in organizations publishing a periodical, have to be registered with local 'organs in charge of publications administration' (Nunn, p. 64). Article 8 of the Provisional Regulations lays down that 'enterprises that publish books or periodicals' shall 'have a definite direction of specialization', and 'shall not print or distribute books or periodicals that violate the Common Programme of the Chinese People's Political Consultative Conference or the decrees of the Government'. Article 9 requires 'enterprises that print books or periodicals' not to 'undertake the printing of books or periodicals the publication of which is prohibited by express Government decrees', and 'before delivery they shall send to the local organs in charge of publication administration one copy each of the books or periodicals printed' (Nunn, p. 62).

These regulations were backed up by a careful sifting of the stocks of publishers and booksellers (Nunn, p. 17) during 1951, and subsequently by a mixture of official and self-censorship. The writer was able to see the latter in operation during the early part of the Cultural Revolution when bookshops rapidly cleared their shelves of anything which might be regarded as 'old', but then brought out such things as Russian technical and scientific books as the atmosphere relaxed. Other observers noted that many works on magic and superstitions remained on the shelves, protected by their connection with the officially-approved traditional medicine.

The work of publishing is officially supervised by the Publications Administrative Bureau under the Ministry of Culture. It organized the first National conference on Publications in September 1950, when it put forward the idea of separating the functions of printing, publishing and distribution. By 1956 the number of publishing houses had been reduced to less than one hundred, and seven major firms were responsible for more than half the national output (Nunn, p. 59). Book distribution was put in the hands of the New China Bookshop (Xinhua Shudian), while periodicals were mainly distributed through the branches of the Post Office.

Distribution and public access

Public access to the written word is probably more limited by production than distribution, though there have been reports of mal-distributions from time to time. The New China Bookshop supplies readers, not only through its own branches, but also through innumerable village stores.

For those wanting to borrow books and periodicals there is a growing library service. In 1958 this was organized as a national system, with national libraries in Peking and Shanghai and local central libraries, in Wuhan, Shenyang, Nanjing (Nanking), Guang-zhou (Canton), Chengdu, Xi'an (Sian), Lanzhou, Tianjin (Tient-sin), and Harbin. Some idea of its scope is given by the following table.

Type of library	Number of libraries	Library holdings in volumes	Number on staff
Public libraries	400	31,090,000	3,714
Higher education libraries	225	33,400,000	3,568
Chinese Academy of Sciences	1,114	6,000,000 (1,750,000 in central library)	632 (232 in central library)
Rural reading rooms	182,960	16,610,000	
Trade union libraries	35,000	34,000,000	

(From Nunn, p. 51, ex. *Union Research Service*, vol. 19, no. 8 and no. 10).

There is an attempt to co-ordinate the work of the various libraries through a Council of Scientific Libraries. Specialization is encouraged, as in the case of the National Library in Peking which concentrates on the social sciences, while the Library of the Chinese Academy of Sciences concentrates on the natural sciences and technology. The Peking National Library includes former imperial collections dating back to the Southern Song dynasty, and includes some 220,000 rare and early books. It is also the national depository library, receiving one copy of all Chinese publications within three days of printing.

Besides exchanging with libraries abroad, and over 8,000 institutions throughout China, the Peking National Library supports a number of branch libraries and mobile libraries within Peking itself. The Shanghai City Library is also known to run over 2,000 'street' libraries. (Nunn, p. 53).

Nunn reports a total of 30 university libraries, with Peking University's collection of 2,020,000 volumes as the biggest.

At the bottom of this pyramid of libraries are the tiny picture-book stalls. Here the readers, mainly children, can for a few fen follow the exploits of the latest hero, or imbibe political lessons through 'real-life adventure' stories. These stalls, which have long been very popular with peasants and schoolchildren, have had their contents carefully scrutinized by the authorities on a number of occasions (SCMP 1102, 1955 and SCMP 2977, 1963).

Newspapers

From the point of view of mass moral-political education the newspapers are undoubtedly the most important medium. Total circulation is still small by the standards of the industrialized nations, reaching a total of 15 million in 1958 (U.S.A. is about 56 million). But newspapers are read to groups of workers and peasants; editorials and articles are carefully copied on to tens of thousands of wallboards; and national and local radio stations read them over the air.

Newspapers are published by such organizations as the Communist Party, the Communist Youth League, and the trade unions. The often-quoted *Guangming Ribao* (the *Bright Daily*) is the official organ of the Democratic League; the *Gongren Ribao* (*Worker's Daily*) is that of the All-China Federation of Trade Unions. The most important newspaper of all is the *Renmin Ribao* (*People's Daily*), official organ of the CC CCP and spokesman of the Government. Its editorials and special articles are reproduced in other newspapers throughout China and are widely discussed in political classes everywhere. Two formerly privately-owned Shanghai papers, the *Da Gong Bao* (*Impartial Daily*) and the *Xin Min Bao* (*New People's Paper*) continue to circulate. The *Jiefang Ribao* (*Liberation Daily*, Shanghai) was widely quoted during the early part of the Cultural Revolution, and should not be confused with the *Jiefang Jun Bao*, the Liberation Army Paper.

In addition to the big newspapers with a national, or provincial circulation there are large numbers of smaller, local newspapers. In 1959 the then Minister of Culture gave a figure of 1,884 for the total number of newspapers, (Yu, p. 108) but analyses made in Hong Kong suggest that a figure of about 800 would include all the widely circulated.

Not only are great efforts made to ensure that the newspapers are widely read and discussed, but it is also official policy to try and involve large numbers of people in writing to them. In a booklet entitled *How to write press and radio scripts*, published in Shanghai in 1963 for workers and peasants, Mao Ze-dong is quoted as saying: 'Our newspapers also must rely on everybody to manage them, rely on the great mass of the people to manage them, rely on the whole party to manage them, and we cannot only rely on a small number of people to manage them behind closed doors.' The booklet argues that everyone is able to and should write something for the news-papers. F. T. C. Yu quotes a much earlier book which makes the same point (Yu, p. 106). And the National Press Meeting in March 1950 issued a directive which stated that newspapers should 'pay the greatest attention to the handling of letters to the editor'. (Yu, p. 104).

An interesting insight into editorial methods is given by the following extract from the *Nongmin Bao* (*Farmers' Daily*, Shanxi (Shensi)):

It has been verified by our experience that only by depending upon correct propaganda policies can our task of uniting closely with the masses be lively, and that only by tying together the actual life and work of the masses with propaganda can our policies be convincing and effective. We have come to understand that peasants have the following habit in comprehension and understanding: they will not accept a theory or principle if it is not coupled with 'facts'; but they cannot see through the 'facts' if no 'reason' or 'theory' is given and therefore cannot raise their level of consciousness. To make newspaper articles appealing and convincing and to strengthen the effect of newspaper propaganda, there must be actual examples together with convincing arguments. (Yu, p. 107).

In the writer's experience this often remains an ideal, and the reality is a steady repetition of general slogans.

All major news stories are the work of the government-operated New China News Agency (NCNA, or Xin Hua She). With roots in the revolutionary past, it operated under its present name from 1937 onwards. Today it has a headquarters in Peking and offices in all the provincial capitals and major towns, as well as some thirty to forty offices overseas. It produces daily news bulletins in Chinese, and also in a number of foreign languages.

Periodicals

From available data it would seem that in spite of the scientific and industrial development which has taken place in China since 1949, the number of periodicals still remains below the peak figure in the mid-thirties (Nunn, p. 30). Nunn records a complaint of lack of space for the publication of scientific papers which reached the columns of the *People's Daily* in 1954, when there was only one periodical for each field. The position in the mid-sixties, with 150 science periodicals, is still unsatisfactory.

Because of export restrictions and other reasons the present position is difficult to estimate. Numerous changes in the number of publishing houses, the titles, and the frequency of publication of journals have taken place since 1949. At the second National People's Congress in 1959 a figure of 818 magazines with a circulation of 537,050,000 was given (Yu, p. 108). The *People's Daily* advertised 315 titles available by subscription through the Post Office in 1960. The Chinese Periodicals-International Holdings 1949–60 gives a figure of 310 titles for 1961, while the International Union List of Communist Chinese Serials lists 601 titles, the majority of them scientific.

Studies of available publication figures show, for March 1958, 19 journals with editions of over 100,000 and 139 journals with editions of less than 10,000. Between these two extremes journals were evenly spread, with a bias towards small editions (Nunn, p. 33). The 19 major periodicals were either directed at the youth, or were general or literary publications. The majority of the small-circulation periodicals were university publications or research journals.

Among the journals well-known to specialists abroad are *Hong Qi* (*Red Flag*), theoretical journal of the CC CCP, until mid-1968 available on subscription abroad, with a reported circulation of

1,363,276 in January 1965; *Xuexi* (*Study*), another party journal; *Zhexue Yanjiu* (*Philosophical Research*); with 26,023 copies in May 1963; *Jingji Yanjiu* (*Economic Research*); with 27,649 copies in December 1964; *Kexue Tongbao* (*Science Bulletin*); *Lishi Yanjiu* (*Historical Research*); and the *Wenyi Bao* (*Literary Gazette*).

Books

Social ownership of the publishing industry was completed, according to the *People's Daily*, in October 1957. At that time there were 97 publishing houses. Of these the following 7 were large, accounting for over half the publication output for the period 1954-7: the People's Press; the People's Education Press; the Cartographic Press; the People's Health Press; the Higher Education Press; the Engineering Industry Press; and the China Youth Press. Over half the houses published less than 6 per cent of the national gross output by value of publications. (Nunn, p. 16).

The number of titles published has first gone up from 12,153 in 1950 to 30,196 in 1956; then down again to 5,180 in 1964, and much lower during the Cultural Revolution of 1966.

Before 1949 the average edition was about 2,000 copies. Some idea of recent editions and prices can be seen from the following selection (*see following page*).

These figures should be compared with the population figures concerned, such as peasants, youth, or primary school teachers and administrators, bearing in mind the possibility of publication by other houses. Prices are only meaningful in relation to money available for spending on books, which is related both to earnings and spending habits. From the writer's limited observations these prices are still high for many potential customers, but are not considered high by many Chinese with whom the question was discussed. Yet another problem is durability of books. All those listed are well printed on strong, thin paper, but all have a paper or thin card cover. In the hands of busy workers and peasants they must have a rather short life.

Published titles are spread over a large number of areas. The strongest areas have been engineering and technology, and literature. Engineering and technology, and agriculture and animal husbandry showed almost a sixfold increase between 1954 and 1958,

Book	Publication date(s)	Edition(s) total	Price in fen*
Village Handbook	1964/2x.1966	600,000	96
Do you know? No. 5 (for peasants)	2x 1965	50,000	29
100,000 Whys, No. 9 (about biology)	1962/1965	130,000	47
Secondary School Physics text-book—translated from Russian	1961/1963	36,000	70
Static Electricity Experiments for Secondary School Teachers	1964	23,000	24
Peking Primary School language book, year 1, term 1	1963/1964	2,115,000	22
Experiences of Part-work Primary Schools—book for educationalists	1965	145,000	50
Lei Feng's Diary (popular hero)	1963/1965	2,631,600	30
Study in Struggle, Use in Struggle (pamphlet on Mao's thoughts)	1966	300,000	22
Ou-yang Hai—(novel about PLA hero)	1966	1,000,000	90

* one fen=1/100 yuan

Note : data on these books have been taken from the covers. It is possible that some of them have been published by other publishing houses, and therefore in greater numbers than is given.

while at the same time literature increased fourfold. In 1963 181 works of literature were published, as against 154 works in engineering and technology, and only 37 in agriculture. From what information can be obtained it would appear that the literature available on agriculture is grossly disproportionate to its size and importance. But one must also take into account that the level of literacy in this area is probably still considerably lower than in other areas of production.

Books specially published for children rose from 247 in 1954 to 882 in 1957, and then fell to 357 in 1963. There are two special children's publishing houses, but about half of the work is done in local publishing houses. (Nunn, pp. 23–5).

Picture books are published in editions ranging from 100,000 to 240,000, and large numbers of new titles appear each year.

As with other fields, textbook publishing reached a peak in 1958, when 1,355 titles were published. In 1963 this went down to 767 distributed as follows: kindergarten, 14; primary, 325; secondary, 296; agricultural secondary, 8; teacher training, 17; spare-time education, 106.

A great deal of work has gone into the production of material written in simple language for the rural areas. In 1956 818 million copies, or 58 per cent of the total New China Bookshop distribution went to the villages. (Nunn, p. 45).

Radio: the spoken word

The radio has been developed extensively as a means of education, primarily for moral-political ends, but also for the propagation of the standard language, and for scientific and technical information.

While China now manufactures its own radio receivers, and a number of different models are available in the city shops, these are still rare and expensive items to be found in rather few homes. Instead collective listening has been developed, loudspeakers of varying quality festooning trees and lamp posts on college campuses and in remote villages.

Technically the system used is simple. A number of loudspeakers are connected to a central point where there is a receiving set and a microphone. The system is operated by a monitor who can relay broadcasts from central or local stations, or make his own announcements through the microphone. In some places the apparatus may be very elaborate. Special organizations, like the foreign language institutes, have a battery of tape-recorders and pick-ups and well-trained technicians, and can relay quite elaborate programmes.

Pressure to develop this system began soon after the new government was formed. In April 1950 the Press Association's Bureau of Broadcasting, at that time in charge of broadcasting, issued 'Decisions Regarding the Establishment of Radio-Receiving Networks' (Yu, p. 125). These, it declared, should be set up in all government agencies, units of the PLA, and the various mass organizations. In September 1951 the Press Administration issued a directive jointly with the ACFTU, 'Regarding the Establishment of Radio Broad-

The moral-political educators

casting and Receiving Networks in all Factories, Mines and Enterprises in the Country'. This urged the setting up of networks in places with more than 300 workers, and suggested that 'in the dormitories of all factories, mines, and enterprises, the administrative staff members, union officers, and representatives of workers' families should work together to organize radio-receiving groups so that all workers and their families can constantly receive political and cultural education' (Yu, p. 126). All organizations were urged to make periodic reports of plans and progress to the ACFTU, to the Radio Broadcasting Bureau, and to the local people's broadcasting stations. Labour unions were directed to 'consider radio-receiving and broadcasting as the major task of the departments handling cultural and educational affairs.' (ibid, p. 126). All this affected the towns. Only in 1955 was attention turned to the villages. The National Conference of People's Representatives then voted that there should, by 1957, be 30,000 radio broadcasting and relay stations in the cities and villages. (ibid, p. 127). In December 1955 the third National Conference on Broadcasting Work, held in Peking, put forward plans for more than 900 line-broadcasting stations by 1956 with a total of some 500,000 loudspeakers, 80 per cent of them to be in the rural areas.

Careful attention has been given to the training of monitors. They are expected not only to handle the apparatus, select the programmes to be relayed, and handle bulletins of local news and information, but also to mobilize listeners, and co-operate in such activities as running local news-sheets, wall-newspapers and group meetings (Yu, p. 125). Various booklets are available to help them with their work. (e.g. *How to write news scripts and broadcast scripts*, Shanghai Education Press, 1963, 1964 and 1965).

The content of broadcast programmes obviously varies greatly from time to time and place to place. F. T. C. Yu reports that in 1951 the Home Service of the Peking station used 70 per cent of its time for political propaganda in the form of news and commentaries, while in 1955 the Central People's Broadcasting Station spent 60 per cent of its time on musical, literary, dramatic and scientific programmes. (ibid, pp. 130–1). A lot of time is devoted to describing model workers, peasants or soldiers, or model factories or farms. Programmes have included: 'Experience of setting up an agricultural co-op'; 'How agricultural mutual-aid teams challenge each

264

other in production races'; and a serialized version of the novel, *The Song of Ou-yang Hai*. After 1956 more attention was devoted to local broadcasting. The fourth National Conference of Broadcasters, held in Peking in July 1956, resolved that: 'while to relay certain programmes of the Central People's Broadcasting Station at specified hours is necessary, a more important task should be to strive to improve locally-originated programmes.'

Local programmes in some areas include work in more than one language. C. MacKerras, describing his visit to Inner Mongolia in 1966, writes:

> Though this commune is in Inner Mongolia, about four-fifths of the population are Han Chinese. There are also a few Manchu families, and the rest are Mongolian . . . Huhehot has two broadcasting stations, one of which uses Chinese, the other Mongolian. The communes relay programmes of news and music three times a day from both stations. Private wirelesses are well beyond the means of most of the peasants here and they listen to the radio through a public address system. (MacKerras and Hunter, p. 39).

In some cities there is television which directly helps local education but the proportion of the population affected is still minute.

The results of these education activities, carried out on a broad front through a number of agencies, are difficult to assess. The extent to which they will be successful in achieving their aims is difficult to predict. They represent, however, a determined effort on the part of the authorities to arouse among the masses an awareness of government policy and to encourage an acceptance of it. In the next chapter an analysis will be made of the background to the Cultural Revolution which was essentially aimed at radical rather than evolutionary change and was for the most part an attack on those who persisted in holding traditional attitudes towards education.

8

Students and the Cultural Revolution, 1966-1968

Why the students?

The students of the universities, colleges and secondary schools were the first to respond to the call 'to make revolution', and appear to have been the last to have settled down to the 'transformation' stage. Many of the more spectacular events of the past two years were of their making. Outside China the question has been widely asked: why the students?

In attempting to answer this question a number of factors should be considered. First, students in China have been deeply involved in political activity since the great upheaval of 4 May 1919, and have always held demonstrations at times of particular stress. But probably much more important: the students, as the future leaders in society, could not fail to become involved in a struggle concerning the nature of that leadership. Then, students are to a great extent uncommitted, and at the same time looking for a commitment, and can be roused by an ideal. Mao's group may have felt that they could best be spared from work to go about and stimulate the other sections of society. And perhaps other sections were less likely to respond in the desired way without the pressure of a student-led campaign.

Which events were consciously instigated, by whom, and on what basis, and which developed in the course of the struggle is impossible to determine at this stage.

Making revolution

The first phase of the struggle, which lasted until the autumn of 1966, might be regarded as a warming-up period in which forces were mobilized and gradually steered in the desired direction. It began slowly, with attacks on a play by Wu Han, the stepping up of political work in the PLA under the direction of Lin Biao, and the attack on three writers of a newspaper column, 'Notes from Three-family Village'. On 11 April the *People's Daily* carried a report of a CCP symposium at the Ministry of Higher Education admitting the failure of attempts to win over the majority of the intellectuals. On 7 May Mao Ze-dong was reported as saying that in addition to their main task of studying students should also 'criticize the bourgeoisie', and that education must be revolutionized. On 25 May the famous poster (*dazibao*) was put up in Peking University by Nie Yuan-zi, attacking the university president, Lu Ping, and demanding the right to put up posters and hold meetings. The text of this poster was broadcast on Peking Radio on 1 June, when the *People's Daily* wrote the editorial, 'Sweep Away all Monsters', spelling out the purpose of the Cultural Revolution.

During this first phase most organizations appear to have been controlled by opponents of Mao Ze-dong's policy, and these either tried to prevent the revolution from developing, or headed it off into attacks against old bourgeois scholars, or young critics of the bureaucracy. The Party sent work-teams into the universities and colleges to supervise the revolution, but in many cases a virtual reign of terror lasted from mid-June to the end of July. Victims were subjected to lengthy 'struggle meetings', threatened, imprisoned, and sometimes beaten.

The second phase saw the beginnings of a clarification of the issues, and the spreading out of the struggle from Peking, and from the schools and colleges to the factories, and to some extent to the farms. The reign of terror was denounced by Mao Ze-dong in a *dazibao* on 5 August, and on the 8 August the CC CCP '16 points' of guidance on the Cultural Revolution were published. The Red Guards emerged and a series of eight huge rallies were held in Peking, involving a total of some 11 million young people from all over China.

Mao's group used the *People's Daily*, together with *Red Flag*, as key organizers of the struggle. During August the *People's Daily* supported the 'revolutionary students' as a 'shock force' whose general direction, if not every action, was correct. At the same time it warned against violence, and urged youth to learn from the PLA.

By the third rally on 15 September workers in the factories were beginning to be aroused and Zhou En-lai had to warn Red Guards and students not to go to the factories and offices, whose workers were to make revolution without disrupting production. (*Peking Review*, 23 September 1966).

The third phase began about the end of January 1967 and lasted until September 1968. It was a period of struggle between various groups, flaring up into violence from time to time in one area or another. When one group took over the running of an organization or area other groups would dispute its authority. Throughout, Mao's group and the *People's Daily* worked to try and bring together a majority against 'the small handful within the Party' who could be proved to be 'taking the capitalist road'. From February 1967 attempts were made to sort out good from bad cadres, and the practice of throwing out all former cadres was condemned. 'Cadres must be treated carefully' warned *Red Flag* (no. 4, 1967). At the same time the call was for three-in-one alliances, to involve representatives of the PLA, the revolutionary cadres, and the masses. But it was not until 7 September 1968 that the *People's Daily* could announce that all provinces, municipalities and autonomous regions had formed such Revolutionary Committees.

Teaching had stopped in all schools and colleges by the summer of 1966. During the spring and summer of 1967 an attempt was made to reopen the schools, and the PLA, who had been going around with those students who were organized in Red Guard groups to keep order, began taking classes in the reading of Mao's *Quotations*. On 7 March 1967 the *People's Daily* called for the reopening of classes in all primary and secondary schools, but this was largely ignored, and the call had to be repeated again in the following November.

In the various third level institutions a veritable state of civil war reigned, with rival Red Guard organizations fighting each other with brush and paper, rival loudspeaker circuits, and sometimes more deadly weapons. In March 1968, after other attempts to win unity had failed, Mao Ze-dong sent the PLA in yet again, this time with clear instructions to enforce unity. By the end of March the press was already claiming results.

However, in spite of these measures and the claimed successes, order was not fully restored in the schools, and in August an article in *Red Flag* announced that on Chairman Mao's directive workers' propaganda teams were to be sent into the schools to assist them to fulfil 'the tasks of struggle-criticism-transformation' (*Red Flag*, no. 2, 1968). In the villages the same task was to be performed by teams composed of poor and lower-middle peasants, 'the most reliable ally of the working class' (*Peking Review*, 30 August 1968). Not only were these teams to restore order and help to establish revolutionary committees in the schools, but they were to remain there permanently to ensure that in the future schools should be run in the interests of the workers and poor and lower-middle peasants.

Criticizing the old

From time to time throughout the Cultural Revolution criticisms of the old education system have been published. While the details have varied, all have centered on the accusation that it discriminated against children of workers and poorer peasants, and trained students to become specialists divorced from the great majority of the people. This was first said in two letters sent from secondary schools in Peking to the CC CCP in June 1966 (*Peking Review*, 24 June 1966). Fervently denouncing 'seeking personal fame, gain and position', the letter demanded an end to the current system of college entrance examinations and the choosing of students after a period of productive work and the granting of some form of 'ideological diploma' by the 'workers, peasants and soldiers'.

In November 1967 the NCNA published an article in which they listed the 'crimes of the bourgeois educational system'. It separated teaching from productive work; separated education from the working people and from class struggle in society; the educational system was too long; the curriculum was over-loaded, and there was too much homework; education produced 'increasing bookishness resulting from studying from concept to concept; and the system put marks in command and book-teaching without character-building took place'.

In December 1967 the *People's Daily* published an article by the Revolutionary Rebel Command Headquarters of the Shandong (Shantung) Provincial Department of Education criticizing the 'little treasure pagoda' system of 'revisionist education'. They quoted a directive of December 1962 to all provinces and municipalities in which they had been asked to select key primary and secondary schools on which they were to devote a higher proportion of their resources. In Shandong (Shantung) this had resulted in the selection of 235 secondary (25 per cent of the full-time) and 1,472 primary (31 per cent of the full-time) schools, and within this group the further selection as 'tiptop schools' of 36 secondary and 162 primary schools. These 'little treasure pagoda' schools had nine and a half months of schooling a year, with one month of productive work in the primary stage, and nine months' schooling with half a month productive work in the secondary stage. The remaining schools had a shorter year, longer productive work and they also did not study a foreign language which meant that their students were unable to enter the better universities. (SCMP 4100, 1967).

The same issue of the *People's Daily* carried an article by the Revolutionary Committee of the China Medical University in which they linked the eight-year medical courses with the 'little treasure pagoda' system. This led to such a high degree of specialization and dependence on the use of expensive equipment that the doctors were quite useless when out on their own in factory or rural clinics.

In January 1968 (SCMP 4109, 1968) two members of the Jing-gangshan Corps of Qinghua University took up the question of the length of courses. They cited the example of the China Medical University, and went on to complain of similar lengthening of their own courses. These had first been increased from 4 to 5 years, and later from 5 to 6 years. They criticized plans made in 1964 to have a 'three-stage rocket' course, which would link classes in the affiliated secondary school with the regular university course and then to the graduate school.

The Revolutionary Joint General Command of the Central Education and Scientific Research Institute attacked the educational system on the grounds that it had just been taken over, with its Japanese and American roots, and that it belittled physical labour and despised practice (*People's Daily*, 9 January 1968).

An article by the Proletarian Revolutionaries of the Science and Technical Commission for National Defence attacking the length of courses spoke of the 'poisonous excuse' that the quality of education should be raised, and that therefore the number of years should depend on the requirements of the particular course. They criticized the view that 'the first and foremost task of education was to impart knowledge', and questioned the meaning of the term quality. What sort of quality was it, they asked, when students complained about having to work hard when they left college and took a job? They went on to criticize the heavy timetable and quoted Lenin's comment about 'encumbering young people's minds with an immense amount of knowledge, nine-tenths of which is useless and one-tenth distorted'. They also quoted with approval Mao's saying that 'reading is learning, but application is also learning, and the more important kind of learning at that.' (SCMP 4109, 1968).

In at least some institutions a great deal of time was spent on discussing education. The Peking Agricultural Institute, which resumed classes on 21 October 1967, held 80 criticism meetings in one month to 'denounce the old education system' and in the course of these put forward 'several dozen tentative plans' for a new one. (SCMP 4071, 1967).

Towards a 'transformation'

During 1968 the number of articles describing changes made in schools, or proposals for changes, greatly increased. Many were in the form of investigations by outside reporters, published in *Red Flag* with a note from the Editor drawing attention to particular problems, or to a solution which might be tried elsewhere. The effort being made to involve as many people as possible in working out solutions is shown by an article in the *Shanghai Wenhuibao* (SCMP 4145, 1968). Attacking students who loitered about instead of returning to classes, it said: 'looking up with outstretched hands, waiting for the Party CC unified regulations, or waiting to share the experience of other schools without making one's own effort—this is by no means a style of the revolutionaries, but is the attitude of a beggar'.

Administration

The exact form which the administration of schools by the workers and poor and lower-middle peasants will take will probably not be decided for some time. In the Shuiyuan Commune in Liaoning Province a committee was formed in each school consisting of representatives of the peasants, teachers and students. Working under the leadership of the commune or production brigade revolutionary committee, the new committees took over powers formerly exercised by the school heads.

The most far-reaching change proposed was that effected in Tongji (civil engineering) University, Shanghai in November 1967. The university was reorganized into the May 7th Commune. Two hundred and twenty teachers and students from Tongji joined 30 designers from the East China Designing Institute of Industrial Building and three engineering teams of 900 men from the Shanghai Municipal Building Construction Bureau (SCMP 4195, 1968). The former departments and teaching research groups were replaced by three new units: the tuitional unit, the designing unit and the building unit. Representatives from each unit were to make up a number of committees which would each control a number of classes. (*Peking Review*, 17 November 1967).

Proletarian schools

Much of the criticism has been concerned with either discrimination against the sons and daughters of workers and the poorer peasants, or with inculcating ideas and attitudes which belong to another class. To alter this situation proposals have been made in three areas: selection and examinations; shortening the courses; and providing local schools.

The suggestion first made by the Peking No. 1 Girls' High School that college entrance examinations should be replaced by some form of 'ideological diploma' granted after a period of productive work has been taken up by others, though the exact form has still not even been proposed.

In November 1967 the Peking Teachers' Training Institute put forward a number of proposals (SCMP 4066, 1967, and *Peking Review*, 17 November 1967). They suggested that the former system of entrance examinations for higher education should be abolished, and that in future a method 'combining recommendations and selection' should be used in its place. 'Young people who are good both politically and scholastically should be selected from among the graduating students and from among the workers, peasants and soldiers for admittance to schools of a higher grade.' No further details were given and it is not at all clear how they envisage dealing with the pressure of good applicants on a restricted number of places.

The question of examinations other than selection examinations was also dealt with by the Institute. They stated baldly that 'examinations are aimed to promote study', and went on to assert that they should test ability to reason rather than memory. They advocated that examinations should be few, and never given as a surprise. In some unspecified subjects they suggested that they might be done away with altogether. They suggested that when necessary they could take various forms: students might be given a choice of questions; they might be allowed to use textbooks, notes and other materials during the examination; or they might be examined while carrying out some kind of practical work.

None of these suggestions are new for China, and it is surprising that no word has come from those colleges where this type of examination has been tried out in the past. Or if it has, it has not been published in the *People's Daily*. Perhaps it had been tried out under the auspices of 'bourgeois authorities'! I. C. Y. Hsu, talking about higher education in the period 1949–61, described how in some colleges teachers went over the scope and essential points of the subject before the examination, and that in many cases students suggested and finally vetted the questions. The students afterwards graded their own papers on the basis of model answers provided by the teacher, who might also grade a few papers as examples. Final grades were settled by class discussion in which a vote was taken, with majority rule applying. In other cases the class divided into groups and exchanged papers before marking. (Hsu, 1964). Belyayev describes how in the N.E. Polytechnical Institute written examinations were evaluated by group discussion among the students before a final grading by the teacher. He also said that evaluation was done by a combination of the Party organization, the teachers and the students, and that it took into account the student's ability to solve specific production problems, his level of theoretical knowledge, and his political consciousness. (Belyayev, JPRS 1176).

Decisions to reduce the length of courses have already been taken. Tongji, May 7th Commune has reduced its course from between 5 and 6 years to 3 years, and Shuiyuan Commune schools decided to reduce the primary course by one year, and the secondary by 2 years. These reductions must be seen together with the accompanying changes in the content of the teaching. Zhou En-lai emphasized their purpose when he told a group of teachers and students from part-work schools that the longer students remained at school the more alienated they became (SCMP 4193, 1968).

The effect of providing more local schools was brought out in the reports on the Shuiyuan Commune, and the Aihui Commune in Heilongjiang (Heilongkiang). The former said: 'As all students live at home, this cuts down on costs for school buildings and the poor and lower-middle peasant can also afford to let their children study in such schools' (*Peking Review*, 27 September 1968). The latter described adding junior high school classes to the village primary school, together with exemption from school fees and special subsidies as a means to the same end (*Peking Review*, 8 November 1968).

The role of labour

Proposals for combining education with productive labour have so far differed in a predictable fashion. Tongji University, where studies concern the practical problem of building, did not find it difficult to propose spending a large part of the course in work on building sites. In the first year it proposed spending half the time, and in the second, two-thirds of the time, in each case linking theoretical work closely with work done on site. The final year was to be spent on more specialized studies, and no fixed proportion of time has been allotted to productive work.

The schools in Aihui Commune, Heilongjiang (Heilongkiang), did 39 days' farm work as members of the ordinary production teams during the first six months of 1968. Under the new poor peasant management they are described as 'production teams and centres for scientific experiments as well as schools' (*Peking Review*, 8 November 1968). It is intended to teach basic farming skills in addition to other subjects, but no indication of time allocation is given.

Red Flag (no. 4, 1968) carried an article on the part-work secondary school of the Wukou Tea Plantation, Jiangxi (Kiangsi) Province, started in 1965. It described how the teaching was closely related to the productive work done in the gardens. Classroom lessons had been reduced to a minimum, and studies included the surveying and laying out of tea gardens, designing of processing workshops and techniques of cultivating and transplanting tea bushes.

The teachers

Something of the suffering and difficulties which a large number of the teachers have undergone during the Cultural Revolution was revealed in an article in the *People's Daily* (SCMP 4063, 1967). It admitted that the poor relationship between teachers and pupils was a big obstacle to restarting classes. 'At first, most of the teachers were unwilling to teach classes. Some of them went reluctantly to teach the classes but could not get along well with the students. Some others asked to be transferred to another trade and to other posts. Some students despised their teachers and reproached them as being "backward and conservative" '. In their November call to resume classes, the *People's Daily* said that the majority of the teachers were 'good and comparatively good' and should be allowed to work provided 'they know and correct their mistakes.' (SCMP 4071, 1967). In December the paper warned that 'revolutionary teachers who have not yet successfully reformed their bourgeois world outlook' should not be struggled against, but should be helped to change gradually in the course of work. The same point was taken up by the editor of *Red Flag* in introducing the report on the Shanghai Institute of Mechanical Engineering. He said:

Those who are really impossible, that is, the die-hard capitalist roaders and bourgeois technical authorities who have incurred the extreme wrath of the masses and therefore must be overthrown, are very few in number. *Even they should be given a way out.* To do otherwise is not the policy of the proletariat. The above-mentioned policies should be applied to both new and old intellectuals, *whether working in the arts or sciences.* (*Peking Review*, 13 September 1968. Emphasis added.)

A number of articles suggest that in the future the size of staffs will be cut and many more teachers will work on a part-time basis, especially in the field of technology. The Peking Forestry Institute report said: 'Reorganization of the teaching research groups and tuition on the basis of specialized company makes it possible to greatly reduce the number of teachers' (*Peking Review*, 17 November 1967). Reporting on changes at the Shanghai Institute of Mechanical Engineering, *Red Flag* reported that workers would in future give lectures, and that 'the great majority [of teachers] should be part-time' (*Peking Review*, 13 September 1968).

Schools on the Aihui Commune selected ten young people of poor and lower-middle peasant origin who had worked on the land for at least a year or two to be teachers. Twenty other similar peasants were invited to become part-time teachers. Old poor peasants gave talks on class struggle; cadres gave lectures on politics; experienced peasants took classes in farming techniques and farm machinery; book-keepers taught mathematics; and health workers taught simple hygiene. (*Peking Review*, 8 November 1968).

Employment

In 1968, as the situation stabilized, the old problem of persuading graduating students from the city secondary schools to accept jobs in the rural areas reappeared. The newspapers again carried articles extolling the virtues of 'integrating with the masses' and 'serving the people' by going to the 'mountains and frontier regions'. In January 1968 the *Wenhuibao* carried such an article, attacking 'the feudal idea that "one goes to school to become a government official" ' (SCMP 4207, 1968).

The major effort is put into persuasion, including conferences like that held in Shanghai in May, attended by 2,000 representatives from 500 secondary schools (SCMP 4207, 1968). But, as a *Wenhuibao* article advising Shanghai youth to return to Xinjiang (Sinkiang) pointed out, the CC CCP had issued a directive that no work permits were to be issued for those who refused to leave the cities after they had been given work elsewhere.

After the Cultural Revolution

1969 may well be a watershed in Chinese education, as the post-Cultural Revolution China settles down to working out the new school pattern. The extent of the changes and their duration will, of course, depend on the degree to which Mao Ze-dong and his supporters are able to consolidate and maintain their political control over the country. The development of the economy will certainly give rise to further problems, and the only certainty is that there will be further changes.

In looking back over the events in the field of education during the past twenty years one thing is clear. The Chinese Communist Party had no detailed scheme which they tried to force through by administrative means. On the contrary, policy attempted to meet immediate needs, and considerable freedom was allowed for experiment. Indeed it is clear that Mao himself, as in the field of politics, is certain only about general aims. Their achievement must be worked out in accordance with 'the mass line', taking into account specific and local needs and conditions. Mao's attempt during 1955–7 to speed up changes in education was defeated during the economic difficulties of 1959–61. 1966 saw the beginning of a more determined effort to find ways of putting his aims into practice.

The most important and controversial area of change will continue to be the part-work principle, and the relationship between theoretical studies and practice. Widely politically divergent groups in China have come to accept part-work schools as the only way to make schooling universal, but they have done so on economic grounds. Mao's argument that productive work is morally beneficial has won fewer adherents, and his ideas on practice as the only road to rational knowledge are probably only accepted in the obvious fields like engineering, where they had always been implemented to some extent. Nevertheless problems such as the relevance of what was taught, methods of selection, and employment prospects have produced a climate of opinion in which solutions along Maoist lines may find widespread support.

Professional objections to the extension of part-work schooling are that it will lead to a lowering of standards and so, until now, it has largely been confined to areas not covered by the full-time school system. But the problem is very complex. Experience outside China has shown that motivation can radically affect the productivity of learning. If China's economy develops and there is a general atmosphere of optimism and progress, the result could be a broadening and deepening of knowledge rather than its limitation.

Perhaps the most difficult problem is that of providing a universal schooling which will on the one hand arouse positive social attitudes in the students, a desire to broaden their general understanding and acquire technical skills, but which will not, on the other hand, stimulate in them desires which Chinese society at this stage cannot satisfy. There is a contradiction here between the need for trained people in order to make technical progress, and the hampering of such progress which can result from trained people being unable to find suitable employment. Over the past twenty years China's secondary schools have continued to produce potential 'officials'. The campaigns to send graduates of the urban schools to work in the rural areas were attempts to cure, when the real problem was one of prevention. But it remains to be proved whether revision of subject-content, and further doses of productive labour will be effective medicines. While a gap in living standards, both physical and cultural, between town and village remains it seems utopian to expect education to 'remould people's thinking'.

It is at the third level of education that the technical-administrative class is trained. Mao's aim of creating a new type of worker-intellectual has so far failed. Changes there have been, but the results have fallen short of the aim, and the practice of the sixties was along traditional elitist lines. The proposals by Mao's supporters for new methods of selection could, if successful, only make a small difference, as already a large number of students come from worker and peasant families. What is vital is the education provided. As for the selection process itself, can a method be devised which will really test social attitudes, or character accurately, and not just the conformist façade?

Changes in the content of third level education are likely to be most drastic in the humanities. Mao has remained characteristically cautious, only hinting in his July 1968 directive when he said: 'It is still necessary to have universities; here I refer mainly to colleges of science and engineering.' (*Peking Review*, 31, 2 August 1968). But it is clear that subjects which have no obvious justification in the world of corn and cotton will come under even stronger pressures than they have in the past, and some subjects may be discontinued at least for the time being.

At the postgraduate level of study the working out of a successful policy in line with Mao's aims promises to be a difficult job. In the training of high-level specialists much depends on their having time to think, on the stimulus of like minds, and on the concentration of physical resources. Yet with the exception of a few fields like nuclear weapons, Mao's policy would seem to be to disperse specialists and resources in an attempt to raise the general level. In the past specialists have spent a considerable part of the time in meetings, or doing administrative work. It remains to be seen whether the policy of simpler administration which Mao advocates will result in more time for productive thinking. It will also be interesting to see how Mao's supporters tackle the problem of keeping specialists and workers socially united. To take an extreme example, can the moral-social benefit of a surgeon taking part in such activities as sweeping the wards, or tending the boilers, justify possible loss of skill, and the failure to use his special talents to the maximum? It is clear that there is much confusion on this question at the present time.

Underlying all these problems is the basic conception of education as primarily moral-political, concerned with human attitudes and ends rather than techniques. This it will remain so long as the ideas of Mao Ze-dong continue to dominate Chinese society, and probably longer, as this is essentially a traditional Chinese concept. The values Mao stresses are deeply rooted in China's past, but must operate in a social-economic context very different from that of Confucian China. Peasant values of hard work and frugal living are to be linked with co-operation and the non-acquisitive outlook of the traditional literati. Mao's *Thoughts* are to teach this, together with a form of scientific method opposed alike to traditional village superstitions and patriarchal authority. How far mass political studies will really contribute to these ends and how far they will remain a shallow ritual remains to be seen. If taken seriously the admonitions to think for oneself and be bold in action might indeed become a 'spiritual atom bomb' whose explosion would far surpass that of the recent Cultural Revolution.

Bibliography

Books

ANALECTS, see LEGGE, JAMES. *The Chinese Classics*, vol. I.

BA JIN (PA CHIN). *The Family*. Peking, Foreign Languages Press, 1964.

BARENDSEN, R. D., *Half-Work Half-Study Schools in Communist China : Recent Experiments with Self-Supporting Educational Institutions*, Washington DC: Bulletin no. F.55. 214. OE 14100, Government Printing Office, 1964.

BARNETT, A. D., *Cadres, Bureaucracy, and Political Power in Communist China*, New York: Columbia University Press, 1967.

BIGGERSTAFF, K., *The Earliest Modern Government Schools in China*, New York: Cornell University Press, 1961.

BODDE, Derk, *Peking Diary*, Jonathan Cape, 1951.

——, *See* FUNG, Yu-lan.

BRANDT, C., SCHWARTZ, B. and FAIRBANK, J. K., *A Documentary History of Chinese Communism*, Cambridge, Mass: Harvard University Press, 1952.

BUNGE, M., *Causality : The Place of the Causal Principle in Modern Science*, Cleveland, Ohio: the World Publishing Company, 1959.

CARROLL, JOHN B., *The Study of Language : A Survey of Linguistics and Related Disciplines in America*, Cambridge, Mass: Harvard University Press, 1963.

CHAI, Ch'u and CHAI, Winberg, ed., *see* LEGGE, James, *Li chi, Book of Rites*.

CHAN, W. T., *Religious Trends in Modern China*, New York: Columbia University Press, 1953.

——, *A Source Book in Chinese Philosophy*, Oxford University Press, 1963.

——, tr., *Reflections on Things at Hand : The Neo-Confucian Anthology compiled by Chu Hsi and Lu Tsu-ch?ien*, New York and London: Columbia University Press, 1967.

CHEN, Theodore H. E., *The Chinese Communist Regime*, New York: Praeger, 1967.

——, *Teacher Training in Communist China*—Studies in Comparative Education Series, no. OE.14058, Washington DC: United States Office of Education, 1960.

CHIN, C. M., *The Song of Ou-yang Hai*, Peking: Foreign Languages Press, 1966.

CHOW, T. T., *The May Fourth Movement*, Cambridge, Mass: Harvard University Press, 1960.

Bibliography

COMPTON, Boyd, *Mao's China: Party Reform Documents, 1942–44*, Washington, DC: Washington University Press, 1952.

CROOK, D. and CROOK, I., *The First Years of Yangyi Commune*, Routledge & Kegan Paul, 1965; New York, Humanities Press, 1966.

DA XUE, *see* LEGGE, James, *The Chinese Classics*, vol. II.

DAVIDSON, Basil, *Daybreak in China*, Jonathan Cape, 1953.

——, *Old Africa Rediscovered*, Gollancz, 1959.

DAWSON, R., ed., *The Legacy of China*, Clarendon Press, 1964.

DE BARY, W. T., ed., *Sources of Chinese Tradition*, (vols. I & II.) New York: Columbia University Press, 1960.

DE FRANCIS, John, *Nationalism and Language Reform in China*, Princeton, N.J: Princeton University Press, 1950.

Doctrine of the Mean, see LEGGE, James, *The Chinese Classics*, vol. I.

DOOLIN, D. J., *Communist China: The Politics of Student Opposition*, Stanford: Hoover Institution Studies, 1964.

Economic Profile of Mainland China, An, see United States Congress, Joint Economic Committee.

ENGELS, Frederick, *Ludwig Feuerbach and the Outcome of Classical German Philosophy*, Lawrence & Wishart, 1963 (1888).

——, *Dialectics of Nature*, Moscow: Foreign Languages Publishing House, 1954 (1935).

——, *Anti-Duhring: Herr Eugen Duhring's Revolution in Science*, Moscow: Foreign Languages Publishing House, 1962 (1894).

——, *see* MARX, Karl and ENGELS, Frederick.

EVANS, Humphrey, *see* TUNG chi-ping and EVANS, Humphrey, *The Thought Revolution*.

FAIRBANK, J. K., *see* BRANDT, C. SCHWARTZ, B. and FAIRBANK, J. K., *A Documentary History of Chinese Communism*.

——, *see* TENG Ssu-yu and FAIRBANK, John K., *China's Response to the West*.

FORREST, R. A. D., *The Chinese Language*, Faber & Faber, 1965; New York: Barnes & Noble, 1965.

FRASER, Stewart, *Chinese Communist Education: Records of the First Decade*, New York: John Wiley & Sons, 1965 (bibliography).

——, ed., *Chinese Communist Education*, Nashville, Tenn: Vanderbilt University Press, 1964.

FREEDMAN, M., *Chinese Lineage and Society: Fukien & Kwangtung*, Athlone Press, 1966 (bibliography); New York, Humanities Press, 1966.

FUNG, Yu-lan, tr. BODDE, D., *A History of Chinese Philosophy, The Period of the Philosophers (from the beginnings to circa 100 B.C.)*. George Allen & Unwin, 1937.

——, tr. HUGHES, E. R., *The Spirit of Chinese Philosophy*, Routledge & Kegan Paul, 1947.

Bibliography

FUNG, Yu-lan, ed. BODDE, D., *A Short History of Chinese Philosophy*, New York: Macmillan, 1938.

GALT, Howard S., *A History of Chinese Educational Institutions*, vol. I: *To the End of the Five Dynasties (A.D. 960)*, Arthur Probsthain, 1951.

GEORGE, A. L., *The Chinese Communist Army in Action*, New York: Columbia University Press, 1967.

GITTINGS, John, *The Role of the Chinese Army*, Oxford University Press, 1967.

Guide to New China, A., Peking: Foreign Languages Press, 1952.

Hanyu Keben, (in Chinese), Peking: Peking Language Institute, 1965.

HARPER, P., *Spare-Time Education for Workers in Communist China*, Washington DC: United States Department of Health, Education and Welfare, Office of Education, 1964.

HINTON, William, *Fanshen*, New York: Monthly Review Press, 1966.

HOOK, Sidney, *From Hegel to Marx*, Ann Arbor: University of Michigan, 1962.

HU, Chang-tu, *China, its People, its Society, its Culture*, New Haven: H.R.A.F. Press, 1960.

——, *Chinese Education under Communism*, New York: Teachers College, Columbia University, 1962 (Bibliography).

HU, Shih, *The Development of the Logical Method in Ancient China*, Shanghai: Oriental Book Company, 1927.

HUGHES, E. R., *Chinese Philosophy in Classical Times*, Dent & Sons, 1942.

——, *See* FUNG, Yu lan.

HUNTER, Neale, *see* MACKERRAS, Colin and HUNTER, Neale, *China Observed*.

JEN, Yu ti, *A Concise Geography of China*, Peking: Foreign Languages Press, 1964.

JENNER, Delia, *Letters from Peking*, Oxford University Press, 1967.

KRATOCHVIL, Paul, *The Chinese Language Today*, Hutchinson University Library, 1968.

LAU, D. C. tr. Lao Tzu: *Tao te ching*. Penguin Books, 1963.

LEGGE, James, *The Chinese Classics*, vol. I: *Confucian Analects, the Great Learning, and the Doctrine of the Mean*, Clarendon Press, 1893.

——, *The Chinese Classics*, vol. II: *The Works of Mencius*, Clarendon Press, 1895.

——, *The Sacred Books of the East*, Part II: *The Texts of Confucianism*, Clarendon Press, 1899, reprinted as: *The I ching*, New York: Dover Publications, 1963.

——, *Li chi: Book of Rites*, 2 vols, CHAI Ch'u and CHAI Winberg, ed., New York: University Books, 1967.

LENIN, V. I., *Materialism and Empirio Criticism* (English translation), New York: International Publishers, 1927.

Bibliography

LENIN, V. I., *Selected Works*, vol. IX: *New Economic Policy: Socialist Construction*, Lawrence & Wishart, 1937.

——, *The Essentials of Lenin in Two Volumes*, vol. I, Lawrence & Wishart, 1947.

——, *Collected Works*, vol. 38, Philosophical Notebooks (English translation), Moscow: Foreign Languages Publishing House, 1961.

Li Ji, See LEGGE, James, *Li chi*.

LIFTON, R. J., *Thought Reform and the Psychology of Totalism*, New York, Norton, 1961.

LIU, Shao-chi, *How to be a Good Communist*, Peking: Foreign Languages Press, 1964.

——, *On the Party*, Peking: Foreign Languages Press, 1951.

LIU, William T., ed., *Chinese Society under Communism*, New York: John Wiley, 1967.

LU Ting-yi, *Education must be combined with Productive Labour*, Peking: Foreign Languages Press, 1958.

MACFARQUHAR, R., *The Hundred Flowers*, Stevens, 1960.

MACKERRAS, Colin and HUNTER, Neale, *China Observed*, Pall Mall Press, 1968.

MAO, Tse-tung, ed. *Socialist Upsurge in China's Countryside*, Peking: Foreign Languages Press, 1956.

——, *On the Correct Handling of Contradictions among the People*, Peking: Foreign Languages Press, 1957; San Francisco: China Books & Periodicals, 1960.

——, *Selected Works*, vols. 1–4, (English translation) of the Chinese edition, 1961), Peking: Foreign Languages Press, 1965.

——, *Quotations from Chairman Mao Tse-tung*, Peking: Foreign Languages Press, 1966*a*; San Francisco; China Books & Periodicals, 1966.

——, *Four Essays on Philosophy*, Peking: Foreign Languages Press, 1966*b*.

——, *Intervention à la Conference Nationale du Parti Communiste Chinois sur le Travail de Propagande* (12 March 1957), Peking: Foreign Languages Press, 1966*c*.

——, (in manuscript) *Remarks to a Visiting Teachers' Delegation*, copied from a wall-newssheet, Peking 1967.

MARX, Karl, *The Poverty of Philosophy*, Martin Lawrence, 1892.

——, *A Contribution to the Critique of Political Economy*, Calcutta: Bharati Library, 1904.

——, *Capital: A Critique of Political Economy*, New York: Modern Library, 1906.

——, *Critique of the Gotha Programme*, Lawrence & Wishart, 1933.

——, *Economic and Philosophic Manuscripts of 1844*, Lawrence & Wishart, 1959.

MARX, Karl and ENGELS, Frederick, *Selected Correspondence, 1846–1895*, Lawrence & Wishart, 1934.

——, *Karl Marx : Selected Works*, 2 vols., Lawrence & Wishart, 1942.

——, *The Holy Family or Critique of Critical Critique*, Lawrence and Wishart, 1957 (1845).

——, *The German Ideology*, Lawrence & Wishart, 1964.

Mencius, see LEGGE, James, *The Chinese Classics*, vol. II

MYRDAL, Jan, *Report from a Chinese Village*, W. Heinemann, 1965, (page references to Penguin edition, 1967); New York: Pantheon, 1965.

NEEDHAM, Joseph, *Science and Civilization in China*, vols. 1, 2 and 3, also vol. 4 pts. 1 and 2. Cambridge University Press, 1954–65 (Bibliography).

——, *The Past in China's Present*, New York: Far East Reporter (reprinted from *Arts and Sciences in China*).

NUNN, G. R., *Publishing in Mainland China : M.I.T. Report no. 4*, Cambridge, Mass: M.I.T. Press, 1966.

ORLEANS, Leo A., *Professional Manpower and Education in Communist China*, Washington: Government Printing Office, 1961.

SCHRAM, Stuart R., *The Political Thought of Mao Tse-tung*, New York: Frederick A. Praeger, 1963.

——, *Mao Tse-tung*, Penguin Books, 1966.

SCHURMANN, Franz, *Ideology and Organization in Communist China*, Berkeley and Los Angeles: University of California Press, 1966.

SCHWARTZ, Benjamin, *Chinese Communism and the Rise of Mao*, Cambridge, Mass: Harvard University Press, 1958.

——, *see* BRANDT, C., SCHWARTZ, B. and FAIRBANK, J. K., *A Documentary History of Chinese Communism*.

——, *In Search of Wealth and Power*, Cambridge, Mass: Harvard University Press, 1964.

SEWELL, William, *The Land and Life of China*, Cargate Press, 1933.

——, *I stayed in China*, Allen & Unwin, 1966; New York; ABC, 1966.

SNOW, Edgar, *Red Star over China*, New York: Grove, rev. ed. 1968.

TENG, Ssu-yu and FAIRBANK, John K., *China's Response to the West : A Documentary Survey, 1839–1923*, Cambridge, Mass: Harvard University Press, 1954.

TREGEAR, T. R., *A Geography of China*, Chicago: Aldine, 1968.

TSANG, Chiu-sam, *Society, Schools and Progress in China*, Pergamon Press, 1968.

TUNG Chi-ping and EVANS, Humphrey, *The Thought Revolution*, New York, Coward, 1966; Leslie Frewin, 1967.

UNITED NATIONS EDUCATIONAL, SCIENTIFIC and CULTURAL ORGANIZATION, (1) *World Survey of Primary Education*, Paris, 1958.

——, (2) *World Survey of Education, Secondary Education*, Paris, 1967.

Bibliography

UNESCO, (3) *World Survey of Education, Higher Education*, Paris, 1966.
——, (4) *Experts Working Group on International Standard Classification of Education*, ISCED/WG/5, Paris, 1968.
UNITED STATES CONGRESS, Joint Economic Committee, *An Economic Profile of Mainland China*, 2 vols, Washington DC: U.S. Government Printing Office, 1967.
WANG, Y. C., *Chinese Intellectuals and the West, 1872–1947*, Chapel Hill: University of North Carolina Press, 1966.
WATSON, Burton, tr. *Hsun Tzu : Basic Writings*, New York and London; Columbia University Press, 1963a.
——, tr. *Mo Tzu : Basic Writings*, New York and London: Columbia University Press, 1963b.
——, tr. *Chuang Tzu : Basic Writings*, New York and London: Columbia University Press, 1964a.
——, tr. *Han Fei Tzu : Basic Writings*, New York and London: Columbia University Press, 1964b.
WIEGER, Leo, *A History of the Religious Beliefs and Philosophical Opinions in China from the Beginning to the Present Time*, Peking: Hsien-hsien Press, 1927.
WILSON, J. T., *One Chinese Moon*, Michael Joseph, 1959.
WRIGHT, Arthur F., ed. *Studies in Chinese Thought*, Chicago: University of Chicago Press, 1953.
WU, Yun-to, *Son of the Working Class*, Peking: Foreign Languages Press, 1956.
XUNZI, *see* Watson, Burton, *tr., Hsun Tzu : Basic Writings*.
YEH Sheng tao, *Schoolmaster, Ni Huan-chih*, Peking: Foreign Languages Press, 1958.
YEN, Maria, *The Umbrella Garden*, Macmillan, 1954.
YU, F. T. C., *Mass Persuasion in Communist China*, Pall Mall Press, 1964; New York, Praeger, 1964.
Zhuang zi., *see* WATSON, Burton, *Chuang Tzu : Basic Writings*.

Articles

ABE, Munemitsu, 'Spare-Time Education in Communist China', *China Quarterly*, 8, October–December 1961, pp. 149–59.
ARENS, Richard, 'The Impact of Communism on Education in China, 1949–50', University of Chicago doctoral dissertation, 1952.
BELYAYEV, A. I., 'The Situation of Higher Education in the People's Republic of China', tr. *in JPRS* 1176 D.C. Regular Series, 19 February 1960
CHANG, Tung-sun, 'A Chinese Philosopher's Theory of Knowledge', *Yenching Journal of Social Studies*, vol. I, no. 2, January 1939.

285

Bibliography

CHEN, Theodore H., 'Elementary Education in Communist China', *China Quarterly*, 10, April–June 1962, pp. 98–122.

DOOLIN, Dennis J. and GOLAS, Peter J., 'On Contradiction in the Light of Mao Tse-tung's Essay on "Dialectical Materialism" ', *China Quarterly*, 19, July–September 1964, pp. 38–46.

FREEDMAN, M., 'The Family in China, Past and Present', *Pacific Affairs*, XXXIV, no. 4, winter 1961–2, pp. 323–36.

GOLAS, Peter J., *see* DOOLIN, Dennis J. and GOLAS, Peter J.

GOLDMAN, Rene, 'Peking University Today', *China Quarterly*, 7, July–September 1961, pp. 101–11.

HOLUBNYCHY, Vsevolod, 'Mao Tse-tung's Materialistic Dialectics', *China Quarterly*, 19, July–September 1964, pp. 3–37.

HSU, Immanuel C. Y., 'The Reorganization of Higher Education in Communist China, 1949–1961', *China Quarterly*, 19, July–September 1964, pp. 128–60.

KLEPIKOV, V., 'The New Curricula of the General Education Schools of China', Tr. Ina SCHLESINGER, *School and Society*, 13 February 1960, pp. 72–4.

——, 'Narodnoe obrazovanii v kitajskoj narodnoj respublike za 10 let', *Sovetskaja Pedagogika* (Moscow) 11, 1959, pp. 119–31.

KUNN, Joseph C., 'Higher Education: Some Problems of Selection and Enrolment', *China Quarterly*, 8, October–December 1961, pp. 135–48.

LAU, D. C., 'The Treatment of Opposites in *Lao Tzu*', *Bulletin of the School of Oriental and African Studies*, XXI (2), 1958, pp. 344–60.

LEE, Robert K., 'The Pao-chia System', *Papers on China—Harvard Seminars*, vol. III. Cambridge, Mass. Harvard University East Asian Regional Studies Seminars, May 1949, pp. 193–224.

MONOSZON, E. I., 'Narodnoe obrazovanie v kitajskoj narodnoj respublike', *Sovetskaya Pedagogika* (Moscow), 2, 1957, pp. 106–16.

MORRISON, Esther, 'A comparison of Kuomintang and Communist Modern History Textbooks', *Papers on China—Harvard seminars, vol.* VI, Cambridge Mass. Harvard University East Asian Regional Studies Seminars, March 1952, pp. 3–44.

P'AN MOU-YUAN, 'Great Accomplishments in Education Reforms at Amoy University in the Last Ten Years', tr. *in JPRS* 1165 DC. Regular Series, 12 February 1960.

POPOV, G. N., 'Higher Mining Engineering Education in the People's Republic of China', *in* Articles on Higher Education in Communist China, tr. *in JPRS* 1176, DC. Regular Series, 19 February 1960.

SHERIDAN, Mary, 'The Emulation of Heroes', *China Quarterly*, 33, January–March 1968, pp. 42–72.

TAO, H. C., 'China', *Education Handbook of the International Institute*, 1938.

Bibliography

ZURCHER, E., 'Buddhism in China', *see* DAWSON, Raymond ed. *The Legacy of China.*

Pamphlets

CR docs. (Cultural Revolution documents)

(1) *Carry the Great Proletarian Cultural Revolution through to the End*, Peking: Foreign Languages Press, 1966.
(2) *The Great Socialist Cultural Revolution in China*, vols. 1-10, Peking: Foreign Languages Press, 1966-7.
(3) *Decision of the Central Committee of the Chinese Communist Party concerning the Great Proletarian Cultural Revolution* (adopted on 8 August 1966), Peking: Foreign Languages Press, 1966.

NPC docs. (National Party/Congress documents)

(1) *Second Session of the Second National People's Congress of the People's Republic of China* (documents), Peking: Foreign Languages Press, 1960.
(2) *Labour Laws and Regulations of the People's Republic of China*, Peking: Foreign Languages Press, 1956.
(3) *The Constitution of the Communist Party of China, adopted by the Eighth National Congress of the Communist Party of China*, 26 September 1956, Peking: Foreign Languages Press, 1965.
(4) *The Constitution of the Communist Party of China, adopted by the Seventh National Party Congress of the Communist Party of China*, 11 June, 1945, *in* LIU Shao chi, *On the Party*, Peking: Foreign Languages Press, 1950.
(5) *Training Successors for the Revolution is the Party's Strategic Task*, Peking: Foreign Languages Press, 1965.
(6) Li Fu chun, *Report on the First Five Year Plan for Development of the National Economy of the People's Republic of China in 1953-1957*, Peking: Foreign Languages Press, 1955.

Further reading

China's history & Chinese philosophy

For the student who wants an outline of events with maps and references for further exploration the 77 pages of 'historical introduction' in Needham's *Science & Civilization in China*, vol. I (Cambridge University Press, 1954) make a good start. Good introductory essays on literature, art, government and other subjects, including China's relationship with the outside world, can be found in *The Legacy of China*, edited by R. Dawson (Oxford University Press, 1964). The tradition is probably best explored under the guidance of *Sources of the Chinese Tradition* (2 vols, Columbia University Press, 1960) compiled by W. T. De Bary, W. T. Chan and Burton Watson. This has useful short introductions to its translations of philosophical and political extracts and a chronological table.

Sociology, politics and economics

Here the best beginning is probably the collection of writings made by F. Schurmann and Orville Schell, *China Readings*, 1, 2, and 3 (Penguin Books, 1967). They cover the period 1644–1966 and can be dipped into as need and interest dictate.

F. Schurmann's *Ideology and Organization in Communist China* (University of California Press, 1966) is a long and valuable study of such questions as government, management of industry, and city and village organization.

For official data and various estimates the most concentrated source is probably *An Economic Profile of Mainland China* prepared for the Joint Economic Committee of Congress of the U.S. in 1967 (U.S. Government Printing Office, Washington). A. Donnithorne discusses problems in *China's Economic System* (Allen & Unwin, 1967).

China's geography

T. R. Tregear's *Geography of China* (University of London Press, 1965) provides invaluable information on physical geography, historical geography, economic and social geography and regional geography. It has good maps, tables of data and bibliography and index.

China in Maps edited by H. Fullard (G. Philip & Son, 1968) conveys an enormous amount of information in 25 well designed pages, and is probably the cheapest and easiest reference book. It includes historical maps, agricultural maps, and mineral and industrial data.

Further reading

For the student of Chinese history the new edition of Herrmann's *Historical Atlas of China* (Edinburgh University Press, 1966) is an attractive aid.

The Chinese language

The best account is *The Chinese Language Today* by P. Kratochvil (Hutchinson University Library, 1968), but the reader must be prepared to use the glossary of linguistic terms provided, or to skip sentences on first reading. Related languages and the history of the language are discussed in *The Chinese Language* by R. A. D. Forrest (Faber & Faber, 1965).

For learning Chinese the series by J. de Francis (Yale University Press) is widely used and has recordings on tape.

Life in contemporary China

In this area the reader is faced with greater problems of bias than in any other, and one must always be aware of the background of the writer. The traveller's tale, however interesting and apparently informative, often tells more about the writer than his subject. Also visitors to any country are told what the host thinks they want to hear: horror stories or sunshine.

Bearing this in mind the selection is endless. The writer particularly likes J. Myrdal's *Report from a Chinese Village* (Penguin Books, 1967) and C. MacKerras and N. Hunter's *China Observed* (Sphere Books, 1968).

For a discussion of the Cultural Revolution of 1966 the best book to appear so far is *Chinese Communism in Crisis* by Jack Gray and Patrick Cavendish (Pall Mall Press, 1968). It contains articles on the background and important documents. Joan Robinson's *The Cultural Revolution in China* (Penguin, 1969) is useful. For a journalist's account see *The Red Guard* by Hans Granquist (Pall Mall Press, 1967).

China's education system

Chang-tu Hu provides an interesting essay on tradition and change, and a short bibliography in his *Chinese Education Under Communism* (Columbia University, 1962), which is mainly a collection of seminal documents. Stewart E. Fraser, in a bigger collection of translations, *Chinese Communist Education—records of the first decade* (John Wiley, 1965) has a splendid bibliography which is classified according to subject. His book is an essential tool. See also his *Education and Communism in China : An Anthology of Commentary and Documents*, (Pall Mall, 1969).

For a discussion of the period from the Zhou to the 5 Dynasties, including detailed notes on the classical sources, and a discussion of educational aims, H. S. Galt's *A History of Chinese Educational Institutions* (A. Probsthain, 1951) cannot be left unread.

Chiu-Sam Tsang, in *Society, Schools and Progress in China* gives a Chinese view of the period covered in the present work.

Chronological table

The items included in this table have either been mentioned in the text, or are especially important in Chinese or world history.

The student may like to consult other tables in de Bary, W. T. Chan, (1963), Fung Yu-lan (1937, 1948), T. T. Chow, and J. Ch'en. Detailed dynastic tables appear in Needham (vols. 1-4).

Dynasty

2,000 B.C.
  XIA

c. 1,520
  YIN or
  SHANG

c. 1,030
  ZHOU
  (Xi'an)
  722-480

                    511-c. 233
  Spring & Autumn '*100 Philosophers*'
  Period
                    Confucius (551-479)
  480-221   Mencius (372—289?)
  Warring States   Mozi (c. 479—c. 381)
  Period   Laozi (?)
                    Zhuangzi (369?-286?)
                    Hui Shi (380-305)
                    Gong-sun Long (b. 380)
                    Xun zi (c. 298-238)
                    Shang Yang (d. 338)
                    Han Fei zi (d. 233)

                    1st unification
                    Li Ji written (?)

211
  QIN   Great Wall built
                    Yi Jing appendices (?)

202
  Former
  HAN   New text school:
  (Xi'an)   Dong Zhong-shu
         (179?–104)
      136 Confucianism made orthodox—
        doctors appointed for 15 classics
      124 More officials selected by written
        examinations
       90 Si-ma Qian's Records of the Historian
        Old text school:
        Yang Xiong
        (53 B.C. A.D. 18)

A.D. 25
  Later   c. 65 First reference to Buddhism in China
  HAN   Earliest known stern-post rudder
  (Loyang) 105 Invention of paper recorded
       175 5 classics and the *Analects* engraved in stone

220
  3 KINGDOMS 2nd unification

265
  JIN

420
  Northern   440 State patronage of Daoism
  and
  Southern
  Dynasties

589
  SUI   c. 600 Invention of block printing
       629 Pilgrimage of Xuan Zang to India

618
  TANG   641 Chinese Buddhist Princess marries first
  (Xi'an)   King of Tibet
        Civil service examinations extended
      725 Clock escapement mechanism invented
        Han Yu (768–824)
      845 Official repression of Buddhism
        Gunpowder first described

907
    Five   932 First printing of 9 classics begun
    Dynasties

959
    Northern   1044 Magnetic compass described
    SONG   *The Neo-Confucians*
    (Kaifeng)   Zhou Dun-yi (1017–73)
                     Shao Yong (1011–77)
                     Zhang Zai (1020–77)

1126
    Southern   Cheng Yi (1033–1108)   Cheng Hao (1032–85)
    SONG   Zhu Xi (1130–1200)   Lu Jiu-yuan (1139–93)
    (Hangzhou)   Yang Jian (1140–1226)

1280
    YUAN   Marco Polo
    Mongol
    (Peking)

1368
    MING   Wang Yang-ming (1472–1529)
    (Nanjing–   Xavier (1549)
    Peking)   Ricci (1601)
                1604 Dong-lin Academy founded at Wuxi
                     Wang Fu-zhi (1619–93)

1644
    QING   1662–1722 Kang Xi reign (Kang Hsi)
    Manchu   Kang Xi dictionary compiled
    (Peking)   1736–95   Qian Long reign (Ch'ien Lung)
                     Imperial Manuscript Library assembled
             1858–1927 Kang Yu-wei

	Internal	*External*
1862	First newspaper in	1839–42 Anglo-Chinese
	Chinese published	(Opium) war
	in Shanghai	
1862–95	About 12 pro-	1850–64 Taiping
	fessional schools	Rebellion
	set up	
1897	First modern	1858–60 Second
	primary school	(Anglo-French)
	established	Opium War

	Largest publishing	1885	Sino-French
	firm starts		War
	First proposal for	1894-5	Sino-Japanese
	general education		War
	on modern lines	1898	Germany
1906	Traditional civil		obtains E.
	service examina-		Shandong.
	tions abolished		Russia obtains
1894-1908	Translations of		Port Arthur
	European political	1900	and Dairen
	works by Yan Fu.		Boxer
			Rebellion

1911		Revolution—Republic declared
REPUBLIC	1916	Chen Du-xiu edits *The New Youth*
	1917	Hu Shi proposes literary revolution
	1918	Lu Xun's *Diary of a Madman*
	1919	May 4th Movement
		Peking University becomes co-educational
	1919 21	John Dewey in China
	1920-1	Bertrand Russell in China
	1921	March–July Peking Teachers' strike
	1921	Communist Party formed
	1919-23	Mass Education Speech Corps
	1920	Y.C. James Yen's Mass Education Movement
	1923	Debate on science and democracy
	1923	7 February, railway strike
	1924	Sun Yat Sen's lectures on 3 People's Principles
	1925	30 May—Student demonstration, Shanghai
	1926	Beginning of Northern Expedition
	1927	12 April—Communists massacred in Shanghai
		August—Nanchang uprising
		December—Canton rising fails
		October—Mao establishes base on Jinggangshan
	1934	January—Metric units adopted as standard
	1934	Jiang Jie-shi (Chiang Kai-shek) launches 'New Life Movement'
	1934	Jiangxi Soviet suppressed. Start of LONG MARCH

1935	LONG MARCH ends—Communist HQ at Yan'an
1935	9 December—Peking students' general strike
1936	Xi'an incident: Jiang Jie-shi kidnapped— agrees to anti-Japanese united front
1937	Marco Polo Bridge incident—Japanese occupy coastal areas
1938	Yellow River dikes breached—floods and course changed
1938	Wartime capital set up at Chongqing
1942	Communist Party rectification movement 3rd Revolutionary Civil War
1945	7th Congress of CCP
1945	2 September—Japan surrendered
1947	20 May incident, student strikes in Peking and Tianjin
1949	Nationalist Government withdraws to Taiwan

1949
PEOPLE'S REPUBLIC

1949	1 October—Declaration in Peking of People's Republic of China
1949–52	Economic rehabilitation
1950	Land Reform
October 1950– July 1953	Korean War
1950–53	Anti-America aid-Korea movement
1951–2	3-anti and 5-anti movement
1952	Patriotic sanitation movement
1953	Gao Gang & Rao Shu-shi dismissed
1953–6	First Five-Year Plan
1954	September—First National People's Congress. Constitution adopted
1956	8 September—National Congress of CCP
1956–7	'100 Flowers' period
1957–8	Anti-Rightist movement
1958–60	Great Leap Forward
1959	Marshal Peng De-huai dismissed
1960	March—2nd National People's Congress
1960	July—Soviet experts withdrawn
1959–61	Poor harvests

Chronological table

1960–1	Winter. Lowest food rations since 1949
	Heroes
1963	Lei Feng
1964	Ouyang Hai
1965	Wang Jie
1966	Liu Ying-zhun
1964	Zhou En-lai announces 3rd Five-Year Plan to run 1966–70
1965	January—3rd National People's Congress
1966	Start of Great Proletarian Cultural Revolution

Transcriptions

The student of any foreign culture is faced with the problem of memorizing names and terms whose written form is a barrier, rather than an encouragement. Chinese words present a problem which is disguised by their apparent simplicity. Short and spelled alike they slide easily out of the mind. Then the careful student discovers that spellings differ according to authority: Wade-Giles, *hanyu pinyin*, Guoyeu Romatzyh, Yale, the French system, the Russian. The more one reads the worse it gets, and nationalistic rivalries perpetuate the problem.

In this book the transcription adopted in the People's Republic of China, known as *hanyu pinyin*, has been adopted, except in the case of a few names of people and places. This transcription is gradually being adopted throughout the world, and has the advantage over the British form of distinguishing certain sounds more clearly to the untrained eye.

The following notes are intended to help those who are not intending to study the Chinese language, but who find the names difficult to remember. Those wishing to learn to pronounce Chinese correctly must go to such books as *Beginning Chinese* by John de Francis, (pp. xviii–xxviii).

Hanyu pinyin

Except in the case of the sounds described here the reader should pronounce as in English.

The following pairs are contrasted in this transcription:

$$p \; - \; b$$
$$t \; - \; d$$
$$k \; - \; g$$

They can be pronounced like their English equivalents, those on the left being more strongly aspirated.

The following should be carefully noted:

$$zh \; - \; j$$
$$ch \; - \; q$$
$$sh \; - \; x$$

zh can be pronounced like *j* in the English 'Joe'; *ch* as in chew; and *sh* as in 'shoe'. *j*, *q*, and *x* are somewhat similar in sound to their opposite numbers, but change when combined with the following vowels:

(1) with *i* $\left.\begin{array}{l} zhi \\ chi \\ shi \end{array}\right\}$ the *i* acts like adding *r*, e.g. *shi* being pronounced like *shr* in 'shrill'.

$\left.\begin{array}{l} ji \\ qi \\ xi \end{array}\right\}$ here the *i* is pronounced as in the English word 'machine'.

(2) with *u* $\left.\begin{array}{l} zhu \\ chu \\ shu \end{array}\right\}$ here *u* is pronounced as in 'rude'.

$\left.\begin{array}{l} ju \\ qu \\ xu \end{array}\right\}$ this *u*, in some cases written *ü*, is pronounced as the German ü. Alone it is written *yu*.

The last group of consonants requiring attention are:

z pronounced like *dz* in 'adze';
c pronounced like *t's* in 'that's';
s pronounced like *s* in 'sound'.

When one of these is followed by *i* the *i* is pronounced like the *e* in the French '*le*'.

The Chinese *r* is difficult for the majority of Chinese, as well as for the foreigner. It is pronounced like a mixture of the English *r* in 'run' and the French *j* in *je*. In *ri* the *i* is something like the *e* in the French '*le*'.

The only other sounds to note are:

ian, yan pronounced like *i* in 'machine' plus *en* in 'men'.
iong, yong pronounced like German '*jong*', or English 'yoong'.
ou pronounced like *ow* in 'know'.

The Wade-Giles transcription

Students wishing to compare transcriptions will find long lists of equivalents at the end of the J. de Francis books, *Beginning Chinese, Intermediate Chinese* and *Advanced Chinese*, and the *Dictionary of Spoken Chinese* compiled by Yale. Here the equivalents of the sounds described above are given.

Transcriptions

Hanyu pinyin	Wade-Giles	Hanyu pinyin	Wade-Giles
p	p'	zh	ch
b	p	ch	ch'
t	t'	sh	sh
d	t	j	ch
k	k'	q	ch'
g	k	x	hs
z	ts	ji	chi
c	ts'	qi	ch'i
s	s	xi	hsi
r	j	zhi	chih
zi	tzu	chi	ch'ih
ci	tz'u	shi	shih
si	ssu, szu		

Map of language families and dialect groups

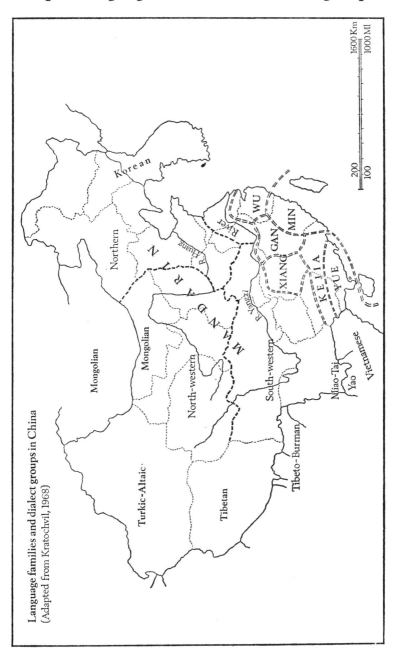

Language families and dialect groups in China
(Adapted from Kratochvil, 1968)

Glossary

Organizations

Zhōnghuá Rénmín Gònghéguó Quánguó Rénmín Dàibiǎo Dàhuì	National People's Congress of the People's Republic of China.
Guówù Yuàn	State Council.
Zhōngguo Gòngchǎndǎng	The Chinese Communist Party.
Zhōngyāng wěiyuánhuì	The Central Committee (of the Chinese Communist Party).
Gāoděng Jiàoyù Bù	The Ministry of Higher Education.
Jiàoyù Bù	The Ministry of Education.
Wénhuà Bù	The Ministry of Culture.
Xīnhuá Shūdiàn	New China Bookshop.
Xuānjiào Bù	Propaganda and Education Department.
xuānchuán	propaganda.
Zhōngguo Gòngchǎnzhǔyì Qīngnián Tuán	Chinese Communist Youth League.
Shàonián Xiānfēng Duì	Young Pioneer Corps.
Tuán zhī Bù	Y.C.L. Branch.

Gāoděng jiàoyù — Higher education

dàxué	university.
xuéyuàn	college, academy, school, institute.
yánjiūsuǒ	institute.
gōngyè dàxué	polytechnical university.
gōngxuéyuàn	engineering college.
nóngxuéyuàn	agricultural college.
línxuéyuàn	forestry college.
yīxuéyuàn	medical school.
nóngyèyánjiūsuǒ	agricultural research institute.
shīfàn dàxué	teachers' training institute.
shīfàn xuéyuàn	teachers' training college.

Glossary

Zhōngděng jiàoyù	**Secondary education**
zhōngxué	secondary school.
chūjí zhōngxué	junior high school.
gāojí zhōngxué	senior high school.
shīfàn xuéxiào	teachers' training school.
Chūděng jiàoyù	**Primary education**
xiǎoxué	primary school.
chūjí xiǎoxué	lower primary school.
gāojí xiǎoxué	upper primary school.
yòuéryuán	kindergarten.
tuōérsuǒ	nursery, creche.

Miscellaneous schools

gōngyè xuéxiào	industrial school.
nóngyè xuéxiào	agricultural school.
nóngmín yèyú chūděng xuéxiào	peasant spare-time primary school.
zhígōng yèyú chūděng xuéxiào	staff and workers' spare-time primary school.
yèyú jiàoyù	spare-time education.
sǎomángmínxiào	people's school for eliminating illiteracy.
shízìbān	literacy class (course).
zhāidiào wénmáng màozi	to doff one's culture-blindness cap, i.e. to become literate.
yīlǎnzi xiǎoxué	village college (day—children; evening—adults).
xúnhuí xiǎoxué	circulating school (teacher goes from village to village).
dānshì jiàoxué	unitary type of teaching (teacher: one-age class).
fùshì jiàoxué	multiple type teaching (teacher: all-age class).
lúntáng jiàoxué	shift classroom type teaching (teacher takes several classes, leaving assistant to maintain order—variant of multiple type).
bànrìzhì	half-day system.
pǔjí jiàoyù	universal education.
bàngōng bàndú	part-work and part-study.

301

gēngdú xiǎoxué	'cultivate and read', i.e. rural part-work school.
zhuānyè xuéxiào	vocational school.
nán nǔ tongxiào	co-education.
hánshou kē	correspondence course.
zǒudú xuéxiào	day-school.
jìkè xuéxiào	boarding school.
rìjiān tuō'ér zhàn	day nursery.

School administration and organization

bàn	to manage, to run (a school, factory, etc.).
guójiā bànde	state run.
jítǐ gànde	run by the collective (commune, factory).
guójiā bàn, jítǐ bāngzhùde	state run, collective aided.
mínbàn xuěxiào	'people operated' school.
jiàoyù chù	Education Division.
jiàoyù jú	Education Bureau.
xué qū	school district.
xuéyuàn	school or college within a university.
xì	faculty, department; course.
zhuānyè	specialty.
zhuānyèhuà	specialization.
jiàoyánzǔ	teaching group.
jiàodǎochù	curriculum division or office.
jiàowù	school business.
jiàowùchù	dean's office, department office.
zhígōng xuéxí xiǎozǔ	staff and workers study group.
xuéxiào zhībù	school branch of CCP or YCL.
xuéshēnghuì	student association.
suǒwù huìyì	institute affairs meeting.
keňqīnhuì	parent-teacher association/meeting.
xiūyè	study (at a school).
xuékē	course (of study); subject.
kēmù bìxiū kē(mù)	subject (of study) required subject.
zhǔ xiū	to major in a subject.
zhǔ xiū kē	major course of study.
xuéfēnzhì	system of academic credits (as in U.S.A.).
xuéniánzhì	system based on school years (cf. Britain).

302

sùchéngkē	accelerated course of study.
kǎoshì	to examine, examination.
kǎoshàng	to pass an examination.
kǎozhòng	to pass an examination.
jígé	to pass an examination.
dé . . . fènr	to get . . . marks.
xuéwèi	academic degree.
xuéshì	B.A.
wénkē shùoshì	M.A.
lǐkē shuòshì	M.Sc.
bóshì	Ph.D.
chéngdù	qualification, degree of attainment.
niánjí	(year) class (e.g. first, second year student).
bìyè	to graduate, graduation (from primary, secondary school or college).
xuénián	school year.
xuéqī	school term, semester.
qīmò	at the end of term.
sànxué	to break up; dismiss school.
jiàqī	vacation, holiday.
hánjià	winter vacation.
chūnjià	spring vacation.
shǔjià	summer vacation.
láodòng	productive work.
shàngkè	classes start; to attend school.
xiàkè	the class is over; after class.
bān	a class.
kè	lesson, class.
yīmén kè	a course (in school).
yījié kè	a class (period) in school.
yītáng kè	a class (period) in school.
xué fèi	school fees.
jiàoshì	classroom.
lǐtáng	auditorium, hall.
túshūguǎn	library.
shíyànshì	laboratory.
xuésù	school building, classroom; class.
sùshè	dormitory; hostel.
shítáng	dining hall, refectory.
sījībān	car pool (lit. drivers' group).
cāochǎng	sports ground; drill ground.
xiàoyuán	school grounds; campus.

Glossary

xuéxiào	school.
wénhuà gōng	cultural palace.

Personnel

suǒzhǎng	head of an institute.
yuànzhǎng	principal, president.
fùyuànzhǎng	vice-principal, vice-president.
xìzhǔrèn	head of department, dean.
jiàoyánzǔzhǎng	head of teaching group.
jiàodǎo zhǔrèn	director of studies.
xiàozhǎng	school head; school principal.
jiàozhíyuán	school administrators and teachers.
zhùlǐ yánjiū yuán	assistant researcher.
jiàoshòu	professor.
jiǎngyǎnzhě	lecturer.
jiǎngshī	lecturer.
jiàoyuán	teacher.
jiàoshī	teacher.
lǎoshī	teacher (term of especial respect).
xiānsheng	teacher (form of address).
zhuānjiā	expert, specialist.
xuéshēng	student, pupil.
nánxuéshēng	male student.
nǚxuéshēng	female student.
xuéchǐ értòng	child(ren) of school age.
xuézhǐ	scholar, student.
xuéjiū	pedant.
jiàoyùjiā	educationist.
jiàoyùzh	educator.
dàoshī	scholar (original thinker).

Education, teaching and learning

xuéshù	knowledge (obtained from study).
xuéxí	to study, to learn; study.
shòuyè	to study a special subject.
yǎngyù	to bring up, to nurture.
péiyǎng	to nurture; to cultivate (e.g. a new CCP member).
jiào	to teach.
jiàoshū	to teach (in a general sense).
jiào (wùlǐ)	to teach (physics).

304

jiàodǎo	to teach, to guide, to direct.
zìxué	to teach oneself.
xùnliàn	to train, to drill.
shòuxùn	to receive instruction or training.
duànliàn	to train; training.
xùn	to admonish.
jiàoxùn	to instruct, to inculcate.
yánjiū	to study, to research; study.
yùxí	to prepare (lessons).
fùxí	to revise.
liànxí	to practise; an exercise.
mòxiě	to write from memory.
bèi	to recite from memory (to 'back' a text); to memorize.
shúdú	to learn thoroughly.
tīngxiě	to take dictation; dictation.
zuò zǎocāo	to do morning exercises.
xué	to study.
dú shū	to study; to read books.
niàn	to read (aloud).
niàn shū	to study (to read a book aloud).
jiàoyù	education.
dé, zhì, tǐyù	moral, intellectual, and physical education.
jiàoyùxué	education, pedagogy.
jiǎngshòu	instruction; to teach.
xiě wénzhāng	to write an essay.
xiě lùnwén	to write a thesis.
láixué	to play truant
taóxué	to play truant.
taóxuézhě	truant.
toūlǎnzhě	truant; loafer.

Index